RICHARD J. SCHONBERGER

World Class Manufacturing: The Next Decade

Building Power, Strength, and Value

THE FREE PRESS

New York   London   Toronto   Sydney   Tokyo   Singapore

The Free Press
A Division of Simon & Schuster Inc.
1230 Avenue of the Americas
New York, N.Y. 10020

Printed in the United States of America

printing number

1 2 3 4 5 6 7 8 9 10

Text design by Carla Bolte

Library of Congress Cataloging-in-Publication Data

Schonberger, Richard.
    World class manufacturing: the next decade: building power,
strength, and value / Richard J. Schonberger.
        p.   cm.
    Includes index.
    ISBN 0–684–82303–9
        1. Industrial management.   2. Production management.
    3. Manufacturing processes.   I. Title.
    HD31.S3387   1996
    670'.68—dc20   95–40876
                                                    CIP

Contents

Preface   ix

1. Industrial Decline and Ascendancy   1

Manufacturing Performance: Down, Then Up   1

Sustained Improvement   4

   U.S. Manufacturers   4

   French Manufacturers   6

   Obstacles and Openings   7

Customer Service   9

   Broad-Based Customer Data   9

   Pooled Customer Data   12

Summing Up   13

   Eras   14

   Japan Decade, American Decade, Global Decade   16

**2. Building Strength Through
Customer-Focused Principles   19**

From Edicts to Principles   20

Customer-Focused Principles   23

   General Principles   23

   Design   33

   Operations   34

   Human Resources   36

   Quality and Process Improvement   39

Information for Operations and Control   41

Capacity   43

Promotion and Marketing   46

3. Best Manufacturers: How They Rate   49

Research Project   50

Scores, by Category   51

High and Lower Scores   55

Intermediate Scores   57

Bottom Group   59

Sector Scores   59

Forging Ahead   64

4. Improvement Pathways   67

1. Gates Rubber, Denver   67
2. Honeywell Scottish Operations, Motherwell, Scotland   70
3. Baxter Healthcare's North Cove IV Solutions Facility, Marion, North Carolina   71
4. Davey Products, Australia   72
5. Baldor Electric, Fort Smith, Arkansas   74
6. Jostens Diplomas, Red Wing, Minnesota   75
7. AlliedSignal, Aerospace Equipment Systems, Tempe, Arizona   76
8. Dover Elevators, Memphis   78
9. Quickie Designs Inc., Fresno, California   80
10. Exxon Baytown, Baytown, Texas   81
11. Varian Associates, Nuclear Magnetic Resonance Instruments, Palo Alto, California   82
12. Alcatel Network Systems, Richardson, Texas   82
13. Ford Electronics, Markham, Ontario   82
14. Rosemount Measurement Division, Chanhassen Pressure Plant, Chanhassen, Minnesota   83
15. Boeing Welded Duct Plant, Seattle Area   84
16. Northern Telecom, Multimedia Communication Systems, Calgary, Ontario   85

17. Johnson Controls, Milwaukee   85

18. Rhomberg Bräsler, Cape Town, South Africa   87

Diverse Pathways—A Summary   87

5. Value and Valuation   91

Product Costing: How and When   92

  Costing for Infrequent Decisions   93

    Product Development   94

    Product Line   95

  Real Needs   96

Motivation to Improve   97

  Open-Book Management (Tripping Over Financial Numbers)   99

  Exception: Small Business Units   102

  Priorities: Customer-Focused Principles and the ABC Paradox   104

  Dual System?   106

Value of the Enterprise   107

  Power Brokers   108

  Genuine Power   110

CASE STUDY: THE COSTING/PRICING PROBLEM AT
HARBOR METAL STAMPING COMPANY   110

Alternative Solutions   111

Modifying the Costing System   111

Modifying the Data Collection System   113

6. The New Mastery of Mass Production— and Its Close Cousins   115

What *Is* Mass Production?   116

Why Mass Production?   116

  Trade Pacts Resize Production Volumes   117

  From Mass-Produced Components to Customized End Products   118

  Japanese and German Mistakes   121

  End Products   123

  Scale Economies Lost   124

  When a Plant Has Too Many Parts   125

How Mass Production?   127
    Standardization   127
    Usage-Rate Production   128
    Agility   129
        Consumer Need or Quirk?   130
        Portability   132
Conclusion: Someone Wants What You Have   133

7. **Strategic Linkages   135**

Product Decisions and Customer Service   137
    Unaware and Unconcerned   137
    Organizational Realignments   140
Building Bridges   140
Multicompany Planning   141
    Quick Response   142
    Vendor-Managed Inventory and Efficient Customer Response   143
    Demand Forecasting   145
Planning with Immediate Partners   146
Internal Multifunctional Planning   147
    Decomposing the Order Book   147
    Capacity Management and New Initiatives   150
Smoothing the Demand Turbulence   151
Forcing the Action   152

8. **Impediments: Bad Plant Design,
    Mismanagement of Capacity   155**

Production Lines: Failure Designed In   156
Too Long, Too Wide, Too Fast   156
Conveyor Removal   158
Arcs   158
Assembly Lines, Station Cycle Times, and People 161
    Maquiladoras   161
    Cut and Sew   162
    Genesis of Modular Sewing and TSS   163

Whole Plants   166
  Flexible Limits   167
  Flexible Automation   168
  Production Support   170
Unconstrained Capacity   173

9. Remaking Human Resource Management   177

Roles   178
  The New Owners of Process Improvement   178
  High-Potential Teams   179
  Organization Charts Lose Their Lines   180
  Associates, Facilitators, and Teamsmanship   180
Motivation and Reward in the Age of
Continuous Improvement   184
  Results   184
  Special Recognition   185
  Negatives to Positives   186
  Performance Appraisal   187
  Quid Pro Quo   188
The Work Force Upgrades—and HR Adapts   192
  Role and Size   192
  Training—to Certification   193
  Line Involvement in HR   194
  Labor Relations   195
  Job Classifications   195
An Example   197
Interconnections   199

10. Quality: Picture a Miracle   201

Pictures   201
Miracles (Accentuate the Positive)   204
Virtual Stability   205
Keeping the Core and Hiring Out   206
The Organization: Bulwark of Stability and Effectiveness   209
  Customer (and Supplier) Stability   209

Employee Stability   213
Quality Individuals Versus Teams   214
Team Stability and Cohesiveness   215
Project Cohesiveness and Stability   219

11. A Ten-Year Plan   225

From Cost to Value   226
Scorekeeping   227
Balanced Scorecard   228
Cost of Quality   229
Renaming Things   230
Throughput   231
Stretch Goals   231
Follow-Through   233
Implementation Tendencies and Necessities   235
Consultants, Advisors, and Trainers   235
Kaizens   236
Application Seminars   237
Points of Light   238
Learning and Training   239
Guessing the Future 241

Appendix: Scoring Against the Principles   245

Notes   255
Index   267

Preface

Roughly forty-five years ago, industry began to lose its edge. Data presented in Chapter 1 show the decline continuing for twenty-five years thereafter. Then, at about the seventy-fifth year of this century, manufacturers began their renewal. The same time-line data show a remarkable pattern of industrial resurgence. One company after another *learned how.* And did it. And are doing it. But they need a continual infusion of energy and commitment, mainly in the form of ideas.

By 1985, the leading edge in the rebirth of industry was composed of two ideas: cycle time (then called lead time) and quality-with-a-small-*q*. My book, *World Class Manufacturing* (I), included an honor role of eighty-four manufacturers that had cut their cycle times at least fivefold (80 percent). A flood of just-in-time books and articles was being published, and George Stalk, Jr., of the Boston Consulting Group was readying his milestone *Harvard Business Review* article, "Time—The Next Source of Competitive Advantage." Deming, Juran, Ishikawa, Feigenbaum, and Crosby, the giants of quality, were invited into the inner sanctums of giant corporations. Now-familiar terms and concepts such as benchmarking, reengineering, activity-based costing, design for manufacture, and total quality management (big-*Q* quality) were unknown or brand new.

The decade piled a dozen important management concepts upon a similar number perfected in Japan in an earlier time period. Or are they all really important? We need a litmus test of significance. And I think we have one—three, actually. By today's standards, a good management concept, application, or plan must (1) serve the best interests of customers, (2) have the commitment of the whole enterprise, and (3) be data (fact) based. This is a book about the group that passes the tests. They form an interacting set of principles, which become manufacturing's action agenda for the next decade.

Management by principles distances itself from conventional management—the planning and control model. In that approach, executives set numeric goals and pass them downward. In Conti's goal deployment version, lower-level teams can recommend goal modifications in light of data obtained through benchmarking, quality function deployment, and other means.[1]

Principles-based management follows two main streams of thought. One is the view that companies are converging on about the same set of customer-focused goals. This is happening before our eyes, as more and more companies embrace internationally recognized standards of excellence (e.g., the Baldrige Award, Deming Prize, and ISO 9000 series criteria).

The other stream relates to how we think about power. We distrust it. We see the ambiguity of motives of executives—those in charge of the conventional planning and control model. Will they go for short-term gain, at the expense of long-term health? Too often, the answer seems to be yes. In North America, this skepticism combines with strong egalitarian beliefs and the Judeo-Christian ethic: We think we all should have a hand in running things. This begins to make sense in learning organizations: companies that educate and train everybody and keep them informed. In advanced cases, the entire work force acquires confidence in its ability to use data to continuously improve in the eyes of customers. These beliefs, along with the tools of improvement, coalesce as stable principles.

The principles approach is not antiplanning. Rather, the number of issues that have to go through the planning process is cut way down. That is, all the issues captured by the principles are no longer candidates for top-down, yes-no decision making. Make things better for customers. No debate. Turn the work force loose on data-based continuous improvement. No debate.

This book provides the principles—sixteen of them (comprising Chapter 2)—plus a tough scoring array that companies may use to assess their standing and progress toward the high reaches of world-class excellence. Some 130 above-average manufacturers already have done so, and their variously summarized scores (in Chapter 3) offer benchmarks. Many of the same companies explain (in Chapter 4) how they have made their way forward.

Those first four chapters lay the groundwork, and the next seven explain what manufacturers must do and not do in their efforts to acquire power, strength, and value. We look at issues from factory floor layouts to the hottest topics in value-chain linkages to assessment practices on Wall Street. We consider ways to reconstruct human resource management and to fix the broken performance measurement system. Along the way several semisacred cows are sacrificed, and senior executives and their tired-out metrics are taken to task. The theme of simplicity is persistent, as is the overarching goal of building a dynasty, not just a flash in the pan.

1

Industrial Decline
and Ascendancy

We've learned more about running a manufacturing enterprise in the eighties and nineties than in all the rest of the century. And the manufacturing renaissance has not yet run its course. In fact, it has spread to less developed countries and out of manufacturing into the service sector. The many new lessons have transformed consultants into educators, invigorated sleepy community and technical colleges, and made employee training a significant budget item.

Training wasn't important in the sixties and seventies. The existing subject matter was stale and simply did not lead clearly to success. Today's is fresh and does drive success. Widely applied new concepts have transformed industry.

MANUFACTURING PERFORMANCE: DOWN, THEN UP

Consider manufacturing performance in just the last half of this century. It takes the shape of a wide V. It declined for twenty-five years and has been rising ever since:

This twenty-five-down, twenty-five-up phenomenon is a global composite, shifting somewhat by region. For Japan the bottom of the V occurred in the mid-1960s. Then total quality control and the Toyota system kicked in, raising Japan to industrial prominence. Prestigious North American manufacturers—Japan's natural target in view of the massive

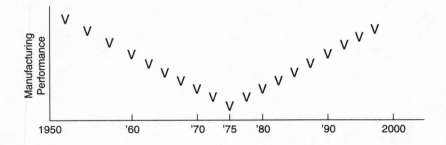

U.S. market—knew they were in trouble by 1975. European manufacturers did not know they had a serious problem until the mid-1980s.

The wide V pattern does not show up clearly in plots of profitability, return on investment, sales, or market share. These "financials" rise and fall with the economic cycle, are influenced by state fiscal and monetary policies, and are easily skewed by protectionist trade practices and internal company manipulations. What, then, might support the wide-V contention?

Anecdotal evidence, for one thing. The research method used by Naisbitt, resulting in his book *Megatrends,*[1] is to pile up stories from the press to indicate trends. In the late 1970s and early 1980s, the U.S. business press was abubble with stories about a "productivity crisis" and the "hollowing of industry." H. Thomas Johnson provides a concrete case-study example: the once-redoubtable machine-tool maker Burgmaster. It's history, Johnson notes, "falls into two phases: twenty years of excellent growth and profitability in the hands of a brilliant, customer-focused engineer who founded the company, followed by twenty years of decline into bankruptcy in the hands of finance-driven, numbers-oriented professional managers." (The company had been a leveraged buyout victim of Kohlberg, Kravis, Roberts in the mid-1960s.)[2]

We need not rely on case studies or news clippings. One statistic extractable from corporate annual reports tells the story with surprising accuracy: inventory turnover (cost of sales divided by on-hand inventory). It happens that when a company manages its processes poorly, wastes in the form of inventory pile up.

Exhibit 1-1 shows the pattern of declining inventory turnovers for several venerable manufacturers. Ford's, Emerson Electric's, Motorola's, Whirlpool's, and Eaton's descents were precipitous. Du Pont's, Eastman

EXHIBIT 1-1
Sample Inventory Turns, 1950–75*

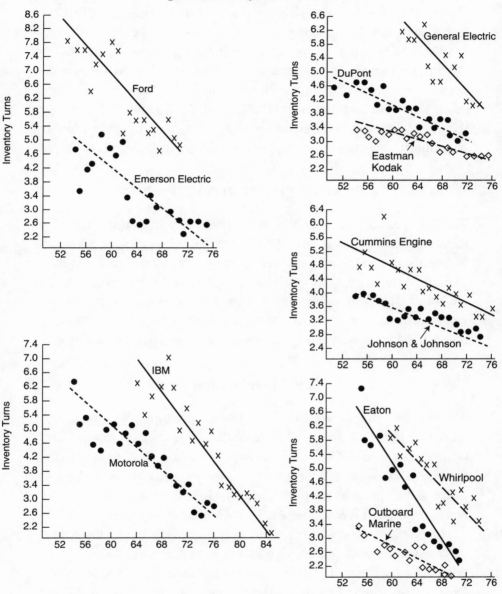

*Most data for Exhibits 1-1 and 1-2 come from the Compustat database, which does not include the years 1950–53.

Graphs were first published in Richard J. Schonberger, "The World Class Manufacturing Company—Ten Years Later," a seminar notebook (Management Research Corp., Spring 1995), pp. 36–37.

Kodak's, Cummins Engine's, Johnson & Johnson's, and Outboard Marine's declines were a bit less sharp but were steady. GE defied the trend somewhat, enjoying rising inventory turnover from 1951 through 1961 (not shown); but then, reverting to pattern, its turns fell steeply.

IBM, however, gets the prize for longest, steepest decline. Its inventory turnover up to 1961 (the inaugural year for IBM's 360-series computer) was spectacular: in the twenties in 1958 through 1961, then down to twelve and eleven in 1962 and 1963. Exhibit 1-1 picks up IBM in 1964 when its turnover was 6.3; from there it plunges, finally bottoming out twenty-one years later at a miserable 2.1 turns.

SUSTAINED IMPROVEMENT

The long period of decline would be depressing were it not for what happened next. By the early 1980s, the Toyota system had reached Western shores. U.S. manufacturers, first to try it, may have had their share of false starts. On the whole, however, the system proved to be eminently transportable. Exhibit 1-2 and the following discussion provides some of the evidence: sustained high rates of improvement, noted in the form of inventory turnovers, for numerous companies.

U. S. Manufacturers

The star performers are Ford, Deere and Company, TRW, Eaton, PepsiCo, and Hon Industries. All have double-digit rates of improvement in inventory turns—from 16 percent per year for TRW to 10 percent for Ford and Eaton. All have been improving turns nearly as long as many of the top Japanese waste cutters—since 1975 for Ford; 1978 for Deere; 1974 for TRW, Eaton, and PepsiCo; and 1980 for Hon.

Honorable mention—for annual turn improvements in the 5 to 9 percent range for at least ten years—goes to Cummins Engine, Outboard Marine, Caterpillar, Black & Decker, General Motors, Motorola, Dover, Honeywell, Emerson Electric, and Timken. General Electric has been improving its turns at a roaring rate but only for about five years, which corresponds well with the ascendancy of GE's common stock price and overall esteem.

EXHIBIT 1-2
Sample Inventory Turns 1975–95

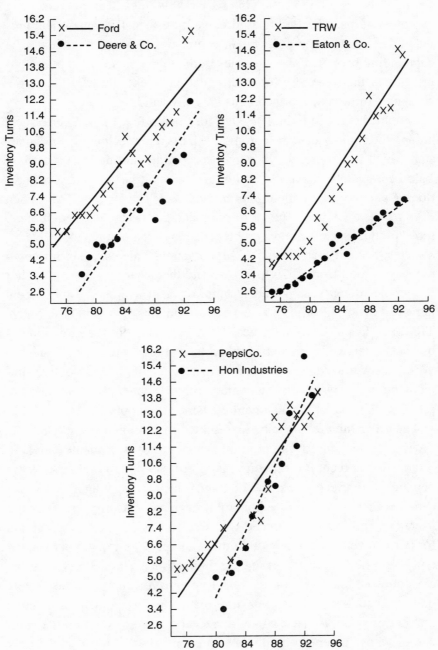

French Manufacturers

The U.S. is not alone in showing remarkable rates of improvement in inventory turns. The Paris-based consulting firm Proconseil has provided data from seven of its client companies plus one nonclient. The data, dating back to 1979, use sales rather than cost of sales in the numerator of the inventory turnover equation. This upwardly biases the computed turnovers, but the trends are fully valid.

Graphic results in Exhibit 1-3 are for the top four French performers among the eight. Valeo, the automotive parts manufacturer, is the superstar, which is no surprise. In a five-year period starting in about 1984, Valeo completely converted its LaSuze radiator, heater, and air-conditioning plant to cells, called *zones autonome de production* (ZAP). Each ZAP has its own mix of metal-forming and plastic-molding equipment, tools, product specifications, problem displays, team of ten to twelve associates (per shift), and technical support staff.[3] Valeo's rate of improvement was good from 1979 to 1989—and then sharply accelerated. For the whole fifteen-year period its improvement averaged 14.9 percent per year (from 4.2 to 13.6), just about equaling that of TRW. Valeo, TRW, and Dana (U.S.) and Lucas (U.K.) are in about the same kind of business—large, multiplant auto parts manufacturers. They are the West's answer to Japan's Nippon Denso. Like Nippon Denso, their implementation of world-class manufacturing has generally been more impressive than that of the major automakers they supply.

The other three companies represented in Exhibit 1-3 have the following rates of improvement in inventory turnover: Renault (cars), an erratic 10.5 percent for thirteen years; Plastic Omnium (auto parts), 8.6 percent for fourteen years; and Legrand (electrical appliances), 8.8 percent for nine years. In the honorable mention category are Carnaud Metalbox (packaging, affiliated with Crown Cork & Seal), 6.4 percent for thirteen years; Pechiney (aluminum and packaging), 4.5 percent for ten years; Le Carbone-Lorraine (carbon applications), 3.6 percent for eleven years; and Peugeot (cars), 3.1 percent for thirteen years. While both Renault's and Peugeot's improvements extend over the same number of years, Renault's rate far exceeds Peugeot's. Of all the companies whose inventory trend data I've looked at, Peugeot is the only

EXHIBIT 1-3
Sample Inventory Turns, 1979–93,
French Manufacturers ("Star Performers")

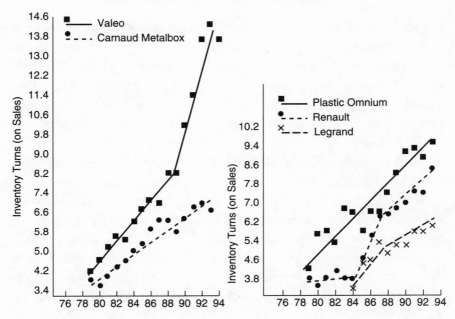

one that experienced a recent several-year decline. Its turns rose steadily from 4.1 in 1979 to a peak of 7.9 in 1988 and then fell for the next five years to 5.8 in 1992 and 5.9 in 1993. Over the last ten years Renault has become a respected, lean, financially sound automaker; Peugeot has survived but not thrived.

Obstacles and Openings

Some companies are doing well despite unimpressive inventory turnover trends—Coca Cola, for example. (Coke is a beverage company. Stellar inventory performer PepsiCo is in a different business, since two-thirds of its sales come from snack food and restaurants.) Companies that are in the midst of global expansion may have to deal with uncertain markets, perverse laws and tax codes, corrupt officials, and lack of infrastructure (good highways, point-of-sale data capture, electronic data interchange, and the like). These factors add up to marketing mistakes, logistics difficulties—and heaps of inventory here and there. In such consumer-goods companies' own developed markets, no excuse.

Other highly successful firms with poor inventory trends have a double difficulty: highly volatile businesses serving those same uncertain world markets. Motorola, Texas Instruments, Intel, and Hewlett-Packard fit the description. This does not necessarily mean that volatile, multinational manufacturers are stuck with static inventory performance. H-P mounted an inventory reduction crusade in 1994 that is off to a good start.

What made the ten star and fourteen honorable-mention companies (U.S. and French) so smart? Westerners were unaware of the Toyota system until about 1980, and it takes a while for knowledge to translate into action. Perhaps a more pertinent question is, why did it take so long for so many companies to see the wastes in front of their eyes? The top ten evidently did see the wastes—some of them well before they learned about the Japanese success story. Notably, however, each considerably accelerated its rate of improvement after about 1985 or 1986 in the United States and about 1988 or 1989 in France. By then, it was no longer the Toyota system. It was manufacturing excellence, or world-class manufacturing, or lean production.

These data are only for top-performing publicly held companies. Their annual reports, and therefore inventory turnover data—are open to scrutiny. Privately held companies, however, seem to be at least as adept as public ones in implementing a world-class agenda. This conclusion is based on data from just a few private companies that were willing to assist in this research. For example, Charles Machine Company, maker of the Ditch Witch line of digging equipment, improved its turns by over 6 percent yearly in a recent decade. Haworth, a maker of office-equipment, improved even more. And Steelcase, the largest office equipment maker, improved its inventory turns by over 12 percent per year. Haworth and Steelcase were not under pressure to compete with a foreign juggernaut. Rather, these improvements took place in a golden decade for the office-equipment industry; each of the majors increased sales at spectacular rates through the 1980s.

CUSTOMER SERVICE

We have seen some eye-opening data on inventory trends and noted the apparent connection between inventory turns and long-range competitiveness. Perhaps, therefore, trend in inventory turnover is a fairly reliable predictor of future success for a company or business unit. Whatever merit that conclusion has, still other indicators beg our attention.

One of the most important, if only it could be measured reliably, is customer satisfaction. During its dominating years, IBM was renowned for its dogged pursuit of customer-satisfaction information. Its excellence in customer service was largely reactive, but in the 1950s and 1960s a well-oiled reactive approach to customer service was world class.

Today's standards are higher. We recognize the need to give equal or greater weight to customers' present and future needs. Since those needs can change quickly and with little notice, speed and flexibility have become mainstream criteria of customer satisfaction. Furthermore, total quality calls for placing more weight on prevention of difficulties and less on recovery when things go wrong. In other words, by today's standards IBM's hand-holding approach was overly narrow.

Broad-Based Customer Data

Today's broadened approach may be found in criteria for prominent quality awards. The Malcolm Baldrige Quality Award in the United States designates 250 of 1,000 possible points for "customer focus and satisfaction." (IBM's business unit in Rochester, Minnesota, was a Baldrige winner in 1990). The European Quality Award puts 20 percent weight on customer satisfaction.

Of all the Baldrige honorees the company with the most comprehensive customer intelligence gathering system may be 1991 winner Solectron, Inc. Solectron specializes in assembly of printed circuit boards and subsystems for makers of computers and other electronic products. Many of its customers are well-known, for example, Hewlett-Packard, AT&T, and IBM. Solectron's customer satisfaction index (CSI) aims at grading the company's performance on five service criteria for *every customer every week.* According to Les Nishimura,

EXHIBIT 1-4

Solectron's CSI Form

✿ SOLECTRON

CSI Feedback Form

DATE: _____

CUSTOMER: _____

PERSON SURVEYED: _____

SALES REP: _____

DIVISION: _____

	A	A-	B+	B	B-	C	D
	100	90	85	80	75	0	-100
Quality							
Delivery							
Communication							
Service							
Overall							

COMMENTS (next page)

10

general manager of Solectron Washington (one of the company's newer business units), "It isn't easy to get that information every week. Sometimes we have to almost pry the information out of the customer." Xerox collects customer satisfaction monthly.[4] A few of the participants in a research project discussed in the next chapter were proud of surveying their customers yearly. Most companies don't do it at all.

Solectron's CSI Feedback Form is shown in Exhibit 1-4. Salespeople administer the CSI and are measured on their rates of completed forms; an 85 percent completion rate is typical. Most CSI responses are conveyed in written form—by fax or E-mail—although Solectron will accept oral responses.

The CSI does not fully reveal the extent to which the system gets at customers' real and changing needs. Both Solectron and most of its customers intend their commitments to extend from product development partnerships all the way through to funds transfer and after-delivery postmortems. Thus, any low CSI scores can trigger formation of improvement teams, often with customer representatives. Solectron's target satisfaction score is 95 percent. Thus, if a customer grades any of the five criteria (quality, delivery, communication, service, and overall) as low as C (zero), an overall score of 95 percent is impossible. This triggers corrective action and a response to the customer.

At the same time, Solectron gets its people into two kinds of teams, both customer-focused. Project-planning teams work with customers to plan, schedule, and set forth specifications and response times. Total-quality-control teams meet weekly to monitor and evaluate production. Walt Wilson, Solectron's president, says, "The teams here are . . . fiercely loyal to [customers]. . . . Ask anyone what team they're on, and they'll tell you. They'll say they work for Intel or IBM or H-P and that Solectron just signs the checks. That's customer focus at its best."[5]

Nishimura has a mental model. It is a four-by-four matrix with customer needs on the x-axis and Solectron's capabilities on the y-axis. He observed that his company's challenge, not always achieved, is to be in the fourth cell (see Exhibit 1-5): all customer needs covered fully by Solectron capabilities. However, Nishimura continued, there is an all-important z-axis: time. Customer needs change, and the changes must be captured and employed to alter Solectron's processes, products, and

EXHIBIT 1-5
Capabilities-Needs Matrix

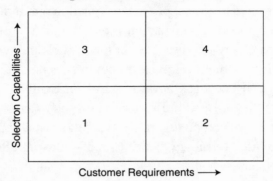

systems. No matter how good we are, he noted, we need to be quick to change.

Few manufacturers plumb consumer satisfaction as deeply as Solectron does. However, help is on the way. Claes Fornell and his colleagues at the National Quality Research Center at the University of Michigan's School of Business Administration have devised a national customer satisfaction index. Fornell first created the index for Sweden in 1989. Germany set up its own similar index in 1992, and several other countries are at work establishing theirs.

Pooled Customer Data

The U.S. version, the American Customer Satisfaction Index (ACSI), began in 1994 using telephone interviews from a sample of about fifty thousand U.S. households. Respondents report on their usage of a company's product, and satisfaction is registered on a scale of 0 (lowest) to 100 (highest). The initial ACSI measured seven sectors and forty industries and included over two hundred organizations. Manufacturers comprise two of the sectors, nondurables and durables, and eighteen industries. (The rest are service-sector organizations.) For example, Procter & Gamble, Unilever, Colgate Palmolive, Dial, and Clorox comprise the personal-care-products industry group.[6]

The index provides a way for a company to compare itself over time, compare with industry averages, predict long-term performance, and answer specific questions. In addition, Fornell believes the index can gauge an industry's and a nation's performance better than such indices as consumer prices can.[7] Consumer prices are subject to currency, trade, and other influences. Marketers may sometimes be able to manipulate customer satisfaction, but not much and not for long.

Not long ago, indices of customer satisfaction would have been less meaningful. Consumers in much of the world might have been fairly satisfied with their own countries' poor workmanship, high defect rates, long delays, and inflexible labor and equipment. Political and trade barriers have that effect. Now, with the globalization of trade, Toyota cars, Benneton sweaters, Mercedes diesel engines, and Compac PCs are everywhere. And global communications networks bring visual portrayal of how others live and work to TV sets in parlors all over the world. Consumers are no longer in the dark. They can judge their local goods against high world standards. Thus, the introduction of customer satisfaction indices is timely.

We have now examined a pair of underappreciated indicators: customer satisfaction and inventory turnover. The two provide overlapping metrics for valuing a manufacturing business unit or company or an industrial sector for an entire country: Customer satisfaction measures quality and value; low inventory turnover reflects costly wastes, delays, scrap, rework, and other negative values.

We must understand, however, that these are aggregated metrics. As such, they can only be watched, not managed. The proper targets of management are root causes: how products and processes are designed, how the work force is trained, how data are used to isolate mishaps, how suppliers and customers are treated, and so on. In Chapter 5 we revisit customer satisfaction, inventory turnover, and other aggregated metrics and put them in their proper places. The real manufacturing renaissance has much more to do with innovations in managing the root causes.

SUMMING UP

We've seen evidence of a general decline in manufacturing performance over a twenty-five-year period beginning in about 1950. The causes were a combination of poor strategies and practices in all of the following functional areas: manufacturing, marketing, performance measurement (accounting), product design and development, supplier relations, and human resource management. In each area the bad strategies and practices led to wastes, which appear on the books as enlarged inventories. The same weaknesses should also show up in the form of lower customer-satisfaction indices. They often do not show up in popular financial metrics. For example, Eaton Corporation, one of the manufacturers featured in Exhibit 1-1 for its long decline and long ascent in inventory turns, had an erratic pattern of earnings per share of common stock. Its EPS was $7 in 1950, fell to $5 in 1954, rose to $9 in 1955, fell to $2 in 1963, rose to $6 in 1979, fell to $2 in 1982, rose to $5.50 in 1984, fell to $3 in 1986, rose to $6 in 1988, and fell to $4 in 1992. (Ford's, GM's, and Outboard Marine's EPS patterns were not much different.)[8] Stock prices and other common financial measures show similar hippety-hop patterns—for Eaton and most other firms.

Savvy company executives have learned how to manipulate most of the closely watched financials in ways that mask underlying weaknesses. Even return on stockholder equity, often thought to be a purer measure of company value, has been assailed. Byron Wien of Morgan Stanley has shown how executives inflate their ROEs by writing off equity through plant shutdowns, employee buyouts, and other well-timed size-downs.[9] Juiced and jumpy financial numbers are not reliable measures of manufacturing strength and value. Over the long run, inventory turnover may be better.

Eras

In my 1982 book *Japanese Manufacturing Techniques,* I traced the decline in manufacturing in another way.[10] I noted how the productivity emphasis during World War II gave way to a marketing emphasis. The reason was that war-related scarcities disappeared, pipelines became filled with goods, and industry ended up with overcapacity problems. (The United States and Canada began to experience overcapacity in about 1950. It occurred several years later in bombed-out Europe and Japan.) What does any company with overcapacity do? It sells, sells,

EXHIBIT 1–6
Eras

1940–50	Shortages	= Production era
1950–65	Excess capacity, national	= Marketing era
1965–80	Concentrated earnings	= Finance era
1980–90	Intercontinental competition	= Quality era
1990–	Excess capacity, global	= Partnership era

sells. A productivity emphasis no longer made sense. The marketing era produced losers in danger of going under and winners with vast accumulations of cash to invest. Naturally, this ushered in the finance era, during which richer manufacturers could make more money by doing mergers and acquisitions than by manufacturing and selling.

We may now update the story. Exhibit 1-6 shows the three old eras plus an update for the past decade and another for the next. By the 1980s Japanese consumer and industrial products were everywhere in the United States. Through superior quality Japanese companies were picking off famous Western brand names one by one. Their names (e.g., International Harvester tractors and Westinghouse home appliances) fade in memory, and it's a shame (see box, "Brand Name—Public Asset). A few Western companies (e.g., Texas Instruments, Motorola, Xerox, Ford, Hewlett-Packard, and IBM) reacted in the only effective way. They adopted their own total-quality commitments.

BRAND NAME—PUBLIC ASSET

To its owners, a well-known brand name ranks in value with the firm's buildings, equipment, and labor resources. A brand name is also a public asset. The company that invests millions to build brand recognition gains sales volume, which cuts unit costs and generates revenue to improve quality and delivery. Consumers depend on the brand, which makes their shopping quicker, easier, and more likely to yield good results. The buying public is the beneficiary—and the loser when a famous brand name bites the dust.

For leading manufacturers the quality era was about a decade long. By 1990 nonconformity and rework rates for Western makers of cars, earth-moving equipment, farm machinery, TVs, computers, appliances, telephone equipment, electric motors, and many more products had plunged to world-class levels. Defectives fell from percentages to double- and single-digit parts per million. Competitive advantage shifted from quality to value: high quality for a low price.

So now value supersedes plain quality. But value is complicated. It requires high quality, timely availability, and removal of non-value adding wastes of many kinds. All this in the face of excess capacity. But this time (unlike the 1950s) it is a global phenomenon. For complex sociopolitical reasons the world is awash in products and capacity to extract, construct, and produce them. A dominant strategy for surviving and thriving is to find external partners who can perform a valued function for you. Internal partnerships across departmental lines are equally important, mainly for ensuring that internal capacity matches market, supply, and financial realities.

Since geographical distance sometimes separates the partners, advanced communications and logistics are supporting elements of the partnership strategy. Technologies such as point-of-sale data capture and electronic data interchange propel real demand data back through supply echelons. The forging of quick-response partnerships among those echelons—including multimodal freight carriers—ranks among the most important management developments of the century. More on this in Chapter 7.

Japan Decade, American Decade, Global Decade

In terms of management innovations the 1970s were Japan's Decade and 1985–1995 America's Decade (the early 1980s were transitional). Japan's innovations include total quality control, just in time, kanban, total preventive maintenance, supplier partnerships, quality function deployment, target costing, employee involvement, cross-careering, and visual management. America's (with some non-U.S. participation) include design for manufacture and assembly, benchmarking, reengineering, quick-response linkages to retailers, point-of-sale technology coupled with electronic data interchange, rapid prototyping, digital design, activity-based costing, cost of quality, peer performance appraisal, broad-band pay systems, reformulated gain-sharing/profit-sharing/bonuses/employee stock ownership, and assorted lesser innovations (e.g., cross-docking and metrics such as the linearity index and the response ratio).

Regional dominance, however, is of the past. The end of the Cold War and the globalization of trade and communications ensures that. Now we are in the Global Decade. Innovations in managing manufacturing companies—and many that are equally applicable in services—will continue to pour forth but from all parts of the world, including the less developed countries.

Amid all the commotion, what companies need is a guide path that will move them forward confidently, step by step. What fits the need is principles-based management, the subject of Chapter 2.

2

Building Strength Through Customer-Focused Principles

Chapter 1 suggests that financial data are not the best indicators of manufacturing company strength and prospects. More basic metrics, such as inventory turnover and customer satisfaction, may be more valid. The two measure differently, however. Inventory turns rise and fall slowly as a result of many activities. Thus, turns assess long-term changes in company strength. Customer satisfaction, on the other hand, can sometimes shift quickly and point to responses needed now. The firm's producers and servers need more such pointers. Many more.

This chapter addresses that need. It provides sixteen principles of customer-focused, employee-driven, data-based performance. (Customer satisfaction is a component of the second principle.) Throughout this and later chapters, I'll usually just call them "customer-focused principles" or "principles-based management," though the other key words, "employee-driven" and "data-based," are equally important. Companies or business units may score themselves on each principle using a tough zero-to-five-point scale. The next chapter provides benchmark scores for manufacturers of various sizes and types, obtained through a research project. Most of the participating companies were hand picked. I looked for companies that have shown some success in implementing the 1986-era world-class agenda. For comparative purposes, the participants also included a few manufacturers that are just starting their world-class journey, as well as a few service companies.

Benchmarking is one use of the research data. The methods of scoring are not so precise or controlled, however, as to yield highly reliable benchmark comparisons. More important uses of the data are the following:

1. For the participant, establish baseline scores and a one-step (one-point)-at-a-time map for broad-based, continuous improvement through this decade and into the next century.
2. Expose blind spots. Even award-winning companies have a few. A low score on any of the sixteen principles raises a flag, which helps combat complacency.
3. Evaluate proposals. If a proposed plan violates any principle, better take a second look.
4. Most important is demonstration: showing the logic, power, and timeliness of management by customer-focused principles. Before examining the principles, let us trace the shift toward principles-based management. Exhibit 2-1 summarizes the evolution.

FROM EDICTS TO PRINCIPLES

Under the poorest mode of management, subordinates take orders from superiors and functional experts. This is management by edict. It is arbitrary, wasteful of the experience and talent of the work force, and lacking in a customer outlook.

EXHIBIT 2–1
Toward Twenty-first Century Management of the Manufacturing Enterprise

Management Modes	Assessments
Management by Edict	Inconsistent, wasteful of talent, and out of touch
Management by Procedures	More consistent and quicker but wasteful of talent; filled with gaps that force-fit poor solutions, adversely affecting customers
Management by Policies	Reflects high-level wisdom but limits broad empowerment and organizational learning
Management by Principles	Customer-focused, employee-driven, data-based; broadly effective, robust, enduring

Standard operating procedures (SOPs) make management more systematic. Procedures remove capriciousness and allow quicker decisions: Just find the best way, authorize and record it, teach it, and expect it to be followed. This is still wasteful of human talents, however, since procedures admit little case-by-case judgment. Worse, procedures-based management has gaps—no procedures to cover certain situations—and it tends to force-fit a procedure where it doesn't belong.

Management by policy partially corrects for these weaknesses. Policies allow latitude within bounds. Those who set policies represent the highest levels of wisdom in the organization. Still, latitude is restricted, and the policies fail to incorporate a wide range of experience. The work force is not yet empowered. Policies are too often misguided and inward looking. Worst of all, policies restrict speedy organizational learning, especially as it relates to customer needs.

Thus, next-decade management must take one more step forward—to management by principles. To be worthy, the principles must take in a full range of world-class innovations. These can be described concisely: customer focused, employee driven, and data (fact) based. The customer orientation must admit both internal and external customers. By employee driven, we mean all employees, acting individually and in teams that cut across functional boundaries. Internal and external data drive continuous improvement in both small increments and big gulps. The underlying rationale is this: Sustained bottom-line success follows when

1. customers are well served
2. employees are fully involved, and
3. actions are based on systematic data about processes, customers, competitors, and best practices.

I am not suggesting there be no edicts, no procedures, and no policies. Of course there should. At times, if no one takes charge and gives a few orders, opportunity slips by. An organization with no procedures will appear random and out of control to the most important target of all: the customer. And policies, if they are fairly stable, can build organizational culture, which helps anchor employees, providers, and customers.

Principles are different. They do not emanate from a select group.

Rather, they are fundamental truths. As such, they procure commitment, deflect skepticism, and endure through thick and thin. IBM's CEO Lou Gerstner put it this way: "[Management by principle] . . . means when a situation arises, you don't go to a manual. You know in your heart and head what to do."[1]

To guide an organization as complex as a manufacturing company, principles must apply to most of the company's business processes. And to make a difference, the principles must be fairly specific. General ones of the customer-is-always-right variety say little. Before presenting the principles, the following points need to be made:

- These are not ethical principles (as are those of Steven Covey[2]) except indirectly. That is, it seems ethically correct—as well as good business—to do what's right for the customer and to build employee competence and achievement.
- This is not intended as breakthrough management. Breakthrough ideas spring forth in mysterious ways. Principles, however, can unify the enterprise in ways that make breakthrough ideas doable.
- These principles do not provide a window to the future (visionary thinking). For every visionary strategy that succeeds (e.g., Motorola's wireless world), there is at least one other, equally admired in its day, that went down in flames (e.g., Control Data's PLATO-based learning). Visionary innovations present themselves often enough. But will the company have the strength and unity to be able to carry them out? Customer-focused principles build that strength and unity.
- These are not principles for managers, per se. They are for everyone, from frontline associates to the most senior executives.
- While the customer's needs and wants are the main focus of the principles, at the same time they meet primary needs of employees, officers, investors, creditors, and suppliers. There is no conflict.
- Principles, including these, apply in nearly every case. But there will be exceptions.
- The principles overlap. Thus, an attribute may be counted more than once. But that is characteristic of good management: Everything connects and intersects.

CUSTOMER-FOCUSED PRINCIPLES

Exhibit 2-2 compresses the sixteen principles and scoring criteria into a four-page array. The following discussion presents each principle, with examples to explain the scoring. Discussion is in extra detail for the far-reaching first principle. The scoring criteria are generally not stated in manufacturing language, since they are intended to apply to all administrative and sales functions, as well as production, and to service organizations as well.

General Principles

Principle 1. Team up with customers; organize by families of customers or products (what customers buy/use).

Under this principle, the conventional way of organizing—everyone hemmed in by functional walls—gets zero points. Forming multifunctional project teams earns one point; getting a client on such teams earns another. Three points requires bringing down the functional walls for key customer or product families. Microsoft's Redmond, Washington, headquarters provides an administrative example. The company's largest family of bought items is computers and workstations, which Microsoft buys at a rate of over one thousand units per month. That kind of volume

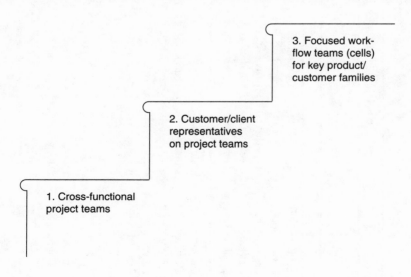

3. Focused work-flow teams (cells) for key product/customer families

2. Customer/client representatives on project teams

1. Cross-functional project teams

EXHIBIT 2-2

Toward Management by Principles: Five-Step Assessment Tool

	Principles of Customer-Focused, Employee-Driven, Data-Based Performance							
	General				Design	Operations		Human Resources
Step	1	2	3	4	5	6	7	8
	Team-up with customers; organize by customer/product family	Capture/use customer, competitive, best-practice information	Continual, rapid improvement in what all customers want	Frontliners involved in change and strategic planning	Cut to the few best components, operations, and suppliers	Cut flow time and distance, start-up/changeover times	Operate close to customers' rate of use or demand	Continually train everybody for their new roles
5	Customer/client representatives for each focused unit	Broad implementation of better-than-best practices for customer service	Sustained yearly QSFV improvement rates of 50% or more in all key processes	Frontline teams help develop strategies and set numeric goals, self-monitored	Average reductions of 90% for all products and services	Cross-functional teams achieve 90% average reductions	Entire flow path for key items synchronized to rate of use or demand	80% certified multiskilled; most also certified trainers
4	Entire enterprise reengineered by customer/product families	All associates involved in customer/competitive/best-practice assessment	95% improvement in Q, S, or F and value (V) in most key processes	Frontline teams plan/implement cross-functionally with other teams	Average reductions of 80% for all products and services	Experts help achieve 80% average reductions	80% of flow path synchronized to rate of use/demand for key items	50% of associates certified as multiskilled; most also certified trainers

3 Focused work-flow teams (cells) for key product/customer families	Systematic customer surveys; full-scale benchmarking for key processes	90% improvement in Q, S, or F in most key processes	Frontline teams continuously plan and implement process improvements	Average reductions of 50% for all items	Associates achieve 50% average reductions across all processes	50% of flow path synchronized to rate of use/demand for key items	25% of associates certified as multiskilled
2 Customer/client representatives on project teams	Gather customer-needs & best-practice data, and non-competitive metrics	80% improvement in Q, S, or F, in a key process	Frontline teams assist in planning and implementing changes in own processes	50% fewer parts/operations and suppliers for all key items	In key processes associates cut get-ready/setup, flow time & distance 50%	Final process synchronized to rate of use/demand—all key products or services	40 hours of just-in-time (train-do, train-do, etc.) training for all associates
1 Cross-functional project teams	Gather customer-satisfaction data and competitive samples and metrics	50% improvement in quality (Q), speed (S) or flexibility (F), in a key process	Frontline associates assist in planning changes in own jobs	50% fewer parts/service operations or suppliers for a key product or service	Train associates in readiness, setup/changeover, queue limitation	Final process synchronized to rate of use/demand for a key product or service	Key managers & teams receive overview training on process improvement

Schonberger & Associates, Inc.

EXHIBIT 2-2 (Continued)

Principles of Customer-Focused, Employee-Driven, Data-Based Performance

	Human Resources	Quality & Process Improvement		Information for Operations and Control		Capacity		Promotion/ Marketing
Step	9	10	11	12	13	14	15	16
	Expand variety of rewards, recognition, and pay	**Continually reduce variation and mishaps**	**Frontline teams record and own process data at workplace**	**Control root causes to cut internal transactions & reporting**	**Align performance measures with customer wants**	**Improve present capacity before new equipment & automation**	**Seek simple, flexible, movable, low-cost equipment in multiples**	**Promote/market/sell every improvement**
5	Profit/gain-sharing; stock/stock options	2.0 Cpk; defects below 10 PPM; rework & lateness cut 99%	25+ mostly team suggestions/associate, mostly implemented by associates	Internal transactions cut 99%; 99% of external transactions by fax/EDI	Second-order metrics (e.g., labor productivity, variances) no longer managed	Operators become technicians; downtime cut 80%	90% of equipment owned by focused teams/cells or is highly flexible/movable	Reverse marketing: Out of strength, you choose whom you sell to
4	Pay for skills/knowledge; team/unit bonuses (no piecework)	1.33 Cpk; defects below 100 parts per million; re-work & lateness cut 95%	10+ mostly team suggestions/associate, mostly implemented by associates	Internal transactions cut 75%; 75% of external transactions by fax/EDI	QSFV are dominant metrics in all processes	Experts teach operators to do repairs; downtime cut 50%	60% of equipment owned by focused teams/cells or is highly flexible/movable	Global/national awards (e.g., Baldrige); over 90% customer retention

3	Investing in employees via training, cross-training, cross-careering	1.0 capability (Cpk)* for key processes; rework, defects, & lateness cut 80%	2 or more suggestions per associate per year	Internal transactions cut 50%; 50% of external transactions by fax/EDI	QSFV are dominant metrics in key support departments	Experts help operators take over their own PM and housekeeping	30% of equipment owned by focused teams/cells or is highly flexible/movable	Registrations, certifications, local awards (ISO-9000, Ford Q1, state award)
2	Variety of low-cost/ no-cost awards to both teams and individuals	Capability analysis for key processes; rework, defects & lateness cut 50%	Frontline teams use process analysis, plot trends	Work-flow, quality, internal scheduling & labor transactions cut 25%	QSFV are dominant metrics in key operations	Preautomation (short flow paths, exact placement, housekeeping, etc.)	10% of equipment "owned" by focused teams/cells or is highly flexible/movable	Positive QSFV trends featured in selling, bids, proposals, ads
1	Systematic, public recognition/ celebration of achievements	Training in & use of "7 basic tools" of statistical process control (SPC)	Training in measurement, visual management, problem-solving teams	Training in fail-safing, process simplification, root cause control	Training in universal customer wants: speed, flexibility, quality, value (QSFV)	Training in total preventive maintenance (TPM) and process simplification	Seek/convert/ upgrade marginal equipment to dedicated or high-flex uses	General advertising slogans ("Quality Is Job One"; "Team Xerox"; etc.)

*or equivalent

Scoring: Score one point for each step, for each of the sixteen principles. Thus, if your organization is at the fifth step for all sixteen principles, the total score is 80—the maximum possible.

Assessment
11–24 points—Eyes open, first steps, early learning
25–38 points—Childhood: Trial and error
39–52 points—Adolescence: Checklists and guidelines
53–66 points—Adulthood: Policies
67–80 points—Maturity: Principles

suggested a product-focused cell. So Microsoft established a co-located team of buyers, receiving associates, and accounts payable clerks just for computers. (This buy-receive-pay unit has since been dissolved and turned over to a reseller—a contractor on Microsoft's premises doing the same thing.) The functional departments—purchasing, receiving, and accounts payable—continued to handle the multitude of lower annual-value items.

By itself Microsoft's focused computer unit would not qualify for three points, since various other administrative processes are still functionally separated. (However, as is the norm in software development shops, Microsoft-Redmond's primary "production" activity is product-family focused: Windows, Excel, Word, etc.)

Reengineering by product families is far more prominent in factories than for administrative processes. Harley-Davidson eliminated the functional shop structure in its Milwaukee engine and transmission factory in the early 1980s. The new structure has layers of product-oriented units. Each provides components to the next layer of internal customers. For example, several mixed-machine cells make gears for other mixed-process cells that make complete gear boxes for lines that assemble transmissions that go to Harley's York, Pennsylvania, motorcycle assembly lines. This structure meets the three-point criteria for plant operations.

Magma International Incorporated, the Canadian auto parts giant, is structured in a way that might qualify for three or four points. Each of its eighty-six plants is product focused and a separate profit center. Its managers have nearly total control, plus very lucrative performance bonuses. CEO Frank Stronach says that the bonus system has made "many of them millionaires."[3]

Sometimes it makes sense for a manufacturer to organize by families of customers instead of products. An example is Microsoft's Dublin software production center serving all of Europe. The center was reorganized into four customer-focused production units—call them focused plants-in-a-plant. One plant is for all English-language customers, another is for German-language customers, another is for French customers, and the fourth is for all other customers. Each of the four plants consists of a few product-focused cells. The customer focus reaches out externally as well. On the supplier side, each plant has its own contract printer; that is, one printer specializes in German-language manuals, one French, and so forth. The printer for all other languages has become adept at running small lots and quick changeovers. For one thing, Microsoft has standardized to a single page size. Also, the printer uses quick-dry inks and has moved folding machines directly against printing presses. On the distribution side, sales is also organized by customer (language group). Thus, nearly the entire European enterprise is aligned by family of customer, which may meet the four-point criteria.

4. Entire enterprise reengineered by customer/product families

Occasionally, a unit can be both customer- and product-focused. For example, if Pope and Talbot (an Oregon-based paper company) got the contract to supply all of Wal-Mart's store-brand disposable diapers, Pope might set up a separate plant-in-a-plant just for that contract. The unit would have all necessary-equipment, direct-labor, staff-support, and customer-service resources and would produce to Wal-Mart's specifications and brand name. The rest of the factory, the high-variety unit, would provide all other diapers for all other customers in a less focused manner.

Principle 2. Capture and apply customer, competitive, and best-practice information.

This principle aims at tapping three vital sources of external information:

1. From the customer, the question is, what products and services maximize satisfaction and minimize dissatisfaction? The firm gets this information in two main ways:

- *Through customer surveys.* Solectron's customer satisfaction index (see Chapter 1) is a good example.
- *Through early and continuing customer involvement.* In effect, the customer helps design and improve the firm's products and services. Boeing's 777 commercial airplane is a case in point. Customers— including British Airways, United Airlines, Japan Airlines, and All Nippon Airlines—had permanent representatives on Boeing's 235 design-build teams. Thus, for the 777 product, Boeing gets good points for customer linkages. Boeing has a reputation, however, for

being insular in other ways: The company did not mount an early, thorough competitive analysis of its European competitor, Airbus Industrie, and it has not engaged extensively in benchmarking outside of its industry. For example, Boeing's current total-quality management and just-in-time initiatives lagged those of other prestigious U.S. companies by nearly ten years. So Boeing as a whole is not at the five-point level on use of customer information.

> 5. Broad implementation of better-than-best practices for customer service

2. The second source of external information is competitive analysis. This is old stuff: Collect samples of competitors' products, reverse-engineer, and categorize and employ the results. Unfortunately, in most companies the product-development people see and study the competitive samples, but nobody else does. In my experience people nearly always overestimate their own company's strengths and underestimate those of their competitors. This breeds a deadly result: complacency. The best counterweight is for all employees to be confronted with competitors' products. I described how this is done at Du Pont's Brevard, North Carolina, plant in another book[4].

3. Best practices, the third kind of external information, go beyond products. The idea is to find and benchmark best ways of doing anything, from generating new products to processing payrolls to negotiating contracts to maintaining buildings. Since competitors may not be best at anything, going outside one's own industry is a must. Xerox, the originator of benchmarking, went to mail-order company L.L. Bean, where they learned improved methods of running a shipping warehouse.[5]

Gathering external information is one thing. Earning maximum points on this principle requires applying that information to good advantage.

Principle 3. Dedicate to continual, rapid improvement in quality, response time, flexibility, and value.

Whereas Principle 2 zeros in on product specifications, this one aims at success in providing the products. And while customers' product preferences vary over time, the targets of excellence in providing the products do not. That is, all customers want ever better quality, ever quicker response, ever greater flexibility, and ever higher value.

Quicker response includes time-to-market, supply-chain reaction time, flow time through the support offices, cycle time through the plant, delivery time to the external customer, and service recovery time when things go wrong. A measure of human resource flexibility is number of jobs mastered; another is the firm's ability to grow and shrink labor capacity as demand rises and falls. Equipment flexibility is measurable as well: speed of setup or changeover, movability of equipment, and reaction time in bringing on new capacity.

General Motors' stamping plant in McKeesport, Pennsylvania, offers an example of a three-point attainment. The plant had been on GM's close-down list. It was small and far from most of its Detroit-area auto-assembly customers, management and labor didn't get along, and performance was below standard. But in 1988 management, under plant manager Bud Bartell, the United Auto Workers, under shop chairman Donn Hicks, and the Pittsburgh community worked out a plant-saving strategy. It was to shift from producing for new-car assembly to the aftermarket. Instead of long runs of a small number of body items, it would be short runs for many more auto models. The key was quick changeover of the massive tandem presses that stamp out auto body parts from steel coil (see Exhibit 2-3). By slashing changeover time, the presses could shift from one part number to another easily and make each in small quantities.[6] The old changeover time was about twenty-three hours. That fell to nine minutes and forty-one seconds, which was the winning time in a nationwide competition called the Die Change Challenge.[7] That much improvement in flexibility (quick changeover on all of its stamping lines) easily meets the criteria for three points on Principle 3.

> 3. 90% improvement in quality, speed, or flexibility in most key processes

Earning one, two, or three points on this principle requires improvements in quality, speed, *or* flexibility. Value, at the four-point level, is a tougher standard. When customers shop for value, they look at how much of several attributes (quality, speed, flexibility, and more) they get for their money. Putting it conversely, value

EXHIBIT 2–3
Tandem stamping press line at General Motors, McKeesport, Pa.

Die sleds on rails permit fast die change: Push old die sets out and new ones in.

is a new code word associated with removal of non-value-adding wastes of all kinds—a never-ending activity.

The criteria for one, two, three, and four points call for percentage improvements; it is left to the company to decide on the time interval. Five points, however, require 50 percent sustained yearly improvements. It's not impossible. Kiyoshi Suzaki cites an example.[8] At Japanese automaker Toyo Kogyo (Mazda), car production per person increased by about 50 percent per year from 1972 through 1981. Capital expenditure per person and work-in-process inventories fell by similar impressive rates. Such results cannot occur without sustained improvements in quality, speed, flexibility, and value (QSFV).

Principle 4. Frontline employees involved in change and strategic planning—to achieve unified purpose.

This is the last principle in the general category. Many companies will meet the one-point criteria: associates assisting in planning changes in their own jobs. The five-point level, on the other hand, requires teams of associates to be involved in strategic planning. One company comes close to meeting this criterion: Zytec Corporation, 1991 winner of a Baldrige

> 5. Frontline teams translate company plans into numeric goals, self-monitored

award. External data (Principle 2) provide the grist for management teams to formulate a five-year strategic plan. Then one-fifth of the work force, from every corner of the firm, critique the plan and, later, translate it into measurable monthly goals for themselves.[9] Overall, I would probably give Zytec about a 4 on this principle, marking them down only a bit on the four- and three-point criteria.

Design

Principle 5. Cut to the few best components, operations, and suppliers.

The design category has just one principle. It is cutting out wasteful practices in product design and delivery. Guidance on waste-free product design comes from Professors Boothroyd and Dewhurst (Englishmen who migrated to the University of Rhode Island). They were the first to codify design for manufacture and assembly (DFMA) concepts such that they could be taught to product developers. Above all, their concepts call for fewer components—in total and in variety.[10] The impact of DFMA is profound, since poor product designs have snowball effects on cost and performance through all later processes.

In an earlier book I extended the Boothroyd-Dewhurst methodology to service processes (e.g., administrative support offices of manufacturers): thirteen design-for-service-operations (DFSO) guidelines.[11] Hallmark Cards offers a good example. Time-to-market for a new greeting card had been two years, as designs bounced from function to function. A card's many-digit stock number had to be entered thirteen times on sixteen documents—a violation of several DFSO guidelines (e.g., minimize number of service operations and number of components). The chances of entering a stock number correctly all thirteen times for card after card were zero. When a number would be entered wrong, some department might merrily work on last year's obsolete card—or a store might receive a big shipment of Valentine's Day cards when Mother's Day was approaching!

Hallmark's Shoebox line of cards was to be the pilot project, making a transition to focused, quick-response management. (Hallmark had sent large numbers of people to my public seminars, where they heard about an earlier, seventeen-item version of the customer-focused principles. The company produced hundreds of pocket-sized laminated cards listing those seventeen principles.) Instead of having artists in one building, verse writers in another, and production in still another (perhaps in a different city), the Shoebox team moved into a single building. A dozen verse writers, a group of artists, several graphics terminals, and administrative processes shared a floor. Result: Stock number entries fell from thirteen to one and documents from sixteen to five. Shoebox's time-to-market fell to about three months.[12] Give Hallmark-Shoebox, say, four points on this principle.

4. Average reductions of 80% for all products and services

Since many services and goods are bought rather than "made," sourcing is another element of the principle. Just as minimizing components cuts many wastes in product and service designs, minimizing the number of suppliers cuts many wastes in purchasing. When there are too many suppliers, there is no time to establish a firm partnership with any of them.

Operations

Principle 6. Cut flow time, distance, start-up, and changeover times all along the chain of customers.

In operations the old management emphasis was on productivity and efficiency. Speed and flexibility counted less (if at all). This principle places emphasis on several measures of speed and flexibility, which embrace much of the just-in-time (JIT) methodology. Training (one-point level) gets things rolling. Maturity (five-point level) requires 90 percent reductions, achieved by teams of associates.

The eighty-four companies or units qualifying for the honor roll in my

1986 book *World Class Manufacturing* had to have achieved at least an 80 percent (fivefold) reduction in production cycle time. Some had achieved 90 and 95 percent. One of the eighty-four is Nashua Corporation (seventy-sixth on the honor roll), a New Hampshire–based maker of toner for copiers. (Nashua had achieved a measure of fame in the early 1980s as the first company—in the new era—with the good sense to hire Dr. W. Edwards Deming.) Having transformed factory operations, Nashua then went to work on other parts of its value chain. With the aid of consultant Dr. Thomas Billesbach,[13] Nashua cut its order-entry cycle time by about 98 percent (from eight days to one hour). If its approach is employee driven and includes other administrative processes (e.g., purchasing, invoicing, engineering changes), Nashua deserves nearly five points on the sixth principle.

> 5. Cross-functional teams achieve 90% average reductions

Principle 7. Operate close to customers' rate of use or demand.

The second principle under operations also is JIT oriented. The snarl of uncoordinated, unsynchronized flow paths that characterizes yesteryear's operations is out. In comes synchronization, first for main deliverables (one-point level) and ultimately for everything (five points).

Synchronization takes two main forms: (1) Produce and deliver in step with actual up and down sales, which minimizes inventories. This requires extraordinary flexibility and often cannot be maintained back through early processes such as machining, molding, and casting. Matching sales spikes tends to be costly since it causes demands on capacity to yo-yo. (2) Produce at the rate of recent average demand. In this case, finished inventories grow when demand falls and shrink when demand rises. At the same time, average-rate production simplifies administration (lowers overheads), quiets demands on capacity (cutting costs), and makes planning easy upstream and down.

The Bernard Manufacturing Division of Dover Industries in Beecher, Illinois (making welding guns) takes the first approach: To synchronize production with demand, production control delivers latest sales figures to the assembly lines four times daily. For key items this triggers the factory's pull system, which includes streamlined delivery of parts from the stockroom to assembly via plastic kanban bins. Quick machine setup provides flexibility. At Bernard manufacturing, one setup time fell from forty-five minutes to five seconds. In addition, focused cells reduced the total flow distance from five hundred feet to seventy-five feet.[14] These achievements add up to about three points on this principle.

> 3. 50% of flow path synchronized to rate of use/demands

The second approach befits products that have steadier, or at least higher-volume demand. OPW Fueling Components identified two such "star" products. One (in four models) has enough demand that its schedule easily converted to a daily rate for each model, fixed for a month. The other product (in two models) was constrained by a long setup at a feeder process where castings are machined for assembly. The setup disruption translates into a less-than-daily-rate schedule: Make a fixed quantity of one model in the first days of the week and a fixed quality of the other in the last days.

Some situations are natural for rate-based, synchronized operations. Charley Lackey, a professor at the University of Texas at El Paso, and I spotted that kind of situation while touring a factory together. It was a Johnson and Johnson plant producing hospital gowns and allied items. These are uncomplex products sold in large volumes, products that go through just four processes, including a trek across the Mexican border and back. Charley and I could not contain ourselves. We took the words out of each other's mouths in suggesting to J&J managers how rate-based processing would work.

Human Resources

Principle 8. Continually enhance human resources through cross-training, job and career-path rotation, and improvements in health, safety, and security.

The first of two principles on human resources both develops and protects. It calls for a continuing high commitment to training—in process-improvement methods as well as job skills. The Institute for Productivity Improvement, based in Oakland, specializes in teaching process-im-provement methods to employees of, typically, small manufacturers. In-stead of concentrated training—too much in too little time—the group employs the just-in-time training method (two-point level): Teach a topic (e.g., quick setup), send the class back to their work places to do it, then review their successes and difficulties first thing next time the class meets. Launch a new topic, and the learning cycle repeats. Leonard Bertain, president of the institute, has written a book describing the often spec-tacular results of this kind of training.[15]

> 2. 40 hours of just-in-time (train-do, train-do, etc.) training for all associates

The protective side of the principle requires upgrading employee health, safety, and security. Failure to develop and protect human re-sources is wasteful of the company's prime asset. In Chapter 9 we exam-ine a scenario that shows the value of this principle even for businesses whose competitiveness seems to hinge on the opposite—spending as lit-tle as possible on its human resources.

Principle 9. Expand the variety of rewards, recognition, pay, and celebration—to match the expanded variety of employee contributions.

In today's superior organizations employees don't just make products and provide services. They master multiple skills and continually improve their own processes. Since employees contribute in many ways, they should re-ceive in many ways: a basket of values. (Instead of emphasizing rewards be-stowed by the employer, I prefer to think of values employees derive from their employment. Empowered employees create many of their own valued inducements rather than depend on management to deliver them.)

The scoring scale for this principle tops out at five points for an ex-panded array of monetary rewards. This does not mean that money is a more effective motivator than other values or rewards. Rather, variable pay mechanisms are the most expensive kind of reward, the most sensitive to fairness issues, and the most difficult to install. Public recognition and praise, on the other hand, are easy to do and thus are at the one-point level. Easy, yes; widespread, no. Rela-tively few companies do this well. (My re-

> 1. Systematic public recognition/celebration of achievements

EXHIBIT 2–4
Wall of Fame and Team Improvement Display
Hewlett-Packard, Malaysia

search shows, however, that companies tend to score themselves high on this principle—higher than they should, in my estimation.) Photos from Hewlett-Packard's Penang, Malaysia, components facility (Exhibit 2-4) show two excellent examples. One is an attractive wall of fame; the other is a display of best ideas from improvement teams (such displays are in each area of the plant).

Quality and Process Improvement

Principle 10. Continually reduce variation and mishaps.

The tenth and eleventh principles concern quality and process improvement. The tenth captures the heart and soul of Deming's thinking: Use statistics, measurements, and facts to drive out variation of all kinds. For plant operations, the process capability index, C_{pk}, captures—numerically—the capability of a process to stay in control and close to the desired specification. Nypro, the large injection molder headquartered in Clinton, Massachusetts, claims a C_{pk} index of 2.0 on all new designs, which equates to 3.4 parts per million defective.[16]

A judgmental, nonnumeric equivalent of C_{pk} will do for less concrete processes, such as administrative work. (After two years of applying its "$C_{pk}2$" campaign to design-related areas, Nypro's plan was to extend "the C_{pk} philosophy to . . . paperwork processes, eliminating attributes such as visual quality criteria.")[17] Metrics that capture variation in process outputs include defects, rework, and lateness.

Generally, quality-award-winning companies (European Quality Award, Baldrige Award, etc.) will score at or near the four-point level on Principle 10. Motorola, a Baldrige winner in 1988, hasn't stopped improving. "At some Motorola factories quality is so high that they've stopped counting defects per million and started working on defects per *billion*."[18] The improvement process has taken root in administrative processes as well. Error rates on billing invoices for domestic pagers fell from 450 to 9, out of some 20,000 invoices—a rate of 450 PPM.[19]

4. 1.33 C_{pk}, defects below 100 PPM, rework & lateness cut 95%

Steep reductions in lateness became fairly common in the last decade and continue to the present. A few of the many examples: Kone Oy Liftworks, Hyvinkaa, Finland (1984 result), 93 percent reduction; United Electric Controls, Watertown, Massachusetts (Shingo Prize, 1991), 86 percent; Timken Company, Bucyrus, Ohio (*Industry Week* Best Plant, 1992), 92 percent; Unisys, Government Systems Division, Pueblo, Colorado (*Industry Week* Best Plant, 1993), 100 percent on time for over four years.

Principle 11. Frontline teams record and own process data at the workplace.

It is often said that responsibility without authority is hollow. If all employees and teams are to take responsibility for their processes (the highest form of human resource development), then they must own the data pertaining to those processes. This means that managers, engineers, and other experts have to give up that ownership. Or at least, they must have secondary, not primary, access to the data.

At the three-, four-, and five-point levels on this principle, employee suggestions and their implementation become concrete measures of process ownership. I've found, however, that many admired companies do not formally count or account for employee/ team suggestions. Continuous improvement is ingrained, they say, so why bother formalizing it? The appropriate answer is the well-known maxim, *You get what you measure.* Putting it differently, the loosey-goosey approach can work for a while. But it will run down and lose steam before long if not formalized.

> 5. 25+ mostly team suggestions per associate, mostly implemented by associates

Some of the highest numbers of suggestions in the Western world come from two Baldrige award winners: Milliken and Company (fifty-two per employee in 1991) and Wainwright Industries (sixty-five per employee in 1994). (The typical poor-excuse-for-a-suggestion-system must be extensively repaired in order to achieve these kinds of numbers. More on this in Chapter 9.) These companies may fall a bit short on the part about "mostly implemented by associates"; still, they deserve close to five points on Principle 11.

Information for Operations and Control

Principle 12. Control root causes of cost and performance, thereby reducing internal transactions and reporting; simplify external communications.

This and the next principle espouse revised thinking about control of operations: Control does not depend on more intricate measures and reports. In fact, common notions of control—and controllers—conflict with employee ownership and root-cause management.

Isn't it true that most internal transactions arise because things are too complex, random, failure prone, or variable? Quality management takes out variation and failures and the many transactions and reports that go with them. Lean manufacturing cuts part-number entries, work orders, move tickets, labor transactions, schedule revisions, expediting documents, engineering changes, storage and inventory transactions, purchase orders, and more. Real-time, visual management of root causes takes over from management by aggregated reports.

For example, in the 1980s Applicon removed its star product from the muddle of other products (CAD/CAM equipment); computer transactions fell from thirty thousand to eight hundred per month. MK Electric, in England, adopted rate-based scheduling for its key products (electric plugs and receptacles), cutting its scheduling transactions from sixteen hundred to one per week. More recently, Johnson & Johnson's Sherman, Texas, plant (medical and personal-care products) adopted kanban, eliminating all work-flow transactions. These examples easily meet the two-point standard.

> 2. Work-flow, quality, internal-scheduling, and labor transactions cut 25%

Today, those companies may have also simplified communications with external partners, meeting criteria for three or four points. The means are electronic data interchange, fax, and various kinds of data links. These technologies convey such data as requirements to suppliers, point-of-sale and after-sale service data from customers, digital design information to design partners, and funds transfers among all parties.

Principle 13. Align performance measures with universal customer wants: quality, speed, flexibility, and value (QSFV).

Under the third principle we saw points awarded for demonstrated improvements in QSFV. Here, however, points are for installing QSFV as the dominant, visible measures of success in operations. Here is a test: Ask your frontline people what they are measured on. If they don't mention quality, speed, flexibility, or value, no points.

Sentrol Corporation, a Portland, Oregon, producer of monitored security systems, has the right idea. Each of thirteen product-focused cells

EXHIBIT 2–5
Performance Charts for a Cell at Sentrol Corp.

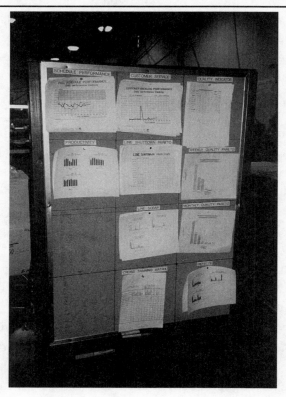

Left column: Pull-Schedule Performance, Productivity

Middle column: Customer-Backlog Performance, Line-Shutdown Pareto, Line Scrap, Cross-Training Matrix

Right column: Quality Indicator, Weekly Quality Pareto, Monthly Quality Pareto, Defects

has its own visual display of results. (See Exhibit 2-5.) It includes a cross-training matrix, defects graphs, line-scrap graphs, a monthly quality Pareto chart, a weekly quality Pareto, a line shutdown Pareto (Paretos show causes, by frequency), a quality indicator, a customer-service graph, and a schedule-performance graph.

These charts, though small (bigger charts have bigger impacts), rate nearly three points (four requires the same kinds of measures in administrative offices). I say nearly rather than a solid three points because speed is

> 3. Quality, speed, flexibility, and value are dominant, visible metrics in key operations

missing. Also, Sentrol gets marked down a bit for including a productivity chart. Productivity is at a higher level of aggregation than the other factors and therefore is less manageable. Keeping a factor that cannot be managed in prominent view diverts attention from root causes.

As the customer-oriented metrics rise in importance, the old inward-looking ones, such as productivity (also efficiency, utilization, and cost variance) fade. At the five-point level the inward-focused criteria are relegated to the waste bin. This may seem extreme, especially to the many managers who cut their teeth on such measures. In Chapter 5 these and other metrics are grouped into four categories: root cause, first-order, second-order, and bottom (and top) line. Effective management of operations focuses on root-cause analysis and first-order results. Higher-order metrics are overly aggregated, and attempts to manage them often have contrary effects.

Capacity

Principle 14. Improve present equipment and human work before considering new equipment and automation.

This and the next principle concern capacity—the firm's human and physical resources. Too often companies treat expensive equipment like kids treat a new toy: Buy it, wreck it, and beg for the next neat toy.

That's where the human resource comes in. The object is to defer the next round of costly equipment and automation. Doing so requires that well-trained equipment operators and technicians follow systematic guidelines of two kinds:

1. Elevate the cost-efficiency of human processes by employing process simplification and standardization. This includes the so-called 5 S's. The S's stand for five Japanese words, but Western companies have chosen their own meanings (see Boeing's, below). Just call it industrial housekeeping.

2. Get more out of existing equipment by practicing high levels of equipment maintenance and eliminating wastes in operation (loading, unloading, testing, setting up, etc.).

Implementation of this principle, at the one-, two-, and three-point levels, is visually apparent in Boeing's welded-duct plant in Auburn, Washington. "TPM [total preventive maintenance] Communications Boards" are mounted throughout. They list "autonomous" maintenance schedules, record downtime and minutes of maintenance meetings, monitor maintenance calls, and specify lubrication and inspection points. Operators maintain their own equipment and keep everything spic-and-span. Everything is labeled, even coat hooks. Painted silhouettes of brooms, mops, and other cleaning implements show where to hang or clamp them to the wall, and all are neatly placed in designated places when not in use. Display boards in every work group extol the 5 S's and show photos of proper and improper housekeeping. (The same displays monitor performance metrics, such as quality, delivery, cost, and customer information.) Boeing's version of the S's are sorting, sweeping, simplifying, standardizing, and self-discipline. At first, the unionized work force reacted negatively to the 5 S's, saying, "It's not my job. My job is making parts." Gradually, some attitudes changed, and then peer pressure took over. Now everyone pitches in to make the plant a showcase of orderliness. Give the plant a firm three points—not yet four, since it takes years of involvement for operators to acquire the expertise of a maintenance technician.

3. Experts teach operators to do repairs; downtime cut 50%

Principle 15. Seek simple, flexible, movable, low-cost, readily available equipment and work facilities—in multiples, one for each product/customer family.

Decisions on capital equipment should not be made in a vacuum. But too often, they have been. The manufacturing engineers doing the choosing justify a fast, complex, monster of a machine that can handle all the product-line's projected demands for the next three years. Not considered are the following customer considerations:

- Customers order many items in the product line at the same time, but the big, fast machine can only make one at a time.
- Each time the behemoth gets set up to run a certain item, many line and staff specialties are involved. So it is uneconomical to produce small amounts at about the same rate as customer usage.
- Large-lot production fills stockrooms and warehouses based on demand guesswork—habitually wrong. There usually is plenty of stock of the unpopular items; best-sellers are on back order.
- Such costly equipment cannot sit idle. So it runs all the time, requiring an overhead empire to store and manage its frequent excesses, further raising costs that are passed on to customers.
- Getting full usage and output from the equipment tempts scrimping on maintenance, which invites breakdowns and undependable service to customers and, contrarily, less output.
- Single pieces of each kind of equipment can't be dispersed and owned by teams operating multiple customer- or product-focused units, the aim of Principle 1.

The ideal is affordable equipment in multiples. Affordable usually means smaller and easier to set up, maintain, and relocate, which is increasingly important as product life cycles continue to shrink.

To be highly customer responsive, the equipment must be flexible— either quick-change or no change. Amtico Limited, a Coventry, England–based producer of premium floor tile, offers examples. Under the tutelage of Phil Stride (a World Class International consultant), the tile-making resources have been reengineered into cells. One type of cell makes high-variety products in low volumes; operators go for flexibility, diligently attacking times to change over from one tile to another. Another type of movable cell makes a single highly popular tile; the equip-

> 4. 60% of equipment owned by focused teams/cells or is highly flexible/movable

ment is dedicated, and highly volume-flexible: When demand surges, run it more hours per day or week; when demand flags, run fewer hours. Amtico may qualify at the four-point level on this principle.

Promotion and Marketing

Principle 16. Promote, market, and sell your organization's increasing capability and competence—every improvement (the results of the other fifteen principles).

Marketing students learn the four P's: product, price, place, and promotion. Customers today seek more than those four. They want continuously improving quality, speed, flexibility, and value. They also want partnerships, open communications, membership on cross-company improvement teams, and dependability. Customer-focused principles, thoroughly applied across the firm, provide these customer wants. Thus, marketers and salespeople may go forth armed with new inducements: evidence of high rates of involvement and improvement on each of the preceding fifteen principles.

Salespeople for the U.S. subsidiary of Lego Systems, Incorporated (Danish maker of toy building blocks) have already experienced the shift in emphasis. Lego's Enfield, Connecticut, sales unit has established quick-response customer partnerships, which feature point-of-sale data shared via electronic data interchange and advance shipping notices. Mogens Jessen, vice president, logistics, describes the effects: "It used to be that salesmen called on customers and talked about promotions, inventory replenishment, and inventory levels. Now staff at the executive level on down sits down with customers and discusses cooperation, including logistics."[20]

The ultimate achievement, at the five-point level, is when the company can pick and choose customers—rather than their doing the choosing. Nypro (mentioned earlier for its C_{pk} emphasis) quickly comes to mind. In the early 1980s Nypro had over six hundred customers for its injection-molded plastic products. By 1993 that number had been pared—deliberately—to thirty-one. Nypro's cherry-picking strategy is to concentrate its marketing "on customers with a potential of providing a million dollars' worth of business in two years." In partnering up this way, Nypro asks the customer, "'Where do you want your molder?' and then Nypro goes there ([setting up its plant] within 100 miles of the customer)."[21] Nypro aggressively promotes its excellence, especially its quality, flexibility, and responsiveness (two-point level); has various customers' highest degree of certification (three-point level) and high customer retention (four-point level). Nypro may deserve close to five points on this principle.

> 5. Reverse marketing: Out of strength, you choose whom to sell to

The sixteen principles just described have evolved over the past ten years. They have been presented in various forms in my books, articles, and public seminars. My advocacy of them, however, has been muted. There was so much to do—the entire TQM or WCM agenda. Companies needed a decade to absorb it all. Now it is time to raise the bar. The principles do just that. At the same time, they reduce the confusion over multiple management initiatives by providing a common easy-to-respect goal linkage: the customer.

The following chapter presents data from managers of over 130 manufacturing organizations that have scored their units using the principles.

3

Best Manufacturers: How They Rate

"I am embarrassed at how low our score is. And we thought we were making progress."

Those words were penned in the remarks block on the scoring sheet of one participant in the management-by-principles research. That company's score was 8.5. By the scoring key printed on each scoring sheet (Exhibit 3-1), the company had not yet opened its eyes and taken its first steps. Another participant—one that scored nearly as low—put it this way: "We aren't even born yet."

There is purpose behind the sobering words in the scoring scale. Prior to about 1980, probably no company would have scored as many as twenty-five points (except for some early achievers in Japan). Few would even score above ten. The many concepts underlying the sixteen principles simply were not on anybody's agenda then. In many cases,

EXHIBIT 3–1

Scoring Scale—Management by Customer-Focused Principles

Assessment (one point for each step, each principle):
11–24 points—Eyes open, first steps, early learning
25–38 points—Childhood: Trial and error
39–52 points—Adolescence: Checklists and guidelines
53–66 points—Adulthood: Policies
67–80 points—Maturity: Principles

---

business practices were nearly opposite to the principles. Take Principle 12, "Control root causes to cut internal transactions and reporting," for example. Under 1970s thinking, control called for tracking everything that happened to a part, a process, or a resource, which generated hundreds, sometimes thousands, of tracking transactions per day. Today, after years of simplifying flows, standardizing parts, removing process variation, and converting to visual tracking, we get more control with a trickle of transactions.

Thus, "eyes open" may be taken literally: We see an altered competitive world—sharply tilted toward simplicity, root-cause control, and a customer outlook. The research shows that, even today, many of the largely handpicked participants have only reached the eyes-open scoring range. For the 130 participating manufacturing organizations, the following shows distribution of scores:

Not born yet, 0–10 points	3 organizations
Eyes open, first steps, 11–24 points	41 organizations
Childhood, 25–38 points	43 organizations
Adolescence, 39–52 points	38 organizations
Adulthood, 53–66 points	5 organizations
Maturity, 67–80 points	no organizations

The scoring criteria are tough and were so intended. The objective is to provide guidance for step-by-step improvement into the next century. Besides summary results—useful for benchmarking—we sent all participants a two-page guide for taking the next steps (see Exhibit 3-2). In following the guide, an improvement task force develops a plan for earning one more point on each principle each year. To be doable, the plan must identify and deal with obstacles.

In the remainder of the chapter, we look more closely at the research project and the results, by category. Included are tables listing names of 127 participating manufacturers (the list omits the three scoring less than eleven points).

RESEARCH PROJECT

The 127 participants have been grouped in the following ways:

- Size: 57 manufacturers with 500 or more employees and 70 with less than 500.
- General industry type: 24 process, 103 nonprocess
- World location: 79 U.S. and 48 non-U.S. (16 South Africa, 9 Mexico, 7 Australia, 5 Ireland, 4 U.K., 4 Canada, 1 France, 1 Netherlands, 1 Brazil); multinational (61) and national (62)
- Industrial sectors—7 of them, such as electronics; and liquids, gases, grains, and powders

The details—industrial-sector data and names of participants in each—come later in the chapter. First, we look at major groupings of participants, how they scored, and what the scores might mean.

Scores, by Category

Exhibit 3-3 shows average scores for each category. The size category refers to the participating unit, which may be a whole company, a division, a site, or a self-contained unit on a site. Of the seventy small units, over half have two hundred or fewer employees. Many of these were one-plant companies. They tend to be in an early growth stage of life and have not had a lot of time to ponder new management ideas. That may partly explain the lower average scores for smaller participants. Otherwise, one would expect smaller units, less encumbered by bureaucracy, to perform better.

Process and non-process industries scored the same. What this says is that the process industries—from foods to detergents to chemicals—may be catching up after a late start. The early birds were in consumer electronics and automotive businesses. People from those industries were dominant in my own public and in-company events in the early 1980s. Then in the latter years of the eighties, half my business was with process-industry firms. Now companies like Milliken (textiles and chemicals) and Globe Metallurgical (metal products) are receiving Baldrige awards, Union Carbide Ethyleneamines and Exxon Baytown (chemicals) are awarded Shingo prizes, and Esso Chemical Canada gets publicity for application of new-wave managerial accounting.[1]

By location, U.S. manufacturers scored higher (33.9) than non-U.S.

EXHIBIT 3–2
Steps Toward World-Class Maturity
Assessing Your Organization's Steps Toward Customer-Focused Principles

Directions:

After each of the eight categories (each containing one to four principles), do the following:

1. For your organizational unit, judge your current number of points (probably zero, if no prior training and implementation). Your unit may be a whole company, a business unit, or a site—not a functional department. State here what the organizational unit is.

_____

2. Estimate attainable points in next twelve months.

3. Briefly state a rough plan for getting there, including likely obstacles to overcome.

4. After all eight categories (sixteen principles), total your points and see where you stand (early learning, trial-and-error, etc.)

	Current Points	Attainable in 12 months
I. General		

   3. Continual, rapid improvement in what all customers want.
   4. Frontliners involved in change and strategic planning.

Plan:

II. Design
   5. Cut to the few best components, operations, and suppliers.

Plan:

III. Operations
   7. Operate close to customers' rate of use or demand.

Plan:

EXHIBIT 3–2 (Continued)

	Current	*Attainable in*
	Points	*12 months*

IV. Human Resources
    8. Continually train everybody for their new roles.
    9. Expand variety of rewards, recognition, and pay.

Plan:

V. Quality & Process Improvement
    10. Continually reduce variation and mishaps.
    11. Frontline teams record and own process data at workplace.

Plan:

VI. Information for Operations and Improvement (Control)
    12. Control root causes to cut internal transactions and reporting.
    13. Align performance measures with universal customer wants.

Plan:

VII. Capacity
    14. Improve present capacity before new equipment & automation.
    15. Seek simple, flexible, movable, low-cost equipment in multiples.

Plan:

VIII. Promotion and Customer Presentation

Plan:

Total points, all 16 principles _____ _____

EXHIBIT 3–3
Average Scores, by Category

Category (number of sites)	Average Scores
Size:	
Large (57)	34.7
Small (70)	30.8
Type:	
Process (24)	31.6
Nonprocess (103)	32.8
Location:	
U.S. (79)	33.9
Non-U.S. (48)	30.5
South Africa (16)	30.5
(five scores under 20, but four over 40)	
Europe: Ireland, U.K., France, Netherlands (11)	24.6
Canada, Australia (11)	24.1
Mexico, Brazil (10)	39.3
Multinational (63)	37.2
National (64)	28.0

(30.5). The non-U.S. contributors, however, are only from English-language countries, or multinational companies located elsewhere whose business is done in English. Nonetheless, U.S. companies *should* score higher. They were under the gun—that is, the quality-driven Japanese export onslaught—first.

Repeal of apartheid laws brought international competition—and people like me—to South Africa. The country's average score (30.5) is respectable but suggests that South African industry still has work to do.

On the other hand, the Latin American participants scored exceptionally high (39.3). Nine are Mexican and eight are maquiladoras on Mexico's border with the United States. (The maquiladora trade law allows a U.S. company to send its fabricated parts to Mexico for final assembly and get the assemblies back for sale in the U.S. market without tariff charges.) I was not surprised. I have visited about twenty maquila plants and found them generally more advanced in world-class excellence than their sister and parent plants in the U.S. A probable reason is, no bad habits: The 1400-odd maquila plants are still young. The parent companies had the opportunity to do it right in Mexico and took it. (The *aver-*

age maquila would probably score low on the principles. However, above-average plants were the target of the research, as well as the kinds of companies that are usually on my plant visitation itineraries.)

Another factor may be plain determination. Doing well in the shadow of big, rich America is likely to be doubly satisfying to the young Mexican managers and engineers that run the plants. I've noted the same thing in Ireland—which has the U.K. as the chip on its shoulder. Ireland's many multinational plants, run by young, well-educated managers, tend to be top-notch.

As it happens, the few Irish manufacturers participating in this research were mostly locals rather than multinationals. Their scores (in the European group) were generally low. This fits with the notable differences overall between multinationals (37.2) and nationals (28.0). It stands to reason that companies competing in multiple countries will have an edge. Locals compete, but usually not with the world's best.

High and Lower Scores

The top eighty-six participants—those scoring over twenty-four points—might be called *flexibly equipped, synchronized, high-recognition manufacturers.* This is a composite description of what the top eighty-six say they are good at—their top three scores. That is, their strengths are in (average scores in parenthesis)

- Gravitating toward flexible equipment in multiples—Principle 15 (3.1)
- Getting synchronized with the customer chain—Principle 7 (3.0)
- Recognizing and praising contributions of their associates—Principle 9 (3.3)

One company in the top eighty-six that fits this pattern to a tee is Precor, a Redmond, Washington–based manufacturer of aerobic fitness equipment. Precor's scores were 4.5 or higher on all three of those principles. There are exceptions. For example, another manufacturer among the top eighty-six (a well-known firm that prefers to go unnamed) scored very high on Principle 15 but very low on 7 and 9. Regarding 7, an executive stated that "on some jobs the schedules are changed thirty times." With frustration, he said, "If the [MRP] system doesn't fix the problem, we should just go off-line and schedule ourselves."

On the other hand, the top eighty-six, on average, are weakest (lowest scores) in

- Capturing and using external data—Principle 2 (2.1)
- Measured improvement in quality, speed, flexibility, and value—Principle 3 (1.9)
- Reducing parts and suppliers—Principle 5 (1.8)
- Reducing variation and mishaps—Principle 10 (2.2)
- Cutting transactions and controlling through simplicity and root-cause correction—Principle 12 (2.0)
- Aligning performance measures with universal customer wants—Principle 13 (2.3)
- TPM and process simplification—Principle 14 (2.3)

Let's take a closer look at what these overall results suggest.

Capacity. The capacity principles, 14 and 15, show the sharpest contrast. Scores on Principle 14 are among the lowest and on 15 among the highest. In other words, manufacturers are doing well on the physical (15) side—dedicating some equipment to focused teams and high-volume uses and upgrading other equipment for flexibility. But they are not doing well in equipment operation and maintenance (14). A typical explanation comes from Wheelabrator (whose shot-blast parts cleaning machines are generic: manufacturers "wheelabrator" their metal parts). The company scored high overall, especially on 15. Regarding 14, manufacturing director Robert Anderson explains that employees in some of the cells are responsible for "doing PMs" (e.g., check the oil) every morning. But the activities are not documented, not formalized. Part of the reason for lagging in this and a few other principles is that business has been very good, which stretches management resources thin. Upgrading and systematizing a TPM effort are on Wheelabrator's to-do-soon list.[2]

Externally critical data. Three low-scoring principles, 2, 3, and 13, deal with externally important information. First, participating manufacturers are not zealous about gathering outside information—from customers, via competitive analysis, and through benchmarking (Principle 2); this is the only principle on which there were no scores of five—and there was only one score of four. Second, achievements in criteria important to their customers, namely, quality, speed, flexibility, and value (Principle 3)—are unimpressive. And third, for the most part, they have not elevated the customer-sensitive measures (QSFV) to prominence—ahead of the usual internal measures (e.g., cost variance and machine utilization).

Simplification and process improvement. The other three low-scoring principles are 5, 10, and 12. On bedrock quality control (Principle 10), performance does not yet measure up to the talk. Low scores on Principle 12 are no surprise. That principle links success in root-cause elimination (through process simplification and fail-safing) to reductions in transactions and reports. This shift—from summary reports to root causes—changes the basis for managerial control in a fairly drastic way.

Principle 5 has both external and internal application: Cut down on number of suppliers (external) and number of parts (internal). A few of the participants are doing well on one but progressing slowly on the other. Fluke Corporation, an Everett, Washington, manufacturer of electronic test instruments sold globally, is a case in point. Fluke has cut down to just one primary supplier per purchased component, about a 90 percent reduction. Its tougher task, since it involves years of product redesign, is to simplify, standardize, and reduce component parts (design for manufacture and assembly). Thus, the company's score on Principle 5 was moderate, though its overall score on all the principles was high. A bit of doggerel in the accompanying box—found posted in drafting rooms some sixty years ago—describes how the "successful designer" thinks.

Intermediate Scores

Scores were very average on the all-important first principle—getting the organization and equipment realigned by families of customers or products. Nine participants, however, scored themselves four or five points on this principle. One is Du Pont's huge Furnishings business, making nylon carpet yarn. Its products had been assigned to plants in the usual haphazard way. A given customer's order might wind up at one plant one time and a different plant the next. Furnishings put to-

---

THE SUCCESSFUL DESIGNER

The designer bent across his board,
Wonderful things in his head were stored,
And he said as he rubbed his throbbing bean,
"How can I make this part hard to machine?"

"If this part here were only straight,
I'm sure the thing would work first rate,
But 'twould be so easy to turn and bore
It would never make the machinists sore.

"I'd better put in a right angle there
Then watch those babies tear their hair.
Now I'll put the holes that hold the cap
'Way down here where they're hard to tap.

"Now this piece won't work, I'll bet a buck,
For it can't be held in a shoe or chuck;
It can't be drilled or it can't be ground,
In fact the design is exceedingly sound."

He looked again and cried, "At last—
Success is mine, it can't even be cast!"

Source: Joseph Harrrington, Jr., *Understanding the Manufacturing Process: Key to Successful CAD/CAM Implementation* (New York: M. Decker, 1984), pp. 88–89 (original source of poem is unknown).

---

gether a multifunctional group to refocus the business for four kinds of customers. Now a marketing segment manager oversees each of the four. Each manager has charge of the people, plant, and equipment necessary to serve the market. For example, the biggest, fastest, highest-volume machines are assigned to residential, which is Furnishing's largest, most cost-competitive market. Two other markets requiring much greater flexibility formerly had been served by nonflexible plants; the new alignment corrects that problem. The refocusing has an important spin-off result: a high degree of interchange between operating people and customers, especially on quality issues.[3]

Bottom Group

The forty-one manufacturers scoring in the eyes-open (11–24 point) group show mostly the same strengths and weaknesses as the top eighty-six. There is one glaring exception: The eyes-open group scores itself high on Principle 16 but only average on 15; it's the reverse for the top eighty-six. Fifteen is getting the production equipment focused (dedicated or flexible, according to product line). Sixteen is presentation of excellence to the outside world. The high-scoring eighty-six are relatively modest about their achievements, while the lower-scoring forty-one tend to claim excellence without having dealt fully with equipment issues. (As we shall see later, the process-industry participants have a lot of influence on average scores for Principle 16.)

For the bottom group, the two weakest areas, on average, are Principles 12 and 13, in the Information for Operations and Control category. This indicates a lack of commitment to getting out of the transactions-and-reports mode of control (12) and getting into the external measures—QSFV—mode (13).

There may be a pattern here. Companies that are rather new to TQM and world-class manufacturing probably have a limited view. They concentrate initially on matching production to incoming orders (Principle 7) and recognizing employee contributions (Principle 9). And they are quick to crow about progress (16) in those areas. Later, they discover the rest of the world-class agenda, which requires physical changes (15) and rethinking the way the business should be managed (12 and 13).

SECTOR SCORES

Of 137 company units participating in the research, four are service businesses that had a TQM effort in process or just starting. One scored well; the others very low. Six more participants are manufacturers that had little familiarity with TQM or world-class manufacturing. They averaged 12.8 points. Some of those managers (and those of two of the service businesses) said they really did not understand much of the language in the scoring criteria. The 12.8 average score and the unfamiliarity with the language make these six manufacturers a surrogate for nearly all companies prior to the "enlightenment" of the 1980s.

The remaining 127 manufacturing units are of further interest. They have been grouped into sectors, such that each has at least ten company units. Exhibit 3-4 shows average scores and participants in each sector. They are arranged in descending order of their scores.

The first three sectors are much alike, both in points and type of manufacturing. Their average scores—thirty-eight, thirty-seven, and thirty-six—are a good deal higher than scores of the other five sectors. Their type of manufacturing spans electronic and electrical assembly, with some machining and sheet-metal fabrication thrown in. Possible reasons why the first sector, electronics, scored highest are these:

- Being light in weight, electronics can be shipped anywhere on the globe without punitive transportation costs.
- Likewise, electronics plants can be located, or relocated, anywhere.
- The industry is high-tech, glamorous, and clean; every country favors start-up electronics plants, and so they proliferate.
- Electronics companies are light-footed and obliged to compete with many others. Competition forces this industry to be customer focused.
- Hence, high scores on the customer-focused principles.

The next two sectors—electrical; and pump, hydraulic, and pressure—increasingly make use of microprocessors, diodes, and other electronic components. Thus, there is a good deal of overlap among the first three sectors. High scores in electrical and in pump/hydraulic/pressure are owed to some of the same reasons as in electronics.

The two lowest scoring sectors—vehicular (except electronic); and machinery, large appliances, and metal components—are opposite to the three highest in one respect: They are heavy and costly to transport around the world. This inhibits competitiveness, customer sensitivity—and scores on the principles.

As an example, ten years ago U.S. white-goods makers learned of innovative Japanese designs for refrigerators and certain other large appliances. They thought they saw the handwriting on the wall: the Japanese

EXHIBIT 3-4
Scores, by Industrial Sector

Sector	Average Score	Participants
Electronic (25 participants)	38.1	Alcatel, Richardson, TX—Telecommunication equipment Aritech Europe, Dusermond, Netherlands—Security equipment ATL, Bothell, WA—Medical ultrasound equipment controls, sensors, recorders Digital Systems Intl., Redmond, WA—Call management equipment Dover Elevator Systems, Walnut, MS—Elevator controllers Eaton Corp., Everett, WA—Optical control devices Fluke Corp., Everett, WA—Electronic test instruments Ford Electronics, Markham, Ontario—Automotive electronics Hewlett-Packard, San José—Opto-couplers, fiber optics, etc. Intel, Fab 6, Chandler, AZ—Semiconductors, microcontrollers Linfinity Microelectronics, Garden Grove, CA—Integrated circuits Northern Telecom, Calgary, Alberta—Telephones Philips Component Group, Juárez, Mexico—Transformers Philips Consumer Electronics, El Paso/Juárez—TVs, transformers, etc. Philips Modular, Plant #4, Juárez, Mexico—Remote control, PC boards Philips Plant #5, TV plant, Juárez, Mexico—TVs Physio Control, Redmond, WA—Defibrillators Rhomberg Bräsler Manufacturing, Capetown—Industrial electronics Sentrol Inc., Hickory, NC—Security equipment Solectron Washington—Electronic manufacturing services Telemecanique-Ireland, Cophridge, Ireland—Contactors Tri-Tronics, Inc., Tucson, AZ—Electronic dog-training equipment United Electric Controls, Watertown, MA—Temperature & pressure United Technologies Automotive, Juárez, Mexico—Wiring harnesses Vectron Labs, Norwalk, CT—Crystal oscillators
Electrical (10 participants)	37.3	Baldor Electric, Ft. Smith, AR—Industrial electric motors Hill-Rom, Batesville, IN—Medical headwall systems Honeywell Home & Building Control, Golden Valley, MN—Heating/ventilation/air-conditioning controls Honeywell Industrial Automation & Control, Phoenix—Central factory/building control systems Honeywell, Motherwell, Scotland—Heating, cooling, microswitch Levical (Leviton), Tecate, Mexico—Wall receptacles, plugs Mine Safety Appliance, Safety Products Division, Murraysville, PA—Safety equipment Mine Safety Appliance, Murraysville plant—Safety equipment Reliance Electric, Flowery Branch, GA—Electric motors Varian, Palo Alto—Nuclear magnetic resonance instruments
Pump, hydraulic, pressure (11 participants)	36.0	AlliedSignal, Equipment Systems, Tempe, AZ—Starters, valves, actuators Bio Clinic, Ontario, CA—Health-care pressure reduction products C. Lee Cook, Louisville, KY—Sealing devices Copeland, Sidney, OH—Air conditioning & refrigeration compressors Dana Corp., Minneapolis—Hydraulic control valves Davey Products, Huntingdale, Victoria, Australia—Pumps

continued

EXHIBIT 3-4 (Continued)

Pump, hydraulic, pressure (11 participants) (Cont'd)		Johnson Controls, Juárez, Mexico—Pressure/temperature devices Johnson Controls, Milwaukee, WI—Valves, screw machine parts Lincoln Industrial, St. Louis, MO—Lubrication equipment & pumps OPW Fueling Components, Cincinnati—Dispensing products Rosemount Measurement, Chanhassen, MN—Pressure products
Textiles, sheet stock (10 participants)	32.6	3M Co., Printing & Publishing, Weatherford, OK—Proofing supplies Albany International, Albany, NY—Paper machine press felts Beier Albany & Co., Pinetown, South Africa—Textiles for filtration, etc. Du Pont Furnishings, Camden, SC—Nylon carpet yarn Herdmans Ltd., County Tyrone, Northern Ireland—Linen yarn Killeen Corr Products, Dublin, Ireland—Paper Milliken, Business A—Textiles Milliken, Business B—Textiles Milliken, Business C—Textiles South African Nylon Spinners, Bellville—Synthetic/polyester polymers
Liquids, gases, grains, powders (14 participants)	30.9	Adcock Ingram, Industria, South Africa—Pharmaceuticals Bonlac Foods, Melbourne, Australia (cheese, dairy powders/products) Cullinan, Oufantsfontein, South Africa—Refractory products Dow Corning, Midland, MI—Silicon intermediates/finished products Dow Corning, Hemlock, MI—Silicone elastomer, tubing, fluids Dulux Australia, Clayton, Victoria, Australia—Surface coatings & paint Exxon Baytown, Baytown, TX—Chemicals FMC Corp., Cork, Ireland—Pharmaceutical & food ingredients Illovo Sugar Ltd., Durban, South Africa- Sugar Lever Brothers, Boksburg, South Africa—Detergents Milliken, Business D—Chemicals National Dairies, Muray Bridge, Australia—Dairy dessert/cheese National Dairies, Tiaree, Australia—Yogurt, yogo, desserts, powder Pilot Chemical Corp., Red Bank, NJ—Detergents
Miscellaneous (18 participants)	30.6	Adcock Ingram, Johannesburg, South Africa—Critical-care products Amalgamated Beverage Canneries, Wadeville, South Africa—Soft drinks Baxter Healthcare, IV Systems, Marion, NC—Intravenous solutions Eddels, Pietermaritzburg, South Africa—Footwear manufacture Gates Rubber, Denver, CO—Industrial belts & hoses Jostens, Denton, TX—Class rings Jostens Cap and Gown, Laurens, SC—Graduation apparel Jostens Diploma Div., Red Wing, MN—Diplomas K2 Corp., Vashon, WA—Skis, in-line skates, snowboards MG Glass, Durban, South Africa—Beverage containers Microsoft, Dublin, Ireland—Software production Midland Communications Packaging, Louisville, KY— Custom loose-leaf binders, etc. Milgard Manufacturing, Tacoma, WA—Windows & doors Olex Cables, Tottenham, Victoria, Australia—Cables Raychem Corp, Menlo Park, CA—Cross-linked polymer products SAD Saf.. East London, South Africa—Self medication & personal care Waterford Crystal, Kilbarry, Ireland—Crystal glasses Wilson Sporting Goods Co., Humboldt, TN—Golf balls

EXHIBIT 3-4 (Continued)

Vehicular products, except electronic (21 participants)	29.3	All Head Services, Braeside, Australia—Cylinder-head reconditioning Autoflug, Luipaardsvlei, South Africa—Vehicle safety restraints Boeing Door Center, Renton, WA—Doors & hatches Boeing Welded Duct center, Auburn, WA—Welded ducts Charles Machine, Perry, OK—Trenchers, underground diggers Genie Industries, Redmond, WA—Industrial vehicular lifts Chief Automotive, Grand Island, NE—Collision repair equipment Cook Airtomic, Louisville, KY—Piston rings Dover Elevator, Mississauga, Ontario—Elevators Dover Elevator, Horn Lake, MS—Hydraulic power units, jacks, etc. Dover Elevator Systems, Middleton, TN—Cabs, entrances, signals Ennis Automotive, Ennis, TX—Remanufacturing armatures, copper motor windings, stators Four Seasons, Coppell, TX—Remanufacturing auto air conditioning compressors, etc. Kawasaki, Maryville, MO—Small vehicle gasoline engines McDonnell-Douglas Helicopter, Mesa, AZ—Helicopters & components Mercedes Benz of South Africa—Passenger cars & commercial vehicles Metalsa, Apodaca, Nuevo León, Mexico—Fuel tanks & pickup frames Munster Simms Engineering, Bangor, Northern Ireland— Water systems for recreational vehicles Pedsa (EWD Co.), Juárez, Mexico—Auto wiring harnesses Rotary Lift, Madison, IN—Automotive lifts, alignment racks Toyota Automotive, South Africa—Exhausts, fuel tanks, seats, chassis, etc.
Machinery, large appliances, metal components (18 participants)	27.5	American Steel, Kent, WA—Steel distribution Arrow Group Industries, Breese, IL—Metal storage bins Arrow Group; whole company—Metal storage bins BPI Inc., Kent, WA—Office furniture Gleason Works, Rochester, NY—Machine tools Inglis, Cambridge, Ontario—Clothes dryers, trash compactors Interlux Louvre, Milton Keynes, U.K.—Louvre controls for lighting Joerns Healthcare, Stevens Point, WI -Nursing home beds, furniture Multibras, Rio Claro Plant, Brazil—Clothes washers Peerless Chain, Winona, MN—Chain and wireform products Power Engineers, Eppinoost, South Africa—Distribution transformers Precor, Inc., Bothell, WA—Aerobic fitness equipment Quickie Designs, Inc., Fresno, CA—Manual & power wheelchairs R.A. Jones, Covington, KY—Packaging machines Servend, Sellersburg, IN—Ice machines, drink/ice dispensers Wheelabrator, LaGrange, GA—Shot-blast equipment Whirlpool Corp., Clyde, OH—Washers Whirlpool Europe, Amiens, France—Washers, dryers

consumer electronics and automobile assault all over again but in their industry. It didn't happen. Nor did innovative U.S. office equipment makers (e.g., Herman Miller, Haworth, and Steelcase) take the world by storm. While there are exceptions (such as automobiles), heavy-goods producers have less pressure to reform than light-goods makers.

The miscellaneous category consists mostly of soft goods (including software and soft drinks) producers. To some extent, low-average scores for this category may reflect national preferences, trends, and sizes (in-line skates, windows and doors, class rings, loose-leaf binders) and regulations (medical devices). These factors tend to restrict geographical competition, which holds down scores on the principles.

Middling scores go to the two process-industry sectors: textiles and sheet stock; and liquids, gases, grains, and powders. These industries tend to be hemmed in somewhat by capital equipment choices made years ago: large, unitary processors that cannot easily be focused by product line or customer family. Accordingly, their scores on getting realigned organizationally (Principle 1) and physically (Principle 15) were low. On the other hand, these two sectors scored rather well on Principle 8, training and cross-training. Process-industry plants usually are operated by a small number of people; so they must be cross-trained and competent, and the entire training cost is not so high. The process-industry participants are different in that fifteen out of twenty-four scored themselves especially high on Principle 16, external presentation of excellence. Perhaps the reason is that they *must* meet purity and other standards to survive. So they do.

FORGING AHEAD

We have judged the performance of a spectrum of manufacturers. The basis is not fleeting financial figures but underlying process strengths. The ratings bear some likeness to other criteria of excellence, such as the Baldrige, Shingo, and Deming awards, as well as total quality management. All of these involve multiple criteria. That would create management complications if they were in conflict. They are not. What is most striking about the principles is that they all line up in the same direction: customers and how to better serve them.

In that respect—customer orientation—principles-based management parallels TQM. We've all seen the occasional item in the press citing a quality prizewinner in trouble or a survey reporting a certain percentage of TQM efforts coming to naught.[4] These are red herrings. As John Ettlie explains, "Surveys report 'average' results . . . , and are accurate to their population of companies." Without looking more deeply, averages can "just hide the real lessons worth noting." In other words, well-managed companies do TQM well and get good results; other companies don't. For that matter, well-managed companies do most things well, and others don't. Ettlie suggests further that "only about 10 percent of all companies are truly outstanding."[5]

"Outstanding" means "standing out from the crowd." Most of the participants in this research do, though they face difficult upward steps on the path from eyes-open to maturity (67–80 points).

The path is strewn with obstacles. As manufacturers make their way—perhaps guided by Exhibit 3-2 ("Your organization's steps . . .)—the best approach is to face rather than ignore the obstacles.

If you compete only locally and have done well at it, your biggest obstacle may be complacency. As we've seen, the research data tend to bear this out. Companies that are somewhat protected from competition include makers of heavy goods or items reflecting national tastes, trends, and sizes; that are located outside the United States; and that operate within a single country. Companies with one or more of those attributes usually have lower scores. Best medicines are benchmarking, plant visits, and getting a critical mass of people educated in the concepts and techniques of customer-centered process improvement.

Among the most troubling weaknesses revealed by the data are in Principles 6, 10, and 14. Average scores on all three were intermediate. Just-in-time fans will be interested in 6: Cut flow time, flow distance, start-up, and changeover times. For many companies, clearing up a multiproduct muddle opens the door to a good score on this principle. Activating other related principles follows. Jostens's diplomas business in Red Wing, Minnesota, is an example. Its difficulty was in handling "add" orders—students who meet graduation requirements at the last minute. The Red Wing solution was a separate "quick-turnaround cell." It has the necessary printing and other equipment (Principle 15—

dedicated equipment) and operating skills (Principle 8—training) to handle the adds. The cell can respond within 24 to 48 hours. Formerly, when add orders were routed through mainstream processing, it took 2 to 2 1/2 weeks.

Applying SPC and cutting out variation (Principle 10) is fundamental Deming, yet progress on this effort is limited. Principle 14, involving process simplification and total preventive maintenance, is a close partner of 10. Both require heavy doses of operator involvement, leading to process ownership. A sound pathway is found in Principle 8, Continually train everybody for their new roles. Tellingly, average scores on 8 were also middling. The prescription, then, is to weigh in on Principle 8, thereby releasing 10 and 14 from bondage. This is not bad-tasting medicine. People like to be trained and feel dignified by having been chosen for it. The trick is to follow the train-do, train-do (just-in-time) training method. All-at-once training, even if extensive, has little staying power.

While Principle 8 deals with training for all, other principles narrow the focus to certain of the experts in staff positions. Low scores on Principles 5, 12, and 13 mainly point to lack of understanding or commitment by some of those staff people. Five—Cut to the few best components, operations, and suppliers—is the prime purview of product developers, process planners, and purchasing people. Specially-focused training, competitive analysis, and benchmarking are means of getting these experts to commit to earning the next point on the three principles.

Strategic change is an outcome of all sixteen principles. Senior executives should not be the sole owners of strategy. Step-by-step attainment of higher scores on each principle transfers strategic powers to the organization and its stakeholders. This is the ultimate challenge.

4

Improvement Pathways

Each company unit participating in the research has its own story on how it reached its current level of achievement. In this chapter we look at the improvement pathways for several of the higher-scoring manufacturers. The sheer variety of approaches, summarized in tabular form at the end of the chapter, is a story in itself. The following brief case studies are for eighteen manufacturers: Gates Rubber, Honeywell-Scotland, Baxter Healthcare's North Cove, Davey Products in Australia, Baldor Electric, Jostens Diplomas, AlliedSignal Aerospace Equipment Systems, Dover Elevators, Quickie Designs, Exxon Baytown, Varian NMR Instruments, Acatel Network Systems, Ford Electronics, Rosemount Measurements, Boeing Welded Duct plant, Northern Telecom Multimedia Communication Systems, Johnson Controls–Milwaukee, and Rhomberg Bräsler–Cape Town.

1. GATES RUBBER, DENVER

Gates is a $1.5 billion, privately held manufacturer of V-belts and hoses in thirty-three state-of-the-art plants employing fourteen thousand people. Gates was a 1993 winner of a Shingo Award in the large-business category. Gates had begun a dramatic change process in the late 1970s, when it began moving manufacturing out of Denver and to scattered small plants. Part of the reason was to avoid unions. It was somewhat of a surprise that productivity improved, though the dispersed plants generated higher distribution costs.

During the 1980s, corporate regularly dispatched quality audit teams to the plants. As was typical of the earlier era, audit results were a basis for "beating up" on plant management. The audits now have ceased. Quality improvement specialists operating in a help mode have replaced the quality auditors.

The help mode is part of a new phase of change that Gates embarked upon in the 1990s. While the company had a reputation for quality and reliability among its customers, world standards had elevated. Gates was feeling the heat. A tortuous evolution toward TQM ensued, characterized by a few go-back-and-try-again cycles. To get a better handle on quality realities in the plants, new criteria called A-1 standards were developed—a composite of ISO-9000, Baldrige, and German VDA requirements. All North American plants are participating in an annual conference centering around the A-1 ratings. Based on those results and related discussion, corporate managers ratchet up the A-1 standards to new levels for the next year. Finally, breakthrough! All thirty-three plants and five distribution centers had achieved at least 95 percent ratings on the A-1 criteria.

This, however, was not a cause for great cheer at Gates. Because there still were unacceptable levels of defectives, relatively high scrap, too many shipments not on time, and so forth. Why? Why, when the factory processes look to be in control, were the overall results still not excellent? After a good deal of gnashing of teeth and probing of the matter, the answer was clear. All the support processes—quality of specifications, order processing, new product development, and others—had to be upgraded. One step was to release a set of ISO-9000 criteria to the staff departments. The reaction of sales and marketing. customer service, purchasing, legal, and the others was, "Huh?" It became necessary to rework the criteria using language the staff groups could better relate to.

Meanwhile, corporate executives were slowly getting up to speed on total quality. They budgeted seed money to explore the use of Baldrige criteria, and they chartered an internal team of about thirty people to assess the entire company against those criteria. The results: dismal.

The reaction of executives—with their traditional management backgrounds—was that the assessment must be wrong. They hired an outside group from the American Productivity and Quality Center in Houston to conduct the same kind of assessment. APQC came in with nearly the same results, except a bit worse. That got the executives' attention. They spent a week in Houston with APQC learning TQM. The experience was convincing enough to get TQM rolling. Quality was defined, including attempts at getting participation in the process. Different vice presidential–level people were each assigned to take a Baldrige category and achieve good scores on it. Within about two months the effort collapsed. The executives hadn't had prior experience in leading such cross-functional implementations with task forces composed of people who didn't report to them.

New approaches were needed. Gates hired Robert Miller, a TQM veteran via his previous employment at Herman Miller and FMC Corporation, as vice president of productivity and quality to regenerate TQM. This time implementation would be pushed downward. Miller spearheaded development of new training materials in the quality-improvement process (QIP) and led benchmarking teams. The revised plan was called the Gates Quality Commitment. In 1992 six thousand employees participated in two workshops over four days. All came out with high expectations, enthused over empowerment but wondering what it means.

In order to preserve and enhance feelings of ownership, TQM at Gates had to be run by insiders. Still, a small amount of outside help was needed to get things going. Gates brought in Destra Consulting of Boulder for training the top managers. Pam Dennis of Destra had helped General Electric with its high-level training, and the Gates training had many of the same features (town meetings, wide sharing of business results, even profit data). A local firm, International Learning Systems (ILS) of Genesee, Colorado, conducted intensive training on development, content, and processes by which Gates could push empowerment down into the ranks. Out of the ILS training came an effective improvement process. Every QIP team goes through a twelve-module training sequence in the just-in-time (train-do, train-do) mode. Among the topics are assessment, chartering, agenda development, and teamwork. About thirty people have been intensively trained as facili-tator-coaches. Their role is as an assigned coach helping a QIP team as it progresses through the modules, leading to completion of improve-ment projects.

Getting there was turbulent, but Gates today is strong in process control (Principle 10), employee and team-driven improvement (4), expanded reward and recognition (9), and measurement in the eyes of the customer (13).[1]

2. HONEYWELL SCOTTISH OPERATIONS, MOTHERWELL, SCOTLAND

Honeywell-Scotland, with 850 employees, is a part of Honeywell's global Home and Building Control sector. The Motherwell improvement journey began in 1988 with the help of U.K.-based Handley-Walker con-sultants (the firm is now a part of the PE consulting group). Handley-Walker worked with Motherwell people for twelve months in setting up the first half dozen cells. John McDougall, director of manufacturing, refers to that experience as providing a "template" that could be repli-cated and improved upon—and the cellular transformation continued.

Closely related to cell development are a few home-grown initia-tives. One is "direct call-off": Operators in cells watch their kanban limits; when reached, an operator keys in the part number on a PC, which sends an order for another kanban quantity directly to the sup-plier, bypassing purchasing. The supplier delivers the parts to the cell—a "direct line feed." This eliminated the central stockroom, re-placed by distributed stocks in the cells. No conventional supplier in-voices or invoice-approval steps follow; instead, invoices arrive monthly by data communications under "self-billing."

In 1989 McDougall and other Honeywell managers attended a Schon-berger public seminar in Glasgow, which was sponsored by World Class International, a training and consulting group based in Denmead in the south of England. The Honeywell group returned with copies of *World Class Manufacturing,* which McDougall says has been influential.

Team attacks on problems follow Home and Building Control's sec-torwide QAS (quality at source) program. Lee Vanbeu, a roving trainer from the sector's Minneapolis headquarters, came to Motherwell to provide the initial QAS problem-solving training, an eight- or nine-day course. Motherwell's train-the-trainer takes it from there.

In late 1994 Motherwell launched its own "teamworking training," which used the services of Martin Thompson, a U.K. specialist in teamwork. Out of an initial group of seventy or eighty people trained by Thompson, a small number with the right aptitudes have become the internal staff charged with training the rest of the work force. The three-day training course will be run about sixty-five times over a period of eighteen months.

Benchmarking, featuring a lot of plant visits, began in 1991. Lucas Industries auto parts business was an excellent benchmarking resource. Honeywell hired, as a manufacturing systems engineer, a Lucas engineer who had considerable cellular experience as both a cell manager and an engineer. A Nissan auto assembly operation in northern England—not so far from Motherwell, Scotland—was a second fine source of benchmarking. Nissan's help included visit invitations to Honeywell managers, which later evolved to visits by Honeywell team leaders and operators. Nissan shared its experiences in continuous improvement, kaizen, supplier partnerships, direct-line feed, and related matters. Motherwell has developed its own internal measures of such competitive factors as quality, speed, and flexibility. There is some expectation that the Home and Building Control group will develop some measures of these kinds for the global group, but thus far corporate oversight is traditional.[2]

3. BAXTER HEALTHCARE'S NORTH COVE IV SOLUTIONS FACILITY, MARION, NORTH CAROLINA

Baxter Healthcare's North Cove plant employs twenty-five hundred associates producing intravenous solutions and bags. The plant was named an *Industry Week* best plant in 1994.

A starting point, for North Cove and for Baxter as a whole, was Philip Crosby's zero-defects program in 1984. This has evolved into an all-company Quality Leadership Process. The Schonberger "world-class manufacturing company" seminar, with related (brief) advisory services, took place on site in 1986. Since then, North Cove has made use of the North Carolina State University extension service for help on quick machine changeover and related topics.

In contrast to other participants in the principles research, North Cove scored fairly well on Principle 15, which involves facility maintenance. The plant got total preventive maintenance (TPM) going with the help of A. T. Kearney consultants. A key step was Kearney's leadership in organizing a Maintenance Alliance, whose members are eighteen prominent companies, including Baxter. Others that have been more or less active in the alliance include Deere and Company, Ford, AlliedSignal, Nippon Denso, U.S. Steel, IBM, Texas Instruments, Sunoco, *Plant Engineering* magazine, and the U.S. Postal Service. Alliance representatives, meeting yearly at different host plants, make presentations on their TPM progress. (John Carter, plant engineering manager, is North Cove's representative on the alliance.)[3]

Recently, North Cove has participated with a few other North Carolina companies in a "knowledge factory" project led by Professors Aleda Roth (Duke University) and Ann Marucheck (North Carolina–Chapel Hill). The project includes validating TQM processes, group learning, and defining the employee of the future as well as measurables of the future.

4. DAVEY PRODUCTS, AUSTRALIA

Davey Products is a 230-employee manufacturer of pumps in Huntingdale, Victoria, Australia. While Davey managers had considerable pride in thinking they were the leading pump manufacturer in the country, a serious problem surfaced in the mid-1980s. This was boom time in Australia—job-hopping opportunities were plentiful, and Davey employees were making the most of it. Employee turnover soared to 70 to 80 percent per year. According to Barrie Dempster, manufacturing manager, the first corrective measure was an employee survey, developed and administered without outside help. The survey showed overall satisfaction to be quite good and working conditions to be okay. On the other hand, says Dempster, results showed that communications were appalling.

This required a large-scale training effort to bring about an atmosphere of trust. Again with no outside help, Davey trained all of its supervisors and developed team briefings on a regular basis. Former problems, such as strict interpretation of work rules by the unions and strict management policies, began to fall by the wayside. Today, regular briefings and communications are part of the culture of the organization. Dempster points out that in 1994 the turnover was only eight people.

Meanwhile, Davey engineers had developed an ingenious new design for a pump: no moving parts! This feat won Davey national recognition: the Australian Engineering Excellence Award, presented by the Production Engineering Society. Then came the next serious problem, high levels of pump returns from customers. The new pumps were supposed to be fully sealed, but moisture was getting into the electronic sensing mechanism. Six technical people worked full-time, at night, and on weekends in an effort to solve the problems. They began to see a pattern of abusive uses of the pumps by some customers. That sent engineers out into the field to find out what the pumps were really being used for rather than just relying on incomplete data from marketing on returns. Among their findings—Australian swimming pools are often finished with a pebbly surface, and pebbles were grinding away in Davey pumps. Some customers were transporting live fish in vessels with Davey pumps keeping the salt water circulating, but the pumps were not made for salt water. Other customers were using Davey pumps in "dog spas," which jammed the pumps with dog hair. In Middle East countries water systems pumped desalinated seawater. This would be no problem, except that for technical reasons the pumps ran only a few hours a day, and the continual starting and stopping and drying out were harmful to the pumps.

The engineering department at Melbourne University ran training sessions in 1993 that were instrumental in getting Davey engineers to spend more time with customers in the field. Key training topics were concurrent engineering, design for manufacture and assembly (using the GE package), and failure mode and effects analysis. Other topics included brainstorming, flow charting, quality function deployment, problem analysis, causal networks, fault-tree analysis, process capability, and tolerance stackup. The engineers concluded that testing of new products had been inadequate. Lab tests were thorough enough, but field tests weren't. They consisted of sending ten pumps to dealers, but usually to those that were likely to be easy on the pumps, and follow-ups were weak. Today, concurrent engineering and other such methods are in common use at Davey.

Along with the engineering and cultural changes, Davey has slashed its cycle times and inventories and put up visual trend charts in key places. Kevin Nestadt of Nestadt Consulting was influential in these changes, especially in the conversion to visual management. Dempster says that Nestadt does not just take notes and write a fancy report re-stating the views of company managers—as some consultants do—but serves a helpful devil's advocate role.[4]

5. BALDOR ELECTRIC, FORT SMITH, ARKANSAS

Baldor Electric produces specialty electric motors in thirteen plants, mostly located in Arkansas and Oklahoma. Fort Smith is home to Bal-dor's headquarters and its largest plant—some nine hundred people. Baldor's climb to excellence is based on two main factors. First, Roland S. Borham, Jr., Baldor's chairman and CEO, has been a cham-pion of participatory management and openness to new ideas since the mid-1970s. That climate began yielding extra dividends starting in about 1987, when Baldor hired four new senior managers, who had al-ready been through a transformation at another Arkansas-based elec-tric-motor manufacturer, Franklin Electric. One was Quentin Ponder, hired on as president to replace Baldor's previous president, who had died. Franklin's closing of a plant in Jacksonville, Arkansas, yielded three other key new hires: Jim Hayes, a plant manager; a senior indus-trial engineer; and a senior systems person. Over the next three years Baldor converted all its plants to "flex flow." Under this method, the cycle times for all of its specialty motors are fixed at five days, ensured by queue limits at every process. Each day another group of five-day motors is started at first operation, and another group started five days before is finished and ready to ship.

The next major step involved quality. The field had always said Bal-dor motors were reliable and sturdy. Now OEM customers were complaining about such nonconformities as paint runs and burrs. Company managers read Deming, met with Juran, and went to Crosby's Quality College. The Crosby approach fit well with the Baldor-Borham culture—more so than the Juran project-by-project improvement approach. Baldor sent seventy people to Orlando for Crosby training, then put fifteen hundred through a follow-on twenty-hour course and fifteen hundred more through an eight-hour version. The results show up as strengths on Principles 8 and 9—training and reward/recognition, respectively.[5]

6. JOSTENS DIPLOMAS, RED WING, MINNESOTA

Jostens Diploma Division, in Jostens School Products Group, has excelled in just-in-time results (Principle 6), employee training and certification (8), and reward and recognition (9). Their successes are tied in with a corporate-driven transformation effort kicked off in 1990. Jostens hired Doug Fletcher, a Twin Cities–based consultant, who was fully versed in TQM, JIT, and related concepts. Now plant manager at Diplomas, Fletcher contrasts the old ways with the new.

• Old (five or so years ago): The plant bought 90 percent of its year's needs for paper at one time, then late in the season submitted an adjustment order for the last 10 percent. File cabinets extended for blocks—what Fletcher likes to call "sneaker net." The plant had just three personal computers. Cycle times were in the order of four to five weeks. Company people did not belong to the professional societies, attend seminars, know about Deming, understand just-in-time (everything was just-in-case).

• New (today): Diplomas has three computer networks with sixty-five people on PCs. It seemed like the cutting edge when the plant put out its modem number on the internet. But the schools are on it, and now orders come in via the net. Cycle times are twenty-four hours, not four to five weeks. Just-in-time is highly beneficial in the diplomas business. Some 30 percent of students on the graduation lists don't make it, and special annotations such as honors (cum laude, etc.) are not known until the last minute.

The transformation began with Fletcher's earlier assignment at corporate headquarters in Minneapolis. He got a group of five plant managers to travel the country with him attending seminars. After each seminar the Fletcher team planned and plotted implementation tactics until the wee hours. Fletcher and a few financial managers attended another seminar on activity-based costing, and the company brought the Schonberger seminar in-house. To kick in the necessary human resources changes, senior Jostens managers brought in the BFR (Belgarde-Fisher-Raynor) group from Colorado. BFR's six-phase renewal program was called High Involvement Work Systems. Each plant has recast the high-involvement message to suit its own needs. Diplomas' version was a two-day training module, later boiled down to 3 1/2 hours. All three-hundred-odd employees go through the training. As all these changes—with emphasis on quality, quick response, and employee involvement—began to set in, pay issues loomed large. Jostens elevated pay from phase 4 to phase 1. (More on the pay system at Jostens in Chapter 9.)

One of the sticky pay issues involved the shift toward teams. Inspectors at Red Wing were a separate group, forty-five people in number. Their end-of-line job was to ensure that the diplomas were right. Operators (of printing equipment) had been at pay grade 5, higher than inspectors who were at grade 3. First steps were to move inspectors to the plant floor, side by side with operators, and to bring their pay up to that of operators. (Plantwide the number of wage bands was reduced from 132 to 28.) The idea was for inspectors and operators to become cross-trained. It was not a quick transition. The inspectors were somewhat resistant. Finally, eight months later, an operator was out sick and an inspector ran the press. Teamwork and cross-training had come of age.[6]

7. ALLIEDSIGNAL, AEROSPACE EQUIPMENT SYSTEMS, TEMPE, ARIZONA

This AlliedSignal plant, with 1,670 employees, produces a variety of accessories for missiles and undersea vessels, such as valves, starters, and actuation systems. It is part of AlliedSignal's Aerospace Sector, which includes over sixty plants. The Tempe site has excelled in getting its equipment and organization aligned with product flows (Principles 1 and 15), in care of its physical plant and equipment (14), and in employee ownership of process data (11).

The improvement process took off in 1990 and 1991. Dan Burnham, now head of the Aerospace Sector, was the main inspiration. His intent was to create a sense of (in his words) "constructive panic," especially over the issue of cycle times. Jim Barrett, then director of manufacturing operations at Tempe, had much to do with translating that sector initiative into action. Barrett, now Tempe site manager, challenged the status quo among the management group. Cutting machine setup times had to be attacked in order to make inroads in cycle times. A local consultant provided initial training. A group of about six manufacturing engineers and industrial engineers became the site's quick-setup roving experts, training others and facilitating one project after another. These were temporary assignments for the ME's and IE's.

Then Lawrence Bossidy took over as AlliedSignal CEO and, as one Tempe manager put it, "kicked in the turbo." Bossidy, who had been a high-level executive at General Electric, brought some of the GE improvement system with him: culture change, TQ tools (brainstorming, general problem solving, etc.), measures of performance, and management by fact instead of opinion. Consultants from Coopers & Lybrand helped develop a corporatewide training program called Total Quality Leadership in late 1992. Cadres of internal "master trainers" and trainer-facilitators took over from there. These are rotating assignments, the belief being that the trainers should have "real" jobs and genuine work experiences to take with them into the training environments. The trainers made up a diagonal slice through the company: managers, technicians, shop-floor associates—anybody. Every company employee went through the four-day TQL training set, and everyone walked out with a project (this is the JIT training method, called for under Principle 8). Some completed their projects in, say, eight weeks; others took eight months.

TQL became TQS (total quality speed) in 1993, which generated another round of training and implementation. Then in early 1995 the original TQL program was recast as TQL-2, which customizes the improvement effort in light of each site's needs. Strategic deliberations identify those needs and set forth desired results. Then "natural teams" (e.g., order entry)—not departments—go to work on the issues while maintaining clear "sightlines" to the site's needs and goals. The number of teams will grow to perhaps two hundred at the Tempe site.[7]

8. DOVER ELEVATORS, MEMPHIS

Dover Elevators is the largest business within the Dover group of manufacturing companies. Headquartered in Memphis, Tennessee, Elevators has plants in Horn Lake and Walnut, Mississippi; Middleton, Tennessee; and Mississauga, Ontario—some 1,260 employees. Collectively, these plants' special strengths are in getting aligned with and synchronized to customer demands for quality, speed, flexibility, and value (Principles 1, 7, 13, and 15) and in bringing the work force into the act through training and expanded reward and recognition (8 and 9).

A beginning, in the late 1980s, is attributable to Charley Chavis (now retired), who was vice president of manufacturing. Chavis had became an ardent fan of cellular manufacturing. Under his influence, for example, the Horn Lake facility—producing hydraulic power units, jacks, car slings, and platforms—was fully laid out in cells, front door to back dock. Inventories fell to about 1 1/2 days' stock. Pipe and tubing were even brought in daily.

In 1989 Johnny Abdon, one of the plant managers, coaxed a few others, including Chavis, to attend a Schonberger seminar in Detroit. Arthur Anderson consultants, doing work on Dover's information systems, also were talking about world-class manufacturing, which steered Abdon onto Schonberger's WCM book. Abdon and the others became avid students (Abdon once even taught a course at Jackson State University using the *World Class Manufacturing* book). Harmon and Peterson's *Reinventing the Factory*[8] was another important source book for the group. Meanwhile, a number of Dover companies were receiving consulting help from the Thomas Group, which specializes in cycle-time reduction.[9] Quick Response Manufacturing (QRM) became the umbrella term for Dover Elevator's factory transformations. The Mississippi Department of Education supplied a person to help develop the

QRM training modules, called DEM (Dover education modules). The individual helped pull together films and various written training materials. One DEM module is called QRM-I, and a second is called QRM-II. The training modules include quick setup, preventive maintenance, and so forth. The company bought copies of Shingo's SMED (single-minute exchange of die) and asked machine operators to read it.

Meanwhile, in August 1990, Dover Elevator invited its top fifty suppliers to a partnering conference, which has led to rigid supplier certification criteria now in effect. An updated partnering conference was held in May 1995. In 1991 a plan went into effect to divide the Middleton (cabs, entrances, signals) and Walnut (controllers) plants into subplants. This transformation applied not only to production but also to the support functions (manufacturing engineering, buyer-planners, etc.), which were split among the subplants. Inventory turns for the three plants all together rose to eleven or twelve per year and later rose to about sixteen (before falling a bit in 1995 when one plant was closed).

These moves were working well—physically. On the human side QRM fell flat. Frontline associates in the focused plants-in-a-plant had new roles, such as setting up machines, preventive maintenance, and quality. Staff experts formerly had done these things. People also thought job elimination was the real agenda. The response to these concerns (in 1991–92) was a new round of training for Dover Elevator employees. The main focus was on *why* the changes were competitively necessary. A gain-sharing plan also went into effect in 1992. Discussions with the work forces led to a company pledge not to lay people off for productivity improvement. Extra time freed up via improvements would be called "pro-action time," during which the extra labor would be invested in improvement projects. The soft-side problems in the plant were getting resolved, and factory costs began to drop—dramatically.

Amid the factory successes was a sour note: Office support functions were still turned inward: While there was some appreciation of the next-process-as-customer viewpoint, the office people had dim sightlines to external customers. To help rectify this, Dover president Hap Hamilton launched TQM for all office people. The intention was to blend TQM seamlessly with the factories' QRM—both focused on the external customer. Dover corporate CEO Gary Robos brought key people from all Dover companies to Cincinnati for a two-day Schonberger seminar in January 1993. (Dover had sponsored familiarization visits by Schonberger to some of its businesses.) QRM/TQM integration and the employee resistance/buy-in issue were items high on the docket during the seminar and during meals. (The Dover companies subsequently purchased a large number of the Schonberger WCM Co. videotapes for continuing education and training in the plants and offices.) Today, each location has a TQM facilitator, and the improvement process continues—with the final customer the prominent concern.[10]

9. QUICKIE DESIGNS INC., FRESNO, CALIFORNIA

Quickie Designs, a subsidiary of Sunrise Medical, is strong in the principles related to employee involvement and recognition (Principles 4, 8, 9, and 11). The 650-employee company's many-faceted Pursuit of Excellence program was developed largely by Richard Chandler, president and CEO of the parent company, Sunrise Medical. Chandler has been scouring the country and the world for several years in his own personal benchmarking effort. These activities include serving as president of the Young Presidents Organization (YPO). YPO's conferences feature presentations by executives from one another's companies as well as invited outside speakers. (I have spoken at two different YPO events and also was invited by Chandler to conduct a seminar at another of the Sunrise business units.) Quickie has had good success in implementing the initiatives that Chandler has developed. As an example, in the employee recognition area Quickie has awarded a new car to an associate at an all-employee awards ceremony annually for the past four years. The award is based on a lottery drawing, but the odds of winning go up for associates whose names go into the hopper for good deeds and good ideas. In 1992 a temporary employee who had fifty-seven pieces of paper with his name on them—for fifty-seven contributions—won the car. That person is now a full-time associate.[11] Chapter 9 elaborates on the Quickie Design/Sunrise Pursuit of Excellence program.

10. EXXON BAYTOWN, BAYTOWN, TEXAS

Exxon Baytown, a 1993 *Industry Week* best plant, has fifteen hundred employees producing some seven billion pounds of chemicals yearly. Exxon, as a company, has been involved with statistical process control since the early 1970s. According to Ray Floyd, site manager at Baytown, SPC fits well with his business. Floyd traces his improvement efforts back to a Schonberger seminar in Greensboro in 1983. The next year Floyd and a few other Exxon managers attended the Schonberger four-day Manufacturing Institute in Aspen, which featured presentations by Edward Hay and Willian Wheeler, then Rath & Strong consultants; David Taylor, then a Hewlett-Packard manager; and guest speaker Tom Gelb from Harley-Davidson. Also, Floyd says they bought "about four thousand copies of your silver-covered book [*Japanese Manufacturing Techniques*]" (probably an exaggeration).

For the most part, Exxon Baytown's improvement efforts from then on have been developed internally. Floyd notes, however, some ongoing contact with Lloyd Provost, of Austin-based Association for Productivity Improvement, and with Ken Case of the industrial engineering department at Oklahoma State University and past president of the Institute of Industrial Engineers. Baytown has developed its own training for operator certification, which is tied to the Occupational Safety and Health Act's PSM requirements. This and other training is the charge of a central thirty-person training staff.

The continuous improvement effort revolves around "natural work teams." Everybody must be on at least one. Typical teams in production include one or more operators, craft people, and an engineer. Office teams focus on such processes as accounts payable. A few special-project teams are chartered by one of the three managerial teams.

Management guidance of the improvement processes is through "goal deployment," one requirement of which is a "quality station" for each team. The stations display the team's goals, plans, measurements, and current activities. The teams can design their quality stations and display media. A staff-support group of senior secretaries, for example, have gussied up their station to have high visual appeal. An instrument electrical craft group, on the other hand, just staples yellow papers to the wall.[12]

11. VARIAN ASSOCIATES, NUCLEAR MAGNETIC RESONANCE INSTRUMENTS, PALO ALTO, CALIFORNIA

This Varian unit, 350 employees strong, was recognized as an *Industry Week* best plant in 1994. Its implementation process included early training via a Schonberger public seminar in the mid-1980s. Recently, a government-assistance program partially funded a seminar held on quality from Lee Mak, a local-area consultant. In view of the low-volume nature of producing NMR instruments, Mak's advice centered on process flows, data collection, and process capability.[13]

12. ALCATEL NETWORK SYSTEMS, RICHARDSON, TEXAS

As a whole unit, the five plants (four in the U.S. and one in Mexico) of this Alcatel 4,500-employee division won a Shingo Prize (in 1994) and received ISO-9001 registration. These achievements have been led largely by people brought in from other companies. Those managers had gained implementation experience at their prior places of employment. Unlike most other participants in the management-by-principles research, Alcatel scored well in the principles related to quality and employee involvement (Principles 2, 6, 8, and 11). The improvement effort has been fed monthly by a set of fifteen internal metrics designed to anticipate customer satisfaction. Actual satisfaction surveys and report cards from customers (e.g., the telephone companies) have validated the internal data set. Furthermore, all employees receive at least forty hours of training, with emphasis on teamwork and SPC. A recent training set on total quality awareness follows the cascading training method: The vice president of operations trains the plant managers, who train the plant work force.[14]

13. FORD ELECTRONICS, MARKHAM, ONTARIO

Ford Electronics, employing 1,850 people, won its Shingo Prize in 1994. Its success story is owed chiefly to the ideas of two managers hired in from other firms (e.g., IBM). In the 1987–88 season, they launched an initiative called "Time as a Strategic Advantage." Most of the firm's achievements spin forth from that program.[15]

14. ROSEMOUNT MEASUREMENT DIVISION, CHANHASSEN PRESSURE PLANT, CHANHASSEN, MINNESOTA

Rosemount Pressure Products is a thousand-employee component of Rosemount Company, a subsidiary of Emerson Electric. While its improvement process is largely home grown, Kelly Hoffman, vice president of pressure products, cites Bill Conway tapes on quality and Schonberger's *World Class Manufacturing* book as being influential. Conway and Schonberger both had conducted seminars at Rosemount in the late 1980s. Conway became a Deming disciple as CEO of Nashua Corporation in the late 1970s. Nashua was the first American company in the modern era to have the good sense to hire Dr. Deming. The Conway tapes provided training for all managers from the top down through first-line supervisors.

Following that, the Rosemount training department developed training in statistical process control. All shop-floor people learned SPC and went back to their jobs charged up. But it didn't work. The problem was that the frontline associates received their training before the supervisors. So the SPC effort was reconstituted. This time supervisors were fully trained and became the trainers for their subordinates—the train-the-trainer idea.

Profit sharing at Rosemount dates back to the company's beginnings some thirty years ago. Usually, profit sharing amounts to about 10 percent. Today, teams are everywhere at Rosemount, doing their part to keep the profit sharing up. Nearly every plant work area has a team called a PIT (process improvement team) crew. Red, yellow, and green status lights, dispersed throughout the plant, provide a source of data for the PIT crews. A typical PIT crew approach to problem solving is to review the "red-light logs," which detail work stoppages and their causes. These reviews set the PIT crews off on another improvement project.

When the crews run into a more complex problem, it may be passed on to a higher-level multifunctional failure analysis team. These teams are able to get going quickly, because Rosemount constantly rotates people—from marketing to operations, accounting to marketing, and so forth. Thus, they can communicate. Formal reporting relationships sometimes blur. For example, one of Hoffman's technicians who had been assigned to a team told Hoffman that a certain engineer was doing an excellent job. Hoffman asked who that engineer's supervisor was, but the technician did not know.[16]

15. BOEING WELDED DUCT PLANT, SEATTLE AREA

The competitive threat from Airbus Industrie to Boeing as a whole may have been the catalyst. At any rate, Boeing's reputation for being aloof and insular was shattered in 1990 when all of its most senior executives trekked to Japan, where they saw the Toyota system and its derivatives, plus other advanced companies, firsthand. Colin Fox and colleagues at the Delta Point consulting firm led this and later Japan study missions. Though by 1990 there were many Western companies they could have visited to learn much the same lessons, there is greater shock value in going to the source, which has refined the refinements. The shock has transformed Boeing in many ways, especially in reductions in cycle times. The Renton, Washington, plant (where the Door Center, another research participant, is located) has cut its cycle to build an airplane from eighteen months to ten months, and the company is now talking about a "six-month" airplane. A corporate Continuous Quality Improvement initiative, with a full set of training modules, has involved every Boeing employee. The Welded Duct plant (and the Door Center) have streaked along quickly, using some of the their own study materials and aggressive timetables.

Welded Duct, in Auburn, Washington, is a business unit of the Fabrication Division. Bill Selby, Fabrication's head at the time, was among the Boeing vice presidents who came back from Japan inspired. At about the same time Pat Day, dynamic leader of Welded Duct, was assembling a team to move the unit from an old, inadequate building to a greenfield site. Day's mission, in line with Boeing's Japan-inspired new mandate, was to eliminate waste. It soon became clear that the team needed a jolt. Bill Selby approved another Japan study mission in 1991 for about fifteen Fabrication Division managers, including key people from Welded Duct. No other Boeing unit has done this. Also instrumental were several books, including Richard Lubin's *JIT Manufacturing,* Imai's *Kaizen,* and two Productivity, Inc., books: Seichi Nakajima's *TPM* and Hirano's *5 S's.*[17] Recently Welded Duct has been receiving benchmarking visitors from other superior companies, who want especially to see the remarkable extent to which it has implemented the 5 S's and TPM.[18]

16. NORTHERN TELECOM, MULTIMEDIA COMMUNICATION SYSTEMS, CALGARY, ONTARIO

The Calgary operation, with 1,250 employees, relied on assistance and information from two main sources: internal corporate consulting and benchmarking, especially with Westinghouse electronics. Westinghouse, a noncompetitor, was open and forthcoming on key concepts and implementation issues in quality and kanban.[19]

17. JOHNSON CONTROLS, MILWAUKEE

Johnson Controls' Humboldt Avenue plant employs 180 people producing valves and screw machine parts. Its journey toward world-class excellence is closely connected to that of the Controls Group, of which it is one of ten plants, and of the entire Johnson Controls company. The Controls Group has been headed since 1986 by Joe Lewis, who in that year attended Philip Crosby's Quality College and returned inspired. He became even more inspired on learning the Deming approach to quality. At about the same time, Johnson Controls headquarters secured the services of an experienced team from 3M Corporation, which provided help with the company's quality implementation, now called Excellence in Customer Satisfaction.

To carry the torch in the Controls Group, Lewis hired a few senior people who had implementation experience at other companies. One of these, Joe Riegel, was as ardent an advocate as Lewis. Riegel was instrumental in bringing the Schonberger world-class manufacturing seminar to the Humboldt site for people from each of the Group's plants. Riegel also hired a small number of new plant managers, including Wayne Canfield, who had gained experience in quality and world-class manufacturing at General Electric. Canfield became plant manager at Humboldt (and now is manager, U.S. manufacturing).

Among Canfield's challenges was breaking through conventional ways of doing things that were ingrained among the plant's managers and professionals. For example, he noticed a purchasing manager sitting at a terminal checking, checking, checking inventory data. In frustration, Canfield "dragged him out to the plant floor to see what was really there—in the kanban containers." (That manager is no longer with the company.)

One of the plants tried using an outside consultant. The consensus of opinion was that it didn't work out very well, and the Controls Group did not bring in any more consultants. Canfield explains that the consultant approach simply did not yield enough buy-in among the people in the plant. Their preferred approach, using inside people, has worked much better.

Humboldt has been bringing in new flexible machines—some CNC and some small machines as well. The small machines, Canfield says, are enablers of automation, which has become increasingly practical, given the availability of fairly low-cost, reliable robots. While the combination of flexible and focused equipment is just what is called for in Principle 15, the plant has been lax in Principle 14, which concerns upkeep of the equipment. Recognizing the deficiency, the plant and group are taking action. For one thing, negotiations with the union are taking place on the matter of including TPM (total preventive maintenance) in the contract. For another, the group has scheduled a four-day TPM workshop at its Goshen, Indiana, plant. The workshop, called "A Maintenance Miracle," is presented by the TPM practice of Productivity, Inc. Why has the plant, and the group, been slow to adopt TPM? Because, notes Canfield, the benefits do not show up quickly, as they do with, for example, kanban and cells. In the first year of operators taking over preventive maintenance—which is essential in TPM—"it actually costs more," says Canfield.[20]

18. RHOMBERG BRÄSLER, CAPE TOWN, SOUTH AFRICA

Rhomberg Bräsler Pty is a hundred-employee, privately held manufacturer of industrial electronics, such as temperature controllers and inductor-sensors. Under managing director Gerald W. Bidder and a strong plant manager and head of quality and with full support of chairman Peter Bräsler, Rhomberg has excelled in such areas as quality, process control, maintenance, just-in-time, and employee involvement. Much of the improvement has taken place in the last two or three years, when, as Bidder put it, "the books and articles became available." He admits to having "fallen into the trap of a long flow line" and just adding more people to it. Instead of continuing in that vein, the plant has been organized into cells with packing at the end of each. A one-week course in 1993 at the University of Cape Town's Graduate School of Business, conducted by Prof. Norman Faull, was helpful, as was a Schonberger one-day seminar. Influential books include Schonberger's *World Class Manufacturing* and Brian Maskell's *Performance Measurements for WCM*.[21] Other than these sources, Rhomberg's improvement effort has been largely home-grown.

DIVERSE PATHWAYS—A SUMMARY

We have seen eighteen examples of how superior manufacturers have advanced toward principles-based management. Exhibit 4-1 summarizes their approaches. The main message is, the destination is about the same, but there are many ways to get there. The few approaches that stand out just a bit are use of outside consultants (mentioned seven times), use of outside seminars (six times), hiring away experience from another company (five times), and use of books and tapes (five times). Spokespersons at the companies that used consultants indicate that the purpose was mostly early training. Gaining cross-fertilization through hiring, along with attendance at seminars and learning through books and tapes, is not surprising, inasmuch as world-class manufacturing is ten years old. Study materials are plentiful, and experienced people are available as well.

EXHIBIT 4-1
Diverse Pathways to Excellence

Company Unit	Product	Implementation Highlights
1. Gates Rubber	V-belts and hoses	Used Baldrige and other assessment criteria. Hired seasoned manager from another company. Outside consultants helped kick off TQM; customized their materials.
2. Honeywell-Scotland	Heating/cooling controls & micro-switches/sensors	Outside consultant, internal and outside trainers, seminar and books, and benchmarking visits provided advice and knowledge transfer. Hired seasoned manager. Adopted corporate quality program.
3. Baxter Healthcare, North Cove	Intravenous solutions	Outside consultants and multicompany alliances.
4. Davey Products	Pumps	High labor turnover led to communications improvements. Field failures & university seminar got engineers connected with customers. Consultant advised on visual management.
5. Baldor Electric	Industrial electric motors	CEO a long-time champion of openness to change. Hired seasoned managers from other companies.
6. Jostens Diplomas	Diplomas	Corporate consultant assembled a team of plant managers to attend seminars. Added in-house seminars, built corporate implementation plan, customized plant by plant.
7. AlliedSignal, Tempe	Aerospace accessories: valves, starters, etc.	Sector executive, site executive, and new corporate CEO were inspirational. Local consultant and national consultant initiated training—taken over internally and now in a third phase.
8. Dover Elevators	Elevators & elevator components	Major impetus from high-level business-unit and corporate executives. Books, seminars, and tapes, plus minor services from outside consultants and trainers, provided materials for formal training.

EXHIBIT 4-1 (Continued)

Company Unit	Product	Implementation Highlights
9. Quickie Designs Inc.	Manual & power wheelchairs	Personal benchmarking and development of implementation plan by parent company's CEO.
10. Exxon Baytown	Chemicals	Quality & safety emphasis endemic to the industry. Seminars, a book, local and national consultants provided materials for internal training effort.
11. Varian NMR Instruments	NMR instruments	Seminar attendance, government-funded local-area consultant.
12. Alcatel Network Systems	Telecommunications equipment	Hired seasoned manager-experts from other companies. Used customer-oriented data to drive further improvements.
13. Ford Electronics	Automotive electronics	Hired seasoned managers.
14. Rosemount Measurements	Pressure products	Two in-house seminars, videotape training, and a book helped launch largely home-grown improvement effort. Train-the-trainer, teams everywhere, and "red-light log books" stimulate action.
15. Boeing Welded Duct	Aircraft ducts	Consultant brought senior executives, and later managers, from this plant, to Japan, where they got an eyeful and earful. A structured Boeing implementation plan, customized by this plant, followed, along with study from a few books.
16. Northern Telecom, Calgary	Multimedia communications systems	Internal corporate consultants and close interaction with a Westinghouse unit.
17. Johnson Controls, Milwaukee	Valves & screw machine parts	Upper executive "got religion" at an off-site workshop, studied, brought in seasoned executives and "help team" from another company. Outside consultant at sister plant not successful, so further improvements done internally.
18. Rhomberg Bräsler, Cape Town	Industrial electronics	Seminar, one-week university course, plus books and articles, led to a home-grown improvement effort.

5

Value and Valuation[1]

Take the entire outpouring of management initiatives of the last fifteen years. Put them on a screen and shake. Many good ideas, in short words and acronyms, sift through. What's left on top is the One Big Idea: Management by the numbers, by financial metrics, by top-down numeric goal setting is obsolete, passé, ineffective. The new, replacement mode, which involves all employees, is managing the processes.[2]

The One Big Idea

Big Idea:
Manage the Processes

TQM
Teams
BPR
DFMA
JIT
Focus
SPC
Kanban
ABC

91

This does not mean that executives should pay no attention to financial numbers. Watching sales, unit costs, productivity, market share, profit, and the like is still part of their job. But only for cash-flow management and for spotting potential problems or opportunities having long-term significance. Not for daily, weekly, monthly, or even quarterly decision making.

Few of today's aging high-level executives are able to accept the obsolescence of what they earned their stripes on. Many others down the hierarchy are converts, however. Their sheer numbers and confidence that they are right gives them power. The following is a case in point.

A *Fortune* 100 multinational had named a new division chief. He was, according to the head of engineering, an ardent proponent of management-by-Deming: Focus on the processes. Watch for patterns. Don't react to single instances. Plant-level people, also Deming fans, were delighted. It didn't last. The next division head was a traditionalist: Make the numbers. However, plant people at one site had their own ideas. The head of engineering told me, "The plant manager and I made a pact: We will do what's right, even though that might not be good for our careers." I said something like, "Bravo. Keep the faith." And he said, "Yeah! We'll outlive the bastard!"

All of the issues taken up in this chapter are related to our changing beliefs about the limitations of money as an object of management. From the shop floor to the executive suite—and even to Wall Street—people are discovering better ways to drive improvement and assess strength and value. We begin with the ferment in product costing. Following that, we look at grander issues—from financial literacy for the work force to revisionists on the Street.

PRODUCT COSTING: HOW AND WHEN?

New-wave management accounting, a decade old, has its settled and unsettled sides. We are settled on needs:

- For improvement, we need expanded customer- and root-cause-oriented measures of performance. This is the mandate of total quality management.

- For product development, we need target costing, which stops the likely losers dead in their tracks before much money has been spent.
- For competitive decisions, we need more accurate product costs.

What are unsettled are certain "how" issues—especially how and how often to report. The usual monthly reports on cost and efficiency won't do. Some data are plain wrong and wrongly used. And some reports are needed much more often, others much less often.

1. Data plain wrong, and wrongly used: According to Peter Drucker, "The most exciting and innovative work in management today is found in accounting theory."[3] He says that "the biggest impetus for this development probably came from GM's failure to get a return on its massive (at least $30 billion and perhaps $40 billion) investment in automation." Bad accounting data is driving some companies to ill-advised automation and other errors (see the box "Whipsawed . . .").

2. Report more often: Customers and root causes are always present and in need of attention. Therefore, report—better yet, display on line—customer and root-cause data while they are fresh. Monthly cost and efficiency reports, on the other hand, are overly aggregated, do not pinpoint causes, and are inward instead of customer focused.

3. Report less often: Since competitive product decisions are made infrequently, report product cost information infrequently. Retaining monthly cost reporting is unnecessary and wasteful for this purpose.

Costing for Infrequent Decisions

For companies well along the improvement path, rather little decision making requires cost data. People's minds have been imprinted with new thinking: that best decisions are those that improve customer service. Customer-focused principles become guides for decisions and actions. Those principles—favoring quicker, more flexible, higher quality, less wasteful practices (Principle 3)—improve service and expand capabilities. They also cut unit costs, but that is a scorecard effect, not part of the decision making or execution itself.

WHIPSAWED BY THE COSTING SYSTEM

McDonnell Douglas Helicopters in Mesa, Arizona, finds itself boxed in by outdated costing practices. Two examples follow.

1. The largest building on the Mesa campus is a warehouse. It holds purchased materials, which park themselves in a state-of-the-art automatic storage and retrieval system. In this age of just-in-time deliveries right to production, I asked "Why?" Finn Waaramaa, my host, answered with a note of irony: "Because the inventory is free." It was the old progress-payments argument: Most of the material is for defense contracts, and the government makes progress payments to contractors as they use materials.

But the inventory is not free. Though the accounting system says it is, we know better. Wherever inventory builds, so do many non-value-adding wastes and delays. They used to be called hidden wastes. By now, however, a hundred books and articles have plumbed the matter. Inventories generate wastes in information systems, scheduling, material control, quality, finance, accounting, budgeting, and administration, to name a few.

2. Another building houses prototyping, mock-ups, and the like. Same people, same facilities for both defense and commercial helicopter models. Formerly, defense and commercial engineering were split. I remarked that consolidating the two customer families has the drawback of requiring a complex costing system. Waaramaa said, "We had it [the complex system] anyway." The system requires that everyone charge time to each job order. Costs get tracked "all the way down to the part number." Government contracts often require this kind of costing overkill (an apt target for "reinventing government"). It's no wonder that the number of accountants, engineers, technicians, planners, schedulers, and so on exceeds the number of direct laborers at the plant.

Product Development

Still, for certain special classes of decisions, cost data can be important. Product development is a case in point. The need is for target costing early enough to kill bad projects and save money or to modify marginal ones enough to be a hit in the market. The method begins with market research and profit estimation. First step is finding out the size of the market at certain price levels. Then, armed with that data, the product strategy team can judge whether the product is worth pursuing. If so, it subtracts a profit margin from the target price to give target cost, which serves as a budget for the product developers. After the development is farther along, if it looks as if they cannot make the target cost, the strategy team may kill the project. Alternatively, they may strike certain costly product features and do another round of market research and target costing.

Target costing is well established in Japan. A 1991 survey reports that over 80 percent of Japan's largest assembly-oriented businesses use it. Another survey reports that usage of target costing is 100 percent in the transportation equipment industry but zero in pulp and paper. Kato, Boër, and Chow state that "the English word 'target' does not fully capture" the essence. A target cost acts more like a budget, they say. Managers participate in the development of the target or budget, then "make Herculean efforts to hit the budget amount, regardless of how difficult the task may be."[4]

Western companies began using target costing in the early 1980s, and now it's old hat for some. Still, most do not do it. Their engineers run with a project until it's well enough defined to estimate the final unit cost, and only then are hard decisions made. Too often, a marginal new product limps into the marketplace only to die an early death there. General Electric has recently begun using target costing in its aircraft-engine business, with the participation of airline customers including American Airlines and the U.S. Postal Service. Along with finding what customers would pay, GE found out that customers of its CF6–80C2 engine for the 747 and 767 didn't need a certain $10,000 valve that regulates airflow. This is simplifying product design, cutting costs, and target costing all at once.[5]

Product Line

Decisions on the product line are another use of cost information. Accurate, activity-based cost (ABC) data sometimes show that products thought to be profitable actually are high-overhead money losers. An example, for a metal-stamping company, is presented as a case study at the end of the chapter. It includes a simple way to correct for the cost system's inaccuracy and interweaves production-control and data-collection issues.

The revelation that the cost system is biased can cause companies to reverse certain competitive decisions and turn a poor business segment into a good one. These are some typical reversals.

- Sales switches emphasis from scratching up new business (many new overhead costs) to retaining existing customers.
- Marketing raises prices on high-overhead, nonstandard products and cuts prices on standard ones. Some competitors may panic and do the opposite: Back away from standard products and plunge forward with their own high-overhead, money-losing models.[6]
- Product development directs its resources toward fewer products and models. The old thinking was to offer more models to widen a product-line's appeal. The new one is to gain even more appeal via low prices. The formula is volume production of a few good products (or mix-and-match modules) with low overhead costs.
- In operations, improvement teams attack non-value-adding wastes for some of the low-volume models. This cuts their costs and turns them into profit makers. (This approach is discussed in the chapter-ending case study.)
- A reengineering project finds a special place for niche products (those worth hanging onto). They get their own business unit and plant-in-a-plant, where improvement teams can isolate and attack wastes and delays.
- For the sake of a well-rounded product line, the company retains other models. But mindful of their high overhead, they get the "virtual corporation" treatment: They are farmed out to a lower-cost job shop.

Real Needs

More accurate cost information may convince managers to make these kinds of reversals. On the other hand, in organizations that have embraced principles, good managers would gravitate toward these decisions without the need for backup cost data. This underlies Thomas Johnson's belief that—even for product-line decisions—cost diverts attention from competitive essentials, expressed as principles (or earmarks, as he calls them).[7]

Furthermore, the above product-line reversals have this common attribute: They are infrequent. Most such decisions would be considered or reconsidered less than yearly. Thus, no need for monthly product-cost calculations.

Bill Bradford, director of finance and administration for one of Johnson & Johnson's business units, agrees: "We do *not* plan to use product costs developed using [activity-based management] to measure manufacturing performance. [Instead, the costs] will enable us to better understand our products and how to position them in the market. These costs will not be recalculated more frequently than once a year unless some significant change has occurred."[8] (See box for further commentary on ABC/ABM.) In some businesses, of course, technologies are in perpetual flux, which would dictate more frequent ABC audits.

Where the costing system is still systematically biased—not ABC-refined—then a suggestion from managers of Schlumberger's Well Services division may have merit: Use informed cost *estimates*. Their thinking is that experienced humans can allocate costs better than any accounting system can.[9] Regardless of costing method, the above reasoning says that collecting costs and assigning them, monthly, to components and products is non-value-adding waste.

MOTIVATION TO IMPROVE

By another kind of reasoning, cost reports provide for control and motivation. In old-style management accounting, monthly reports are supposed to tell whether managers are diligent or lax in controlling costs. Laxity brings finger-pointing, blame-shifting, and recriminations. Diligence furthers managers' careers.

In the TQM-enlightened firm, however, by the time a cost report comes out, project teams are already sifting causal data and experimenting with solutions.[10] Laxity shows up in the form of plateaued trend charts (no recent improvement in throughput time, flow distance,

---

WHEN ABC/ABM IS NVA

Glowing reports on the power of activity-based costing—upgraded to activity-based management—have made their mark in the accounting and business press. But much of it is pure NVA (non-value-adding) waste:[11]

Item: "At one company [ABM showed] the cost per purchase order to be abnormally high. Investigation disclosed that more than 15 separate forms were required to be completed for each purchase."

Retort: Is it necessary to do a cost study to prove that 15 separate purchase-related forms is waste? I think not.

Item: "ABC tracks scrap and rework to the responsible party, whether a vendor, a process, or engineering. ABC is integrated with the quality reporting system. The cost of poor quality is assigned to its sources."

Retort: ABC doesn't track scrap and rework to its sources. ABC only costs it once it's identified. Uncosted scrap and rework are obvious wastes in and of themselves. Proving that each time the wastes occur is redundant waste.

Item: "ABC highlights and quantifies design decisions that create overhead costs."

Retort. Design for manufacture and assembly guidelines do this more directly, and multifunctional design teams see overhead impacts that isolated designers would miss. DFMA and design teams serve us well. No need to see the overheads in monetary terms, too.

---

changeover time, rework, and so forth). Diligence is rewarded in many ways: The performance chart that scolds static performance or backsliding praises each advance. Improvement teams value the chance to present their findings and results. Managers look for extraordinary results and bring the proud teams to awards ceremonies. "Walls of fame" (as they are called at Baxter Healthcare and Milliken and Company) display photos of top achievers. The house organ and, occasionally, the local press add to the hoopla. Simple rewards, such as T-shirts, a best parking place, ball-game tickets, and dinner for two at a fine restaurant, set the motivational hook more securely. Monetary rewards—such as pay for suggestions, gain sharing, profit sharing, and company stock—add to the "basket of values" that is a part of well-rounded TQM.

The basket-of-values concept (a modern twist on J. Stacy Adams's equity theory)[12] calls for multiple ways for associates to give value to the company and, in turn, receive values from it. If the basket contains the right mix, each value in it provides an added increment of motivation.

Open-Book Management (Tripping Over Financial Numbers)

Sometimes things thought to be of value have unintended adverse effects. Traditional accounting reports—on cost, cost variance, productivity, efficiency, output, sales, market share, and profit and loss—fall into that category. The hope is that they will highlight good work, thus motivating in the right direction. The trouble is the accounting reports are twice or three times removed from real events. Therefore they will frequently admonish good performance, reward the wrong work unit, and pass out blame or praise in this period for what people no longer with the company did in a previous one. Operating people know these things and scorn the reports—see *At Alcoa* box. To minimize the disruptive effects, managers at one 3M plant set forth this policy: "No one below our level [just below the plant manager] will be responsible for unit costs." On the other hand, the management team at Du Pont's massive nylon carpet yarn plant in Camden, S.C., has an opposite policy: "We are trying to make all employees business managers."[13]

AT ALCOA-AUSTRALIA:
TQM IN, VARIANCE REPORTS OUT

As part of an eight-stage TQM-related overhaul of its management accounting function, Alcoa-Australia interviewed people companywide. Customer satisfaction, clarification of problems, and needed improvements were the issues. Respondents vented their spleens on "the despised monthly comparison of actual to budget, together with the analysis of subsequent unfavorable variances. Decision-makers almost universally regard this report as an absolute waste of time (though their opinions were usually expressed in less polite terms)."[15]

The main motivational values of traditional accounting reports are general. They show long-term trends, which can create beneficial tension and combat complacency. Better yet compare your own aggregated metrics against those of competitors. (This has been called strategic benchmarking, as opposed to process benchmarking.)[14] Presenting such data to the work force every month, however, implants too many destructive false signals: "We slashed nonconformities, cut setup times, and tore out a stockroom, and what did it get us? Higher unit costs on the cost report!"

Something like this happened at Zytec Corporation. A 1991 Baldrige quality prizewinner, Zytec is an innovator. Its trailblazing includes being one of the first companies to implement activity-based costing—in 1986—and one of the first to use production cycle time as the ABC cost "driver." Cycle-time-based costing gave Zytec's decision makers more accurate product and component cost data. But according to case study writers, "the new system was dominated by confusion. Everybody wanted to compare the old and the new numbers. . . ."[16] In retrospect, it is not hard to see what went wrong. Zytec was using the ABC cost data not only for infrequent competitive decisions but also as the new basis for its monthly product cost reports. At the same time, Zytec had a sound visual measurement system—wall charts that track causes on the spot. The charts would show continuous improvement in various customer-sensitive metrics, but the monthly costs bounced around. For example, if sales of a certain product went down, the monthly cost report would show unit costs going up. A long-term average cost means something; the monthly ups and downs don't.

Such are the problems when the work force pays as much (or more) heed to second-order results (e.g., productivity) and bottom- and top-line results (e.g., costs, sales, and profits) as to root causes. Exhibit 5-1 distinguishes between these different levels of results, and how—and how not—to report them. As is suggested, what's worst is making the higher-order results a centerpiece of visual management, on display in main traffic ways continuously (e.g., cost, productivity, and sales charts on the walls along with primary data). The natural assumption will be that the score-card metrics are upper management's real concern, rather than primary results of local improvements. This leads to "short-

EXHIBIT 5-1
Communicating Improvement Activities and Results

	Real-time Wall charts in workplace	Frequently Main traffic ways & the press	Infrequently All-company meetings
Problem-solving (e.g., Pareto chart)	X		
First-order results (e.g., defect rate)	X	X	
Recognition (e.g., waste-cutting team of the month)		X	
Second-order results (e.g., productivity)			X
Bottom-line results (e.g., profit)			X

Explanation.

Collect and display problem-solving data in the workplace, ongoing with the process.

Summarize primary results of the problem solving periodically (e.g., weekly). and display those results, along with related recognition for achievements, in the workplace and in public places.

Second-order and bottom-line results (e.g., productivity, profit, sales growth) have many causes, some
beyond the control of company people. Communicate such results to the associates infrequently—
perhaps quarterly in an all-company meeting, as is the practice at Hewlett-Packard.

termitis": To make the next management-sensitive number look good,
cut back on training, maintenance, and project work.

Quality science has a name for this kind of behavior. It's called tampering. The tableting machine produces too many tablets that crumble,
so the operator sweetens the mixture—and the next batch won't solid-
ify at all. This is reacting to a higher-order metric, rather than understanding, controlling, and improving the process. Our managers, from
senior executives to process owners, fall into the same trap when they
try to steer the boat by watching the wake.

A crisis situation is different. In 1991, Mack Trucks was veering toward bankruptcy. Responding to the threat, a new management team at
Mack's Winnsboro, South Carolina, plant wanted to "turn our employees from spectators into players." They started with the leadership of
the United Auto Workers, then went plantwide. "We sent out bulletins
on personnel changes, our market position, our financial situation, and
our priorities for internal improvements." Detailed monthly performance fact sheets followed. Results: Hours to build a truck were cut by
41 percent, and both inventories and break-even volumes were halved.

By 1993 sales were up 38.5 percent, which included taking back some market share.[17]

Mack Trucks is back on track. So, should the company continue to intensively communicate the state of the enterprise to the work force? Probably not. At least not so frequently.

Instead, the best way to feed higher-order results back to the work force may be in an all-company quarterly meeting, as is done as Zytec. Hewlett-Packard has generally followed this pattern for years—now with simultaneous communication by satellite to H-P sites worldwide. Robert Galvin, former chairman at Motorola, had his own way of shifting emphasis away from third-order results: For regularly scheduled senior staff meetings he said, "Topics related to quality now would come first on the agenda." He announced, further, that he intended to leave the meetings after that agenda item, "confident that if quality was in place, the financial results would follow."[18]

Exception: Small Business Units

It is the big, multisite, multiproduct businesses that need to handle second-order and bottom-line information with care—à la H-P. In a small, self-contained business unit, on the other hand, any kind of outcomes information may be okay. Visibility makes the difference. Daily display of profit and loss may not send false signals because causes and effects are clear, visible, and separable. This would be the case for a fast-food restaurant, men's shoes in a department store, or a small manufacturing unit with its own products and resources.

Jack Stack's Springfield (Missouri) Remanufacturing Company (SRC) has achieved some fame for its daily financial reporting system. Stack has encouraged other companies to do the same thing. Other adopters of frequent financial feedback to employees include small companies such as Electronic Controls Company in Boise, Idaho, which is owned 100 percent by its employees. Adopters even include a large, publicly held organization: Du Pont's multiplant nylon carpet business with four thousand employees.

SRC, at over seven hundred employees, is not small. It acts small, though, in that it is actually eight separate companies, each remanufacturing a different line of products (heavy equipment, engines, etc.). Every employee gets a financial report weekly, a summary of the daily reports that are posted in the companies. The small size of each company lends visibility to the daily events that cause ups and downs in revenue and expenditures. Corporate overhead is *not* allocated to the companies, which avoids a major source of confusion.[19] (In most cost accounting systems, certain costs are retained as corporate overhead and not allocated to products. The idea is to give operational decision makers information only on costs they have some control over. For some decisions, such as pricing and bidding, the corporate overhead must be added back in on a percentage basis.)

Larger producers might be able to do something similar. For example, a small trend is for a plant to split off service parts from its larger new-products business. Say that, for a machined products manufacturer, fifteen machines (with tooling and blueprints), six operators, a buyer-planner, and a customer-services rep move into a separate building to handle service parts. The new, small company-within-the-company contains all direct and nearly all overhead costs. (In effect, this kind of reengineering creates cost-containment centers.) Everyone participates in every order. Bad days—when a tool breaks, scrap is excessive, or few orders come in—are no-profit days. But everyone knows exactly why and reacts properly: Chalk it up to a need for better preventive maintenance, process control, and closer customer contacts to encourage smoother ordering patterns. On very good days, when profits soar, everyone cheers but knows it's a statistical blip.

But why would even a small unit want profit-and-loss and related information as often as daily or weekly? It's the trends that should be acted on, not daily events. The Jack Stack philosophy is instructive. He believes that every employee needs to learn how to be a business manager and therefore must see the numbers and know what they mean. SRC grows by occasionally adding a new company; then, as that company's employees become more "economically literate," SRC transfers ownership of the new company, in percentage increments, to its employees. (Currently, employee ownership ranges from zero for some newer companies to 49 percent for others.)

Thus, in the small, self-contained business unit that reports profits daily, associates see all the blips and average them out in their own minds. And when an H-P–sized company reports financial results to its associates quarterly, the statistical blips caused by daily events are averaged out. No harm done in either case. The in-between frequency—the typical monthly financial report—is where the problems are, as the aforementioned Zytec example illustrates.

One further thought about daily reporting: Before long, won't associates become numb to daily financial results? They go up, they go down (like the stock market). So what? What associates should be watching, diligently and without end, is variations in processes and their root causes. In employee-owned companies the main value of frequent financial reports may be taking them home and showing them to the family—who have an ownership interest but no role in company success. By this reasoning, daily financial reports appear to be helpful in strengthening a climate of open communications but hardly a way to manage a business.

Priorities: Customer-Focused Principles and the ABC Paradox

A final issue is prioritization: picking the right improvement projects. Looking at potential cost savings *can* help, if the cost data have been made accurate and precise.

In mainstream TQM (predating activity-based costing by several years), however, nonmonetary process data are the lifeblood of improvement projects. Associates collect and categorize the data using process flow charts, check sheets, fishbone charts, Pareto diagrams, process control charts, histograms, and scattergrams (the "seven basic tools"). In addition, they measure flow distances, videotape machine setups, calculate throughput times and response ratios, monitor rework, and use customer survey data. These and still more methods tell what needs to be done and, to a large extent, prioritize those needs. Cost data are not a part of that improvement methodology.

TQM clarifies objectives and restates them as universal principles of good business practice. Less rework, flow distance, setup time, throughput time, process variation—the common stuff of continuous improvement—*always* are cost-beneficial. Picking which of the many cost-beneficial projects to pursue next is partly based on incidence (e.g., most checks on the check sheet or tallest bar on the Pareto chart). In addition, improvement teams will also consider—by reckoning and approximation—likely impacts on cost, importance to customers, ease of implementation, and so on. This works best when the team is cross-functional so that various experts (e.g., in costing and customer service) are included.

High technology can obscure the correct course of action: Should the circuit board be machine loaded or handloaded, surface mounted or installed through the hole? These kinds of questions seem to beg for pinpoint decision making. Refined ABC data has seemed, to the electronics industry, to partially answer the need.

Hewlett-Packard's Andover, Massachusetts, plant tried it. According to an H-P insider, "It was my personal expectation . . . that continued use of ABC would drive out most high unit-cost elements of boards. . . . [But] reality fell short of personal expectations. . . . Overall, improvements have been made to board designs but ABC has not radically changed the engineer's design process." A key reason is that "design engineers must balance requirements other than cost improvement. Time-to-market, functionality, and high quality all bid for an engineer's resources."[20]

Often, the tough part of getting results lies in implementation. Some frontline associates, staff experts, and managers are aggressive proponents of eliminating non-value-adding wastes. Others are footdraggers. Therefore, the highest priority improvement project may be where the eager beavers are. If a high potential (high savings) project is situated where resistance is high, there is little point in giving it high priority.

Thus, ABC data are unlikely to be sufficient for prioritizing or otherwise managing the improvement effort (often referred to as activity-based management—ABM). Still, can't ABC data at least help sharpen the decision making?

Not necessarily. One reason is the ABC paradox. If the method employs few drivers, the cost data may be too imprecise to be useful at the level of an improvement project (though precise enough for ABC's main use: competitive product-line decisions). Cost analysts will want to employ many drivers for greater precision. Then, however, the ABC methods become too complex to be understood, believed in, and willingly and confidently used by the improvement team.

Moreover, cost analysts are precision fanatics. They tinker with the drivers. A good decision made based on today's ABC costs may look bad when one or more drivers change next month. A good example, detailed in my earlier book, comes from circuit designers at Hewlett-Packard's Roseville division.[21]

For these reasons, applications of ABC data for design engineering decisions perhaps will grow to a peak and then fall off as poor results show up. This may already have happened.

This is not to say that activity-based management has no value. Paul Collins, a director at World Class International, a U.K.-based consulting firm, finds that senior managers in many of his client companies still are wedded to the pound (or mark or dollar). Getting them interested in process improvements requires first getting their attention in monetary terms. That task becomes an early phase of a consulting project: Gather process-driver data, feed them into a PC, and use the cost outputs to reveal startling process weaknesses.

Dual System?

The traditional management accounting role was to collect, manipulate, and report monetarily. Today's requirements are for much less of that and much more on nonmonetary, customer-focused results. Even as cost precision increases through ABC methods, needs for cost data in decision making fall in frequency and in scope. Nearly every overhead function (e.g., quality, purchasing, human resources, production control, and management accounting) is shrinking in size (number of people, budget, etc.), though the importance of the functions are increasing. New methods push much of the functional responsibility to the front lines, while a smaller core support group plays a vital facilitating role.

Amidst the continuing flood of new, sometimes conflicting management ideas, it is difficult to decide what to do. We can agree at least that the conventional accounting system, with its overhead allocation biases, doesn't tell a straight story. What does, at the operational level, are process data. The companies to emulate are those whose employees immerse themselves in process data—and show the results by papering the walls with process improvement charts. This becomes the new information system in operations.

And what happens to the old one—the monthly cost variance reports and their close kin? Few managers have the nerve to kill the reports, so perhaps the practical answer is to retain a dual system. Let the high relevancy of the root-cause system instill growing confidence. And let the redundancy and inadequacy of monthly aggregated numbers cause the old system to atrophy and sink under its own weight.

Still, there is an essential role for accurate cost information. Product teams need it to make intelligent product-line decisions. But since product-line decisions arise infrequently, product costs need to be reviewed only infrequently. Thus, instead of trying to spiff up the old monthly cost reporting system with ABC-enhanced accuracy, an as-needed ABC audit is sufficient.

And what of senior managers—who earned their spurs by watching the monthly reports and cracking the whip? Send them to the front lines. That's where the valued information is—and, in today's best companies, where much of the management takes place. (But see the accompanying box.) Even Wall Street is beginning to understand this, as we see next.

VALUE OF THE ENTERPRISE

Alexander Blanton picks stocks for the machinery and capital goods industry. He is an analyst for Ingalls & Snyder, a Wall Street money management firm. Unlike most all the other analysts in his sector—any sector, for that matter—Blanton has learned how to size up a firm by probing underlying strengths. In 1991 his *Weekly Notes* said, "Buy Timken," the roller bearing company. In six single-spaced, small-typefaced pages, he explained about Timken's world-class manufacturing initiatives: how the company has installed cells, slashed inventories, implemented kanban, and so on.

Later, others (outside of Wall Street) noticed Timken. In subsequent years two of Timken's plants were named as *Industry Week* magazine's best plants. In 1994 Timken's Gaffney, South Carolina, plant was

---

SOME EXECUTIVES *DO* MANAGE THE BOTTOM LINE

I've been fascinated in watching how executives in two or three companies manage key financial numbers. These are firms that have had years
of uninterrupted increases in earnings and revenue. Maintaining the
string is the overarching goal: Doing so involves maintaining a tight
ship. (A fleet admiral or a wing commander—taking early retirement to
run a business—would be good at this.) The financial system closely
tracks all expenditures and receipts. Cash-flow projection is so refined
that, months before year's end, it's clear what needs to be done: Cut off
certain ongoing expenses, shut down a facility, sell off a marginal business, take a charge against earnings for unloading some obsolete inventory, coax a key account into taking early delivery, and so on.

It works. These manipulations keep the string going, which stabilizes
the upward trend in common stock price. Too bad about the lost opportunities that would have made the company and its stock even more
valuable:

- We laid off 500 people and cut the payroll but lost a key materials sci-
  entist, two young, high-potential managers, and several top-notch machinists and welders.
- Two years after selling a subsidiary, that business is a roaring success—and is backward-integrating into some of our remaining product lines.
- We cut the training budget in midyear, which effectively killed the
  budding TQM effort in six plants.

---

awarded a Shingo Prize. Also, if you had bought Timken in early 1992
at 23 (as I did), you would be more than satisfied. Timken common
stock was trading at above 45 in August 1995.

Power Brokers

Most analysts are numbers people. They pore over quarterly reports
and plug in conventional money-management wisdom: "Acme Amalgamated is in a cyclical business. There's cyclical risk here. Don't buy
right now." Most visit companies; sometimes they walk through plants.
They see but do not understand.

Few of these numbers-driven analysts are likely to change their ways. But they might at least learn to seek out some of the relevant first-order metrics, especially customer satisfaction and inventory turns. (Not one of the sixteen principles or scoring criteria presented in Chapter 2 includes the word *inventory.* Yet success in applying most of the principles has inventory reduction as one result. Thus, inventory turnover is a first-order result.)

While most financial publications pay little attention to inventory data, which is available in company financial statements, one does: *Investor's Business Daily.* Its detailed evaluations of companies include the usuals (earnings, return on equity, etc.), plus two inventory metrics: number of days of inventory and inventory turnover. Even so, few financial analysts give inventory its due; therefore, few manufacturers do so. Inventory reduction crusades arise from time to time but rarely stick.

Alexander Blanton got interested in world-class excellence in the 1980s. He attended one of my two-day seminars and then persuaded a few other analysts and pension-fund managers to attend in various cities around the United States. I usually had breakfast with these unconventional attendees and learned a little about what went on inside their businesses. They, in turn, picked up a few pointers on what to look for and ask about when they visit manufacturers. Of course, they also heard about what not to be enthused over: legions of white-coated end-of-line inspectors, powered conveyors feeding stock into automated storage racks, computer systems that track every event, and large automated warehouses.

Regarding warehouses, one of Blanton's *Notes,* in 1992, pointed out that Trinova "is closing warehouses and distribution centers at a rapid rate (40–50 . . . in the past few years)." Meanwhile, a somewhat similar company, Parker Hannefin, "presented slides showing 24 distribution centers in the U.S., 42 in Europe, and 212 in Latin America. A different, and more expensive, strategy, in our opinion." (However, Blanton had a few counterbalancing good things to say about Hannefin.)

Ingersoll-Rand became another Blanton favorite. Ingersoll had been reducing inventories sharply and steadily. That raised earnings and generated a lot of cash, which could be put to use in acquiring another company. Clark Equipment fit the bill. Ingersoll could borrow $700 or $800 million to secure a controlling interest and pay off the loan soon out of cash flow from continuing inventory reductions in both companies. Ingersoll tendered an offer for 50 percent above the market and, after a few skirmishes, had Clark's agreement to be acquired.

Genuine Power

The real world revolves around processes. The artificial one turns on monetary representations of process outcomes. It remains for the legions of believers in the power of process management to convey and convince the powers that be.

CASE STUDY: THE COSTING/PRICING PROBLEM AT HARBOR METAL STAMPING COMPANY*

At Harbor Metal Stamping overhead is charged to products based on machine hours. A result is that the high-volume parts stamped out on Harbor's 600- and 750-ton presses are overcosted and overpriced. Production and inventory control (P&IC) costs—a component of overhead—are part of the problem. Even though it is clear that the large presses require little P&IC support, the machine-hour method allocates a good deal of P&IC costs to parts made on the big presses. (On the other hand, the high-volume parts require a lot of technical support, another main component of overhead; the machine-hour method allocates those costs rather well.)

Conversely, most low-volume parts are undercosted and underpriced. They require most of the P&IC support but don't get charged for their share. Low-volume parts also are responsible for most of the data-entry and computer transactions and for related costs of computer hardware, software, and staff. But those costs aren't a part of the burden (overhead) cost pool at all. They are treated as sales, general, and administrative (SG&A) cost.

---

*This case study is a nearly word-for-word copy of a report that I presented to the company based on a plant walk-through in 1987. The company name is disguised.

ALTERNATIVE SOLUTIONS

If Harbor's costing system were modified to reflect true costs (further comments later), probably numerous low-volume parts and products would show up as moneylosers. That might suggest (1) weeding out the losers or (2) raising prices and hoping that that won't drive too many customers away.

A better remedy is first to simplify Harbor's production and inventory control system, including slashing the number of production transactions. For Harbor, best methods of cutting transactions and material move-and-store actions include

- formal kanban, using labeled containers (rather than detachable cards)
- temporary work cells for medium-volume work (avoids the need for labeled containers)
- more permanent cells for higher-volume "star" products or standard component parts (may eliminate need for containers—until the packaging step)
- regularized, daily-rate schedules for star products and components
- work-in-process stock on the factory floor (close down the stockrooms)
- tear out the MAPICS on-line reporting stations
- reassign resulting excess staff people to production, technical support, sales, supplier development, and factory renewal and reorganization projects

After those (and other) simplification projects, proceed with product-line "rationalization." Using a more accurate method of allocating burden (see below), check costs, revise prices, and weed out money-losing products. In simplifying the system first, many currently unprofitable products probably can be saved. (Some money losers should be saved if they are indispensable to a product-line package.)

MODIFYING THE COSTING SYSTEM

Harbor's present costing system is a good deal more accurate than that of most companies. Charging overhead to products based on machine hours is, for machine-intensive companies, a modern idea. (Over 95 percent of industry still allocates overhead by direct-labor (DL) hours, which, in view of the shrinking DL element of total product cost, can be grossly inaccurate.) Still, the Harbor cost system needs to be modified.

First step is to split factory overhead in two:

1. Technical support (die design, die maintenance, machine setup, manufacturing engineering, etc.)
2. Production and inventory control (P&IC) support (scheduling, materials, handling, dispatching, etc.)

Next, split computer information systems (IS) in two:

1. Administrative support
2. Factory support

Finally, recombine. The old and new overhead allocations are shown in Exhibit 5-2.

As indicated, P&IC + factory IS should be allocated by product (or component) manufacturing cycle time. This requires, for random samples of products, a monthly audit of cycle times (from the purchased material stockroom to finished, packaged products). At CalComp, the

EXHIBIT 5-2
Overhead Allocation at Harbor Metal Stamping

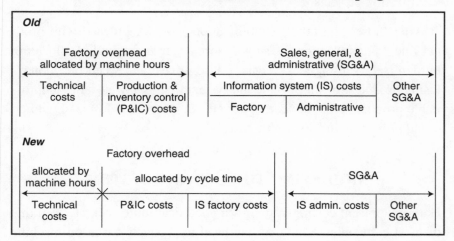

manufacturer of electronic plotters, the method is to wand a bar code when a key component leaves the purchased-parts stockroom and again when the item becomes a finished good; the difference is cycle time.

A possibility for collecting data on technical support costs is for Harbor to install piece counters on all machines that have a "stroke" action. An occasional audit of piece counts, converted to machine hours, then serves as the basis for allocating periodic technical support costs.

MODIFYING THE DATA COLLECTION SYSTEM

Regarding data collection, I'll offer three very broad comments (many details need to be worked out):

• There is no good purpose in costing, costing, costing. The real need is to be able occasionally to do a good cost audit on selected products to find out if pricing is right, to bid on similar business, to do feasibility studies for new equipment or new products, and so on.

• Don't try to pin down all costs. It's futile and too cumbersome and costly to try to do so. An inaccurate product costing system (the kind in most companies) should not be used to appraise managerial performance or to motivate improvement. Instead, drive costs down and quality, response time, and flexibility up by plotting quality, cycle time, setup time, etc., on large visible charts on the wall. That is the most effective way there is for upper managers and line employees alike to size up results and take pride in accomplishments.

• Abandoning the present system (and planned upgrades) at Harbor of collecting labor and units produced for each operation is not gutting its cost system. Usual cost collection by expense categories (payroll, direct materials, etc.) is still there, as are budgets and budgetary controls. Operation-by-operation costing must be seen as non-value-adding duplication and waste, not as valid and necessary for control.

6

The New Mastery of
Mass Production—
and Its Close Cousins

The first derivative of mass production is mass customization,[1] or agile manufacturing. The core concept is not high flexibility extending backward through all processes, for that is far too costly. Rather, it is mass-producing the components, after first designing them for quality and ease of building into other products. This drives down unit costs, and it sets the stage for wide-variety finishing, and hip-hopping from one product generation to another.

In this chapter we examine high-volume production—wrong way and right way. We see that when the critics assail mass production, they really are attacking yesteryear's feeble attempts at it. The old way was to thunk out large quantities, all right. But the method was to break those quantities into separate heaps, made sporadically in far-flung departments. The many stages of production were unsynchronized, so that partially completed components—often the wrong ones—piled up all over factories and spilled out into warehouses.

We are finally mastering mass production and are spinning off innovative derivations of it. And just in time, too—since global trade pacts are creating mass markets magnitudes larger than what we are accustomed to.

WHAT *IS* MASS PRODUCTION?

Our image of mass production is one of high volumes, uniform output, low unit costs, and few surprises. Cement making may be the purest example of it. In goes the limestone and clay (or shale). Kiln heat at 2700°F, grind with gypsum, and out comes portland cement. It goes on twenty-four hours a day, seven days a week, with uniform output. And it continues for maybe six months, until a formula change or a stop to rebrick the kiln.

We think of many other industries as being mass production even though they fall far short of the image. A refinery or an assembly line may be high volume and yield low unit costs and few surprises, but the outputs usually are not uniform. Refinery formulations keep changing, and assembly lines produce a variety of models in varying amounts. (It seems that no other manufacturing has such unchanging output for so long as cement making. Unless you want to count electric power generation, starting with continuously mined coal moving by trucks to furnaces whose steam spins turbines in a 500-megawatt plant, all situated in a Wyoming coalfield.)

What about makers of piston rings, gears, file drawers, pumps, bolts, wire and cable, writing pens, apparel, and floor tile? These and tens of thousands of other industrial and consumer products are often made in what some call mass production. Volumes may be large per lot and massive per year. Yet outputs are constantly changing as to quantity and type, unit costs are high, and it's a surprise when schedules and other plans hold up for as long as a couple of days. This is the kind of mass production (dubious to so label it) that leads to being eaten alive by more adept competitors. Firms operating this way need to become effective mass producers. The remainder of the chapter explains why and how.

WHY MASS PRODUCTION?

Mass production is not dead or dying. In fact, it is enjoying rejuvenation. One reason is that lesser forms of high-volume production are ineffective. Another is that we've learned to apply mass production, with all its advantages, to early production stages—and save customization to the last stage. Still another is that the world's densest populations, now relatively unfettered by trade and power-bloc barriers, generate massive demands. We take up these reasons in reverse order.

Trade Pacts Resize Production Volumes

If you are an adult, you can still remember a time when the United States was the world's only open-for-business mass market. The markets of Europe, Asia, Africa, South America, Canada, and Mexico were small and restricted in comparison. Trade pacts have changed this, and trade blocs continue to grow and to become increasingly open.

Multinationals—most of the big ones being American—generally have an advantage. For many years Ford, IBM, Coca Cola, and scores of other *Fortune* 500 companies have been big spiders trying to spin webs around Western Europe. Wherever there is a weakened bug, they swoop down for the kill. The bugs are one-country companies, stuck making a wide diversity of products in small volumes to meet their countries' restrictions. (National companies had distinctly lower aver-

---

MASSIVE MASS MARKETS

1980
- One mass market: United States, 240 million people, $4,200 billion GNP
  Next largest: Japan, 120 million people, $1,200 billion GNP

1995
- North America (3 NAFTA countries): 365 million people, $5,900 billion GNP
- European Union (17 countries): 350 million people, $5,000 billion GNP
- Association of Southeast Asian Nations (ASEAN—7 countries): 425 million people, $410 billion GNP
- MERCOSUR (4 South American countries): 201 million people, $498 billion GNP
- China: 1,190 million people, $393 billion GNP
- India: 920 million people, $240 billion GNP

age scores than multinationals on the management-by-principles research, as reported in Chapter 3.)

Paris-based Groupe Schneider was one of the weakened bugs—until M. Pineau-Valencienne took over as CEO in 1981. A major hurdle, he says, was that standards and regulations forced makers of electrical products to produce them in the countries in which they were to be sold.

As reported in a news magazine, Pineau-Valencienne transformed "that chaotic, debt-ridden conglomerate of the '60s into an $11 billion world electronics power that now generates 50 percent of its sales from international operations."[2] To exploit the economic melding of Europe and passage of the General Agreement on Tariffs and Trade (GATT), he built up a technology-based core—electrical distribution and industrial controls—and sold off the other diverse businesses.

A key acquisition was Square D, a venerable U.S. maker of circuit breakers and allied products. Square D's factories were well along the path of driving down costs via the new mode of mass production: synchronized, rate-based production in dedicated, product-focused cells. (Its old mode was conventional: separate shops producing in chopped-up volumes with stockrooms in between.) The knowledge and experience of Square D managers was a valued part of the acquisition: twenty-seven of its top thirty-two managers remained on board.

Schneider's new product strategy builds on regulatory standardization occurring in today's enlarged markets. Pineau-Valencienne explains that his new products are "such that we [can] manufacture 95 percent of them for world use and change the last 5 percent at the end of the process for use in a specific country. This new concept was a huge breakthrough in cost structure."[3]

From Mass-Produced Components to Customized End Products

Groupe Schneider recognizes where the costs are: 50, 80, 90, sometimes 95 percent of most products' costs are in their components. Recovering those costs typically requires offering a product in multiple variations and extensions, with plenty of add-on options. Therein lies a success formula: Mass-produce components that can fit together in a wide variety of combinations.

Johnson Controls has applied the formula to its car-seat plants. The seats come in a broad array of models for various automakers, but it holds down costs through "commonization" of components across its product lines (Principle 5).[4] If Johnson commonizes five parts, the new, standard part has five times greater annual volume. Production costs go down, which makes Johnson more competitive and increases its volumes still more. At some point along the trend line of growing component volume, production flips over. It leaves the irregular batch mode and arrives at the ultimate in low-overhead simplicity: Make the part in the same quantity every hour of every shift in a dedicated cell with no material handling, no storage, no work orders, no job setups (or just simple within-a-family setups), and no tracking in-process labor or WIP. The hourly quantity is a smoothed representation of the downstream usage rate and changes no more often than monthly (Principle 7, operate in synch with demand). The rate extends backward to suppliers, who can realize the same benefits, and who deliver right to points of use.

General Motors is working along the same lines as Johnson Controls. We know about the lean-on-people part, and it's not just plants that have been downsized or shuttered. Under CEO Jack Smith, GM's headquarters bureaucracy was trimmed from 13,000 to 1,300 people. But there's more to lean than that. In 1988 GM's midsized models came out in 1,900,000 combinations. Plans are in motion to have that down to 1,000 combinations by 1997–98.[5]

Other industries are commonizing, too.

• Machine tools. Ingersoll Milling Machine Company crows about design simplicity for its next-generation machine, called the octahedral hexapod. The part count for its working prototype is only about a hundred. "Compare that with the thousand or so in the conventional machine tool," says Dennis Bray, vice president of technology.[6]

• Consumer electronics. This industry probably leads all industries in simplifying designs and cutting components. Thousands of design engineers at Motorola, Texas Instruments, Hewlett-Packard, IBM, and the other majors have been to design school. They've absorbed the Boothroyd-Dewhurst DFMA (design for manufacture and assembly) lessons and put them to use.[7] A good example is the IBM LaserPrinter. The design team's charge included following the full set of DFMA guidelines, plus another dozen special ones.[8] The final criterion was to design the printer for assembly by IBM pick-and-place robots. The product turned out to be so simple that it was "cheaper and easier to make them by hand."[9]

In electronics, driving down component costs via fewer parts with higher volumes is critical. Pittiglio Rabin Todd & McGrath (PRTM), a consulting firm specializing in the industry, corroborated this in a study of printed-circuit-board assembly. The study, involving a select group of thirty-five electronics companies in the United States, Europe, and the Far East, showed that unit costs are "extraordinarily sensitive" to volume.[10]

• Apparel. Carole Little, a Los Angeles–based women's wear maker, has experienced difficulties in dealing with major department stores, which now make up 95 percent of sales, up from 60 percent a decade ago. President Leonard Rabinovitz says, "In order to provide exclusives for the big stores, you have to give them a bigger mix. . . ." Marie Beninati, director of retail market strategies at Kurt Salmon Associates, apparel industry consultants, explains the industry's response to this trend: "What apparel makers are moving toward is mass-produced styles, individually customized for specific retailers."[11]

• Aerospace. A door for a Boeing 737 airplane has 637 parts in it, and the sixteen doors made in its door center have 6,000 parts. McDonnell-Douglas has designed a new airplane door with a small fraction of the typical numbers. Fabrication shops can stick to just a few parts, made at aircraft assembly rates. With too many parts, fabricators are forced into the mode of making fifty of one kind this week, fifty different ones next week, fifty more the third week, and so on, which results in completions badly out of synch with aircraft build rates.

In Boeing's and McDonnell's old approach, different engineering groups passed the design project back and forth. Each added more parts to meet their own requirements (e.g., structural engineers worrying about structural integrity), which were complicated by other groups' requirements. Boeing's team approach in designing the 777 aircraft eliminates much of the problem of group after group adding more parts and greater manufacturing difficulties.

• Process industry. Most of the so-called continuous processors—chemical plants, sheet processors, and so on—really aren't. They cycle through a wide mix of products, grades, and order sizes. The lesser ones interfere with the greater ones. Milliken's new Blacksburg, Virginia, chemical plant was designed differently: two reactor groups instead of just one. The larger group, which handles large orders, can act more like a pure mass producer; the smaller reactor group concentrates on small-batch orders, which formerly were aggravations.

• Remanufacturing. Even remanufacturers are finding places to commonize parts, though they have no role in original design. Four Seasons, the automotive climate-control division of Standard Motor Products, found that by porting holes originally closed in some air-conditioning compressors, the replacement compressor eliminates six GM part numbers. This benefits customers (auto parts stores), because it reduces numbers of SKU's (stockkeeping units) to maintain.

This is not to cast aspersions on GM. Those compressor parts were designed years ago, well before Boothroyd and Dewhurst laid down the canon of design for assembly. Actually, it is the Japanese automakers that give Four Seasons fits—because of many different models for the same family of cars. "Sometimes, the Japanese will implement a [compressor] design change in midyear," claimed one Four Seasons manager, rolling his eyes.

Japanese and German Mistakes

I was not surprised to hear this about Japanese compressors. Beginning in the mid-1980s, while U.S. automotive and electronics engineers were off applying DFMA, Japan was off in the opposite direction. Germany, too. When the smoke began to clear, the enormity of the errors could be tallied:

• Matsushita had developed six thousand models of stereos and portable tape players.[12]

• Nissan tallied 28 different types of chassis,[13] 87 of steering wheels, 110 of radiators, 200 of ashtrays, 1,200 of floor carpets; and engines of 2, 2.3, 2.4, and 2.5 liters.

• Nissan's practices ripple back to Calsonic, a major supplier and close partner of Nissan. As a business news reporter put it, "Mindless variation by carmakers forces Calsonic to make no less than 2,000 kinds of mufflers alone, the majority of which are used at a rate of only a few units a year." Calsonic president Yukio Miyamori, sums up the consequences: "We have to maintain the presses, dies, and inventory on all those different kinds of mufflers for the lifetime of the cars. That's nine or ten years. It's terrible!"[14]

• In a study of seventy-one automotive-supplier plants, the University of Cambridge and Cardiff Business School, along with Anderson Consulting, found a similar situation in Germany. "Germany struggles under the weight of . . . tremendous product variety. . . . German seat plants average more than thirty thousand live part numbers, a consequence of what the Germans proudly term 'mass customization.'"[15]

I do not mean to paint all Japanese or German manufacturers with the same broad brush. There are plenty of exceptions, both in the past and the present. For example, in the early 1980s Honda and Yamaha went to war over the motorcycle market. Willard Zangwill explains that upstart Yamaha was gunning for first place in market share, and Honda would have none of it. Honda's rallying cry, *"Yamaha wo tsub-*

MASS CUSTOMIZATION

First version (worth a million dollars): Like the Mississippi River barge fleet with great pilots and quick reflexes in the steering and engine controls so it can maneuver around shifting sandbars and carry any cargo in quick time. Everything is flexible and quick.

Second version (worth a billion dollars): Like the barge fleet that invests in standardized boats, barges, and load/unload facilities and in dredging a dependable channel to haul huge loads carrying any cargo in quick time. Flexible and quick at the customer interface; standardized, routinized, and ultralow in cost for foundation processes.

usu!" translates roughly as "We will crush, squash, and slaughter Yamaha!" During a brutal eighteen-month period, Honda came out with a new model of motorcycle nearly every week. Yamaha had to wave the white flag and content itself with a lesser market share.[16]

How could Honda do what it did? According to Don Clausing of MIT, each new Honda model contained 75 percent of parts from previous models. The 25 percent that were changes were on the outside, so that the new model looked very different to customers.[17]

End Products

From components come end products. Or, in rare cases, product. Consumers who buy a videotape of, say, *The Lion King* are not looking for variations. People in other industries think, we should be so lucky.

Appliance maker Whirlpool made its own luck. The product in question is a clothes washer. As everyone in the industry knows, German consumers demand front-loading machines, while the French prefer top-loaders. In manufacturing the difference is immense.

Not to be dissuaded, Whirlpool-Europe probed these preferences. Through research, they found that "Europeans of all stripes would gladly trade their assorted preferences for superior overall performance . . . a reliable machine that cleans well, is easy to use, and economizes on water, detergent, and energy. Meet these criteria, and the door's location gets less important."

Whirlpool took the data to heart and devised a more uniform product line, which eliminated the need for fourteen of thirty European warehouses. A few regional organizations handle sales rather than separate national offices. Against the advice of its ad agency, Whirlpool mounted an all-European advertising campaign: "Whirlpool brings quality to life." The uniform product line and the ad campaign were rousing successes: Whirlpool held the line on prices and boosted profits. Chairman Hank Bowman concludes, "Consumers across the Continent share more in common than people assume."[18]

Japan is catching on, too. Omron plans to slash 30 percent of its product line—some thirty thousand products—within three years. A spokesperson for Matsushita says, "Consumers no longer want bells and whistles," which translated into hundreds of variations of the same items.[19]

Scale Economies Lost

I've found that breaking free of conventional thinking tends to come easier for piece-goods makers like Whirlpool than in the process industries. A European candy-bar maker comes to mind. The situation was that its single, wide-belt production line divided its time between two popular candy bars. The difficulty and cost of cleaning out one product and starting up another called for monthlong production runs. That's a lot of candy pushed into the pipelines. Long intervals between runs made it hard for the company's salespeople to keep retailers' shelf stocks fresh. This was a serious matter in view of the firm's reputation as a stickler for watching freshness codes. Inbred thinking was that the wide-belt, twenty-four-hour-a day operation gave them enviable scale economies. It might have been so had production not been in large, widely-spaced lots.

Those issues arose during a seminar I was conducting. I offered a few options:

1. A crash quick-changeover/smaller-lot-size campaign. This would help but probably only modestly.

2. Consider dedicating the line to just one of the two bars and building another line for the second bar (following Principle 15 on dedicated capacity). This would yield true economies of scale. For this to be feasible, the company would need to pump up sales to where one bar would keep a single line fairly busy. I had already heard company managers talking about expanding promotional efforts along the Mediterranean and points east, where candy-bar-eating habits were weak.

3. In future expansions, don't build all lines to maximum widths. Instead, build an occasional narrow-belt line. The capacity of a narrow line would come fairly close to matching sales of one popular bar within a given sales territory.

As I laid out these options, I looked around the room for allies. I expected at least a few of the managers in the audience to be bright eyed and nodding their heads in agreement. None were. A joint marketing-manufacturing strategy—raise demand to equal optimal production-line capacity—apparently was too extreme an idea for this group. So, too, was the idea of building a line to equal typical sales of a key product. The high costs of a production line are obvious. Perhaps the high costs of being out of synch with demand were not.

Recently this company has lost market share. Customers complain about poor fill rates. Outside observers say much of the problem is the company's firm policy of maximum asset utilization.

Exxon's Baytown, Texas, chemical plant is a good example of scale economies captured. It's a massive plant with massive equipment producing massive amounts of mostly the same things—some 7 billion pounds yearly. Ray Floyd, site manager, believes the equipment is right for the job—and he's correct.[20] If the plant's mission were to produce a variable mix of products and product quantities, however, the scale economies would be lost. As noted earlier, Milliken Chemical has met the challenge of a variable mix by two reactor groups, one smaller sized.

The point is that only a small number of the world's manufacturing facilities have the right set of conditions to profit from scale economies. The chief condition is that they produce "superproducts"—super because the whole world wants it (Apple's original Macintosh) or because the sales volumes are huge and stay that way "forever" (Honeywell's round thermostat). How many such products are there in the world? Maybe no more than ten thousand. The other 99.999 percent of products call for a different manufacturing and marketing concept. In other works, I've called it *economy of multiples.*[21]

When a Plant Has Too Many Parts

The manufacturing book of the nineties, so far, is *The Machine That Changed the World.*[22] Based on a study of ninety automotive plants (final assembly only) in seventeen countries, the book's message was that being competitive in auto assembly required getting lean. But those that are lean by the book's tough standards are fat by an even tougher standard: number of parts per plant.

I often judge a plant by a quick look-around just after entering for the first time. If I see conveyors winding through and above the work centers, fork trucks and mini-tractor-trailer trains filling the aisleways, and big islands of storage racks, the plant has too many parts. The obvious evidence has just been ticked off: non-value-adding conveyors, fork trucks, and so on. The nonobvious wastes are the extensive staff and information system required to keep track of all the movement and stocks.

Off-loading parts to supplier subassembly plants rids the final assembly plant of the non-value-adding wastes. When the number of parts is right, handling and accounting for them requires scarcely any costly storage, handling, and tracking apparatus or staff.

One of the more intriguing speculations about the future of manufacturing is along these lines. Future car assembly, according to the speculations, will involve small numbers of preassembled modules instead of thousands of piece parts. One prediction, in 1989, came from the National Center for Manufacturing Sciences in Ann Arbor. The center's source materials were translated Japanese auto-industry documents, which painted a scenario of multiple small-car plants, each assembling a grand total of just thirty-seven modules.[23]

Anthony Vecellio, a GM engineer and inventor, has patented a similar idea: consolidating the fifteen thousand parts found in an average car to fifteen integrated subsystems. Fifty or so small $10 million assembly studios would replace one massive $2 billion highly automated assembly plant. (His plants would incorporate various other ideas and inventions of his.)[24]

The future may have arrived. The new Mercedes-Benz venture in Tuscaloosa, Alabama, follows the modular idea. The plan is for most of the vehicle's parts to arrive in about twenty modules for bolting and welding together. For example, the cockpit will be a single module, complete with steering column and air bag, air conditioning and heater, and built-in audio system. The plant's target cost is only $540 million versus the estimated $1.9 billion that GM has sunk into its Saturn complex in Tennessee.[25]

The new mode of auto assembly dovetails with the industry's strategy of relying more on the expertise of suppliers. Let the supplier of cockpits become the cockpit expert, the seat manufacturer the expert in seats, and so forth. Levels of expertise will be raised, unit costs for parts will fall, and suppliers will become strong and durable rather than competitive pushovers (Principle 1, partnering up).

The advantages of modular assembly apply not just to cars but to all products high in parts counts: mass spectrometers, mainframe computers and copying machines, and airplanes, to name a few. For example, Boeing's engine buildup factory in Kent, Washington, has shifted from loose parts to preassembled modules. One result is a sharp reduction in assembly defects. The specifications for hundreds of parts that had to be hung on the engine were too many for the assemblers to master. Staying sharp on the assembly requirements of the much smaller number of modules is no problem.

HOW MASS PRODUCTION?

Mass production is not a yes or no proposition. Rather, it's a matter of degree. Large-quantity producers making sporadic lot sizes operate too far from the high end of mass production to be effective for long. They need to look diligently for parts and processes to standardize and to put on rate-based schedules. And they need to seek out flexible, agile equipment and methods to apply especially at final stages of production. The quest for agile manufacturing capabilities arises from needs to respond quickly to product-life-cycle shifts and dodges. These matters—standardization, rate-based production, and agility—are the chapter's final topics.

Standardization

Among practitioners of world-class manufacturing, standardization is a familiar topic—one that needs little elaboration here. Kiyoshi Suzaki's book *The New Shop Floor Management* devotes most of a chapter to the matter.[26] Among other things, good shop-floor management requires standardizing—spelling out numerically—the amounts of work-in-process at every work center. Robert Hall's books and writings are also excellent on standardization. His lists of things to be standardized include number of parts, product line, equipment, tooling, methods, and training.[27] Roy Harmon makes the same kind of point for warehouses, which he says should "[trim] the unnecessary bells and whistles, concentrating on machines suitable for specific purposes, and forgetting the elusive goal of universal flexibility."[28] Standardization can apply to pricing and scheduling as well, as is explained next.

Usage-Rate Production

Value pricing is not just for consumer-goods makers like Procter & Gamble. Carmakers have their own version: offering a standard vehicle package at rock-bottom prices with no dickering. For example, for $13,995, GM offered a 1995 Pontiac Grand AM SE sedan equipped with air-conditioning, radio and cassette player, and tilt steering. "That's $1,450 below what it would normally sell for if the same options were ordered for a base vehicle, GM said. And it's $4,155 less than . . . a similarly equipped Honda Accord LX."

Why would GM do this? Two answers. One is standardization of option packages, which is easy to understand. The other is more subtle and perhaps not fully exploited by GM: The possibility of scheduling that standard model as if it were the only car GM makes—something like Ford did with its basic black Model T over fifty years ago. There are two ways to do this in final assembly:

1. If the sales volume is sufficient, make the Grand AM SE on a single dedicated assembly line. Produce it at the sales rate, same quantity every day. Adjust the rate only once a month as new sales figures come in and to account for any promotions or rebate deals. For this option to be profitable, sufficient volume might mean, say, one and a half to two shifts of demand. The many advantages of a dedicated line easily justify letting the line go dark for the rest of the twenty-four hour day.

2. For a lesser volume intermix a regularized schedule for the SE with irregularity for other models. ("Regular" means repeating the mix, or in this example, repeating the dominant item in the mix. An alternative, oft-used term is "leveled," but level might be interpreted just as the same number of units per day with no regard for the mix.) Among the ways of doing this are the following:

A. Run the SE on Mondays and Thursdays and other models the rest of the week.
B. Run the SE for one shift, same daily quantity, then change to an irregular mix of other models for the rest of the day.
C. Run to a mixed-model schedule, in which the SE repeats in a regular cycle and other models fill in the gaps. For example, where X is any other model:

SE   X   SE   SE   X
SE   X   SE   SE   X

Etc.

For the sake of hundreds of subassemblies and component parts, options 1 and 2C are best. They allow the daily regularity to be passed backward, becoming the production and delivery schedules for hundreds or thousands of parts. Some of this regularity passes back through more than one echelon of supply.

Whenever schedules can be regularized, quality and efficiency improve. Certain pieces of equipment can be dedicated, which eliminates model-to-model changeover costs. Sometimes the dedicated equipment is a small, simple, low-cost machine. (Nondedicated equipment, in contrast, tends to be larger and equipped with costly, complex changeover features.)

More importantly, various overhead costs plunge. It is sometimes possible to eliminate work orders and related baggage, such as work-order accounting and completion transactions. Thousands or even tens of thousands of computer transactions per month can disappear.

But what about all the irregulars—especially irregular demands that are unexpected? That situation calls for agile manufacturing.[29] (Flexibility is said to be the ability to react to planned changes, whereas agility is the ability to react to unplanned changes.)

Agility

In general, high agility is being able to respond quickly to life-cycle shifts. In many industries product lives have been steadily shrinking, which raises the stakes. But many products' lives are hard to predict because products are a bit like people. Some age gracefully. Others get sick and die suddenly.

When a product runs down slowly, the supply chain can react—without much need for agility—and avoid costs of obsolete stocks. And producers can introduce new products or models to keep capacity busy. When a product sickens and drops dead, however, the costs and losses can be very high.

Consumer Need or Quirk?

Sometimes, a little common sense can suggest when a product is likely to die suddenly. Some years ago my son wanted a bicycle to ride to college classes. I tried to steer him to the practical kind with straight handlebars. He scoffed because at that time—when adult biking was the new, green thing to do in the United States and Canada—"nobody" would have such a bike. It had to be the kind with downward-thrust racing-bike handlebars. To no avail, I pointed out that in mature bike-riding countries, such as the Netherlands and Japan, everyone except racers had bikes with sensible straight handlebars.

Within a few years, the racing-bike fad died. Straight handles were—and are—all any casual cyclist wants. The temporary popularity of the low-slung handlebars was a style quirk.

This fad involved handlebars. It would be no problem for Panasonic's bicycle division to deal with a sudden shift in handlebars. The company's technology for turning out customer-tailored bicycles is a frequently cited example of agility. The starting point is the bicycle retailer's store, where clerks take the customer's measurements and preferences. The data speeds electronically to the factory, whose semiautomated final assembly cells fill the order—with an assembly lot size of one.[30] This degree of agility is backed up, however, by mass production of common frame components and smaller parts. Without the foundation of mass-produced, standardized parts, the Panasonic feat would be a technological marvel but a financial disaster.

Robert Hall is articulate on the subject of agile manufacturing. He cites the likely development of technology in which a man can order a "custom-designed suit that is built to exact body measurements" and

MORE STYLE QUIRKS

The point about bike handlebars is, when a craze doesn't make sense, it is probably wise to expect it to die precipitously. Contingency planning for quick product deaths is a necessary part of agility. (Here we are talking about staples and durable goods; no one needs cautionary advice about items known to be faddish, such as teenagers' apparel.)

Consumer electronics provides another example. The gadget-happy Japanese were the style setters who kept putting more rows of tinier buttons on the controls of the stereo, VCR, or TV remote. Manufacturers might have foreseen a backlash, because the trend didn't make sense. They finally responded with simpler devices with bigger buttons about the time that comedy-club wags had made standard shtick of the VCR-programmable-only-by-a-kid.

I sometimes wonder if the driver's cockpit in today's automobiles hasn't become as silly as racing handlebars on recreational bikes. Intruding upon the driver's ability to shift position now and then are severely bucketed low-to-the-floor seats, knee-cracking dash and steering columns, and ever larger consoles for the gearshift apparatus and various pigeonholes. Oldsmobile's 1994 Aurora goes one step further, featuring a rounded dash that seems to surround the driver. No wonder so many people buy a minivan or jeeplike vehicle instead. Andy Rooney, please investigate.[31]

---

have it ready the next day. He wonders, however, "how many men will want immediate delivery [and] how many will actually prefer to design their own suit." He wonders further, "How many off-the-rack buyers will order a customer-fit version of something on the rack?" "No one knows," Hall says, "whether such a market will be limited to connoisseurs, or whether the vision will be shaped by a new movement in customer roles and tastes." Hall concludes by saying that "In any case, it's wise to begin with a vision that allows for flexibility depending on customer preferences. . . . "[32]

Yes. And we need not restrict that vision to fancy technology. The sure road to agility is mass-making modular components, then (where it makes sense) employing data communications and gee-whiz production technology at the end to put them together as the customer sees fit.

Agility has multiple dimensions, the most obvious of which is ability to change over from one product to another on a dime. Industry understands and has worked on this dimension for a long time. Movability, another dimension, has not received much emphasis.

Portability

The cofounder of Sealed Air Corporation, maker of bubble mailing envelopes, however, was thinking about it—many years ago. His vision was of an extruder on the back of a truck that pulls up to a customer and runs off the customer's order on the spot.

Such visions of portability are becoming a reality in, of all places, the machine-tool industry. Ingersoll's octahedral hexapod, designed for agile manufacturing, is one example. Giddings & Lewis has its own version—the Variax. Both machines have geodesic dome–like frames, which provide a high degree of stability without the need to bolt them to a thick concrete floor. The hexapod and the Variax have several features that make them agile:

• Because the hexipod is so self-contained, Dennis Bray, Ingersoll's vice president of technology, sees it as a natural for machining in low-gravity, such as in space or on the moon. The machine's mechanical simplicity along with its foundation independence provide other advantages. These, Bray says, include the ability of users "to quickly reconfigure production lines, with the easy option of storing the machines disassembled when they aren't needed.[33]

• Paul Sheldon, vice president of R&D at Giddings & Lewis, touts the Variax's portability. In moving the machine from a plant to its headquarters, "We had a truck in Milwaukee at seven in the morning, and at five that evening the machine was running in its new location." In contrast, Sheldon cites an aerospace manufacturer's relocation of a machine tool: "It involved three months and $150,000, and I'm not sure that included the cost of the factory-floor space that was being used as a pit [for the tool's foundation] until they filled it with metal reinforcement and concrete." In addition, the Variax contour-cuts five times faster than a typical machining center and accelerates faster as well.[34]

CONCLUSION: SOMEONE WANTS WHAT YOU HAVE

If volume production of standardized components is so attractive and so fitting with market trends, why do we hear from so many experts that mass production is dying? One reason is carelessness about the definition of it. Growth of sales and production volumes are what every business wants. But when product volume is chopped up and unsynchronized—yesterday's approach—we have a job shop, not mass production.

Another reason may be perspective. The well-off Westerner who writes books and articles on the future of manufacturing sees commodity goods as unappealing and thus sees variety as the future. An executive with Chetak-Bajaj in India, however, would see things differently. Bajaj sells a few million motorbikes a year in only a few models. And a few hundred million Indian citizens look forward to when they, too, will have enough money to buy a Bajaj.

7

Strategic Linkages

Medieval castles have a characteristic architecture: fortified inner buildings with towers interrupted by window slits that allow inhabitants to see out without being easily seen—or targeted; and extremely thick outer walls with defensive ramparts and watchtowers. The business enterprise, especially the manufacturing company, is like that.

We all know about the inner fortifications. Instead of castle towers, the favored metaphor is silos, representing functional departments.[1] Looking at the manufacturing company more closely, however, we see the shape of a castle—actually two nearby castles with the same owner. One specializes in production; the other in distribution. The two communicate at a distance, feebly. The communication dysfunctions are leading causes of the same serious problems: misguided product and capacity decisions and poor service to best customers. Products get made and shipped but often the wrong ones or at the wrong times. Three approaches can help bring the crossed strategies into alignment:

1. Multi-echelon collaboration (supply-chain reengineering): Manufacturers harness point-of-sale data to force joint action back through the supply chain. This approach, originating in the United States in the mid-1980s, was labeled *quick-response* program; a later version is called *vendor-managed inventory;* another version is *efficient customer response.*

135

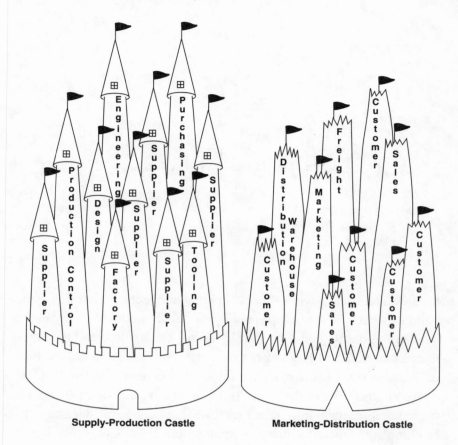

Supply-Production Castle   **Marketing-Distribution Castle**

2. Next-echelon partnering (immediate suppliers/customers). A producer plans jointly with next-echelon suppliers and customers. Few companies have done this as well as Boeing did on the design of its 777 passenger aircraft.

3. Within-company multifunctional collaboration. A company gets its divergent functionaries to team up and work out collectively beneficial strategies. A commonsense result involves favoring certain classes of customers and products over others—as has been done at Queen City Treating Co., a small job shop.

Where applied together, as in such leading-edge organizations as Milliken and Wal-Mart, multi-echelon, next-echelon, and within-company collaboration are mutually reinforcing. Discussion of the three approaches comes later in the chapter. First, let's look more closely at a few examples of the two-castle problem.

PRODUCT DECISIONS AND CUSTOMER SERVICE

Managers at Thomson, the French-based manufacturing giant, had a descriptive way of referring to a deep-seated functional rift within its television manufacturing group. I was conducting a seminar in Paris for managers of the group. Thomson had been on a buying spree and had become the owner of several TV brands. These included its own marques in France, Telefunken in Germany, Ferguson in the United Kingdom, RCA in the United States, and so on. In chatting with some of the attendees before the program began, I was told, "We are two companies in one."

"Are you referring to the European TV companies and the U.S. companies?" I asked. "No, no, monsieur. We mean the production company and the distribution company." I nodded, knowingly.

Motorola's recent misread of its market for cellular phones shows that even a Malcolm Baldrige prizewinner—steeped in TQM and customer consciousness—tends still to be a house divided. In February 1995 the company's stock plunged 10 percent on news that its production unit had swamped dealers with inventory they didn't need. Distributors were reported to be offering to sell their overstocks at below cost. Rakes Sood, analyst at Hambrecht and Quist Inc., said, "Motorola should have known that orders were going beyond demand."[2]

Unaware and Unconcerned

Most manufacturers have the same problem. Sales and marketing—the distribution company—live with customers in their own high-walled castle, blissfully unaware of and unconcerned about productive capacities and capabilities. Production, in its castle, has no access to final customers' needs and seeks none. It plans to suit its own interests, which are to meet its own internally set schedules and to maximize resource utilization.

Small organizations are the exception. Their managers and professionals wear several hats. Engineers and production managers meet with

PRODUCTION CASTLE: THICK OUTER WALLS

TQM and reengineering have made their marks in manufacturing. Final producers partner up backward, deep into the supply chain. Via quick-change artistry, basic materials suppliers—of polymers, metals, dyes, fabrics—make and deliver in smaller lots more often. Component makers reengineer to create plants-in-a-plant and work cells. JIT processing extends from receipt of basic materials to shipment and forward from one stage of manufacture to another, all the way to the final product. Each stage builds quality in, which avoids quality-hold areas and inspection delays at customer plants.

Freight haulers reengineer as well. Operating with advance shipping notices, satellite navigation, backup vehicles, and electronic data interchange, they pick up at suppliers' docks to the hour and deliver to point-of-use docks at customers' plants.

The effect is to create highly synchronized chains of customers. Timing is tight, like an Olympic-class relay team. Each stage of manufacture achieves close to 100 percent on-time performance. The trouble is, it's on time against manufacturing's own schedules. They, in turn, are based on off-target forecasts, orders that have been batched too many times, and an internal fixation on capacity utilization. Fast-changing industries, such as consumer electronics and apparel, suffer the most. Early stages of production (e.g., semiconductors and fabric makers) can be 100 percent on time but 180 degrees out of phase with what final users are actually buying or want to buy. Even final producers can be well out of phase, since both the production and the distribution castles fill their grounds with warehouses of made-on-a-guess finished goods—the responsibility for which is ambiguous.

and relate to customers. Marketers, sales staff, and distribution people interact with production planners, schedulers, and supervisors in booking and filling orders. When companies grow, however, each profession proceeds to organize around itself—the towered citadels within the castle. Later, they form two superfunctions (two castles). Fog shrouds sightlines from the product development, purchasing, and production side (one castle) to the distributor-customer functions (other castle).

The production-distribution misconnection is harmful not only for the company but also its customers. Consumer goods—tobacco, household supplies, foods, and the like—offer many highly visible examples. Quaker Oats is typical:[3]

- Production Company. At Quaker's Shiremanstown, Pennsylvania, plant, the credo was, Keep the machines running full tilt. It took up to six weeks to run all nine flavors of Instant Quaker Oatmeal cereal. Dominant flavors, such as apple-cinnamon, were produced in huge batches.

- Distribution Company. Sales and marketing's strategy was to offer deep discounts, especially to meet quarter-end sales targets and garner bonuses.

- Consequences. Quaker had to carry huge inventories to bridge the gulf between production's even output and distribution's spikey sales strategy. Food stores and their customers were the real losers: They had to carry huge stocks and pass both Quaker's and their own higher costs—and aging inventories—onto final consumers. This is not an example of large retailers using their high sales volumes to obtain quantity discounts—a rational business activity. Instead, it is a practice pejoratively known as *trade loading* or *channel stuffing*,[4] in which suppliers use their name-brand clout to push overstocks upon customers.

DISTRIBUTION CASTLE: CUSTOMER SENSITIZED, IN A WAY

Marketing and distribution are finding excellent uses for modern improvement tools. Reengineering projects forge tighter, more responsive linkages forward from company distribution centers (DCs) to customer DCs and onward to final use points. TQM projects include zero-defect ordertaking, 24-hour customer-service hot lines, benchmarking tours of the world's best-managed DC's, just-in-time shipments, and simplification of shipping and receiving paper to eliminate non-value-adding steps.

At the same time, marketing continues to indulge in promotions, specials, negotiated delivery dates, and end-of-period sales bonuses. These and other initiatives create great waves of demand. The waves slosh backward, alternately flooding and drying out the neighboring manufacturing/supply-base castle.

Organizational Realignments

There are notable exceptions to this state of affairs. Leading-edge manufacturers are forging strategic linkages several echelons back through their supply chains and forward along their chains of customers (Principle 1). The three kinds of collaborations previously listed—multiechelon, next-echelon, and multifunctional-internal—bring about closure: one company instead of two-in-one.

These agreements employ reengineering and total quality management and direct them toward organizational realignments (instead of just an overhaul of processes). This may be thought of as the third phase of an industrial transformation. Earlier phases aimed first at operations, then at back-office support.

Exhibit 7-1 elaborates on the three phases. We'll look closely at the third and newest phase, strategic collaboration.

BUILDING BRIDGES

When the walls of a besieged castle could not be breached, attackers used ladders and built siege towers to abut and bridge over them. The same thing works—but in a cooperative rather than an attack mode—when disunity between production and distribution is the barrier. Companies in the chain of customers build the bridge. The underpinning is final user demand.

A start on final-demand-based bridge building was made early in the 1980s. Benetton, the Italian clothier specializing in multicolored garments, used its retail sales data to schedule factories making the garments. Wary of the uncertainty of the fashion business, Benetton produced 25 percent of total output *undyed;* then it colored the garments "at the last minute" based on very current sales data. The remaining 75 percent was produced (with color) and shipped based on forecasts, which provide a longer planning horizon. This system partially closes the production-distribution gap, since factories can run most of their production to a fairly stable plan and still react to spurts in the marketplace. Benetton could do it alone since it owns or controls both the globally scattered Benetton outlets and the apparel plants in Italy.

EXHIBIT 7-1
Industrial Transformation: Three Phases

Phase 1, since early 1980s—Customer-focused operations. Production functions (e.g., molding, circuitry, assembly, and packing) are broken up. They emerge reengineered as plants-in-a-plant, work cells, and flow lines. Each focuses on a family of products or services—what customers buy or use—and is measured based on continuous improvement in generic indicators such as speed, conformance quality, and flexibility.[5]

Phase 2, since mid 1980s—Customer-focused support functions. Walls around functional support departments (e.g., purchasing, receiving, and accounts payable) come down. Reengineered units encompass entire critical processes (e.g., a colocated order-entry team), one for each focused production unit.[6]

Phase 3, since late 1980s—Strategic collaboration.
- **Multi-echelon.** Firms in supply and customer chains collaborate. They jointly plan, schedule, and ship based on recent sales to final consumers (rather than each independently managing customer demands based on internal efficiency and capacity utilization). The joint goal—and name for the approach—is *quick response*.
- **Next-echelon.** Planners from one's own organization, plus next-echelon suppliers and customers, team up to generate novel options that each would be unlikely to consider independently.
- **Multifunctional, within-company**. Divisive functions (especially the production and distribution core functions) unite. They form multifunctional product strategy teams, which jointly make planning and demand management decisions formerly made independently (e.g., longer-term decisions on new products and markets and immediate decisions to restrict or divert sales when demand exceeds capacity).

A few other companies, such as The Limited, have followed their own tailored variations on Benetton's approach. But what about the vast majority of firms that function in a long chain of independent companies?

MULTICOMPANY PLANNING

The need was for multicompany planning. Milliken and Company, the privately held textile and chemical giant, led an effort that puts all other examples of reengineering to shame.

Milliken had been among the first companies to mount a Philip Crosby zero-defects crusade, which grew into full-scale TQM and culminated, in 1989, in a Malcolm Baldrige national quality award. In 1986 a company team headed by CEO Roger Milliken invited several leading apparel houses, plus four of the largest U.S. department store chains, to a meeting in Chicago. The Kurt Salmon consulting firm had done a thorough study showing that the industry was losing the most profitable sales of all: resales of popular garments in the same season. Many-week lead times from fabric to retail had made same-season resupply of sold-out stocks impossible.

Quick Response

The Chicago textile-apparel-department-store cabal hammered out an audacious plan. They would synchronize the entire supply chain (or, from Milliken's position, customer chain) to recent sales at the four big department stores. Point-of-sale bar-code technology made the plan eminently feasible, although a crude version of the plan could have been carried out using telephones and fax machines. What was most important was the agreement among the diverse players in the chain of customers to use retail sales as the basis for *getting synchronized* (Principle 6). They called their creation "quick response" (QR) program. When implemented, QR had the effect of linking production and distribution companies at several echelons in the chain all at once. A response-time target of three weeks from fabric ordering to receipt in the department store—down from eighteen weeks (sometimes much more)—has been achieved through a few of Milliken's customer chains.

Within a few years many other sectors had forged similar chain-of-customer linkages. An annual Quick Response convention and exhibition emerged to tout the concept and the technology. Quick Response '93, held in Atlanta, included special sessions devoted not only to textiles and apparel but also to housewares, health and beauty aids, footwear, menswear, consumer electronics, toys, tools, hardware, and jewelry; attendees came from dozens of other business sectors as well.[7]

Basic QR requires only that producers receive point-of-sale data from selected stores. This is like election predictions. By sampling key precincts, pollsters can predict election results with high accuracy. Similarly, manufacturers—even if several echelons away from final sales points—can use recent POS samples as their production schedules. In contrast, conventional scheduling is always weeks or months out of date.

Though a manufacturer started QR, retailers have largely taken it over. Wal-Mart has gone so far as to publicly announce that it would cease doing business with distributors and would deal only with manufacturers. Manufacturers, in turn, provide freight haulers with advance shipping notices, and satellite-navigated trucks hit loading docks to the hour—or even within a fifteen-minute window. The retailer's own distribution centers don't stop and store but speed the goods onward via cross-docking. The following describes this no-stop way of getting the goods from the maker to the stores:

> Every truck in industry-leading Schneider National's fleet has sprouted a jaunty little satellite antenna. . . . You look in the cab and see generally not a Teamsters truck driver but an 'associate' with a merit pay plan and an on-board computer that links him with headquarters. . . . When Schneider's tractor-trailer pulls up with a cargo of appliances, for example, Sears' home delivery trucks are lined up across the loading dock, scheduled to bring them to customers expecting delivery that day.[8]

Vendor-Managed Inventory and Efficient Customer Response

In the next step—beyond basic quick response—retailers confer to producers the management of retail inventories. Under this plan, called vendor-managed inventory (VMI), first-echelon producers receive POS data from their retail customers daily by electronic data interchange and have access to retailers' inventory files. For example, by 1992 Kmart had developed two hundred suppliers as its VMI partners.[9] These makers are responsible for more than their own production. They must also ensure that the retailer's needs are included in the replenishment plans of producers down into the supply chain.

Efficient customer response (ECR) is sometimes used as a synonym for VMI. Alternatively, ECR provides additional supply-chain linkages in four main ways:[10]

- Efficient replenishment. These are the practices already described for QR and VMI.
- Efficient assortment. Retailers use sophisticated "category management" software to stock store areas with what consumers want most. The twin aims are more sales per square foot and improved customer satisfaction.
- Efficient promotion. Order, produce, ship, and stock exactly what sells. Cease forward buying, trade loading, and BOGOS (buy one, get one free), which pay little heed to real customer needs or usage.
- Efficient product introduction. Product development is a joint effort. Producers, distributors, brokers, and retailers team up to get the right products to market quickly.

Regarding efficient promotion, Ronald Zarrella, GM's new head of sales and marketing, has introduced a radical idea: Advertise and promote car models throughout their life cycle instead of spending lavishly in the introductory year, then starving the model after that. Zarrella, formerly president of eyeglass maker Bausch & Lomb, had no previous experience in autos to becloud his views on good promotional practices.[11]

We have seen the power of QR/VMI/ECR for goods that can be tracked all the way to the retail sales point. What about the vast number of manufacturers making industrial products or items supplied to myriad downstream-user chains? In this category are bearings, fasteners, coil and sheet stock, chemicals, polymers, and many more. Makers of these products need to invent their own versions of QR. The current method—making everything to forecasts and orders from immediate customers—is delay-prone, uses capacity poorly, and is blind to real usage patterns. The answer is to form quick-response partnerships with major customers and a sample of their customers' customers. A few manufacturers have taken the first steps. Kennametal, for example, manages inventories (and tool testing as well) for companies like GM's Saturn.[12]

Although the simple, early versions of QR could have come about with phones and faxes, we are now beyond that. We have entered the important new age of electronic commerce. Internal electronic systems for planning, scheduling, and control have often been disappointing, creating complexities and wastes even as they deal with other complexities. The promise of electronic commerce is that it links external partners up and down supply chains in ways that immediately snuff out long-standing delays, wastes, and tendencies to operate at cross purposes.

Demand Forecasting

A manager attending one of my public seminars wondered if I was saying that manufacturers using QR no longer had to forecast. One answer is that the point-of-sale data from the stores is the forecast, which is the production schedule. In this early stage of QR, however, only certain of a manufacturer's products or models are likely to be covered under QR. For now, the rest require traditional forecasting.

POS-based forecasts are reasonable where the POS data are based on valid sampling, or a 100 percent sample, and for even-selling products. Where sales are uneven because of store promotions or the manufacturer's sales promotions, a familiar demand-forecasting method enters the picture: the sales force estimate. That is, the manufacturer's salespeople keep tabs on upcoming sales promotions, which merge with POS sales data to produce the forecast. That forecast may become the production schedule. In my experience the biggest beef between the production castle and the distribution castle has always centered around demand forecasting, which production people always say is way off the mark. Inasmuch as QR is by definition right on the mark, QR is a momentous invention.

We have been referring to model-mix forecasting, which is the part that QR can replace. Aggregate forecasting is another story. Forecasting the aggregate of all models several quarters and several years into the future will always be necessary. The midterm and long-term purpose is predicting needs for labor, equipment, and plant. Happily, aggregate forecasting has a built-in accuracy-improving factor: Aggregate demand is a mix of items that are likely to be overestimated and underestimated. The over- and under-estimates tend to cancel out, which improves accuracy.

PLANNING WITH IMMEDIATE PARTNERS

It isn't easy to get multiple layers in the supply chain together. An easier starting point may be special-purpose linkages with one's immediate supplier or customer. These limited partnerships usually address production-supply problems, quality and warranty issues, new technologies, product design, and other issues. (In contrast, multiechelon partnerships have a single-minded focus on shared demand data.)

Boeing's development of the new 777 commercial airplane is a notable example. While all of its prior aircraft had been developed with virtually no external inputs, this time Boeing established 235 design-build teams, which included, in addition to assorted Boeing functionaries, the airlines and the suppliers. Among the many design innovations emerging from the teams are hushed lavatory doors and toilet seats. Shin-ichi Nakagawa, leader of a group of 250 engineers from Japanese supplier companies, says Japanese companies "are familiar with teams of design and production engineers, but they haven't experienced Boeing's all-embracing teams that include customers, suppliers, and support teams."[13]

The Boeing teams designed an entire aircraft having some 3 million parts. Joint projects between suppliers and customers usually are narrower in scope.

For example, I listened to a presentation by a team of Wal-Mart and Johnson & Johnson people.[14] They described joint studies leading to such things as price reductions in Wal-Mart stores that would increase sales, market share, and production volumes while smoothing demand. Revenue and net income would be raised for both partners. In other words, marketing people at each company would not be setting prices independently. Nor would finance people at each set financial targets independently or production people at J&J set production rates and plan capacity independently. The prices J&J would charge Wal-Mart and Wal-Mart its customers were worked out by the cross-functional team representing both companies: accountants, operations managers, and marketing representatives. The process altered both companies' financial plans for the product line, as well as, in part, J&J's production and capacity plans.

Another example of close partnership involves Xerox Corporation, the developer of benchmarking. What are the most advanced and potentially most important uses of benchmarking data? It may be deciding which suppliers to partner with and providing those partners with advice on how to meet world standards. Xerox uses its voluminous database of benchmark metrics for just those purposes.[15]

INTERNAL MULTIFUNCTIONAL PLANNING

Close supplier-customer planning may eventually become common—at least for superior companies. But what if, right now, your company can find no willing partners upstream or down? Can anything be done internally to link the production and distribution companies?

Yes. First step, which many manufacturers have already done, is to create plants-in-a-plant and work cells. Each is organized around a product family. This is reengineering at the operational level.

At higher managerial levels, however, fractionated functional management generally persists. When business is slow, that may cause little apparent grief. But separatism creates havoc when business gets brisk and demand exceeds capacity. This is when profit-making opportunities and competitive risks are at their peak. On the risk side, this is when service deteriorates and customers, even long-standing ones, are most likely to defect. To take advantage of the opportunities and avoid service deterioration, collaborative response becomes essential.

Decomposing the Order Book

To do it right, each product family must have its own cross-functional team—call them *multifunctional product strategy teams*. At a minimum, team members should come from sales and marketing, finance, and production; also, in some cases, product development, purchasing, and human resources. One of the team's roles is to act as a superordinate master planner. In that capacity it meets often, perhaps weekly. It decomposes the order book or recent sales, which nearly always will contain a mix of high-profit, low-profit, and loss items—to good customers, average customers, and pain-in-the-neck customers. See Exhibit 7-2.

EXHIBIT 7-2
Decomposing Recent Sales or Orders

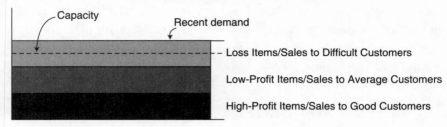

Capacity

Recent demand

- - Loss Items/Sales to Difficult Customers

Low-Profit Items/Sales to Average Customers

High-Profit Items/Sales to Good Customers

When business is slow, the company gladly does business with difficult customers. It will sometimes even sell at a loss—to help cover fixed costs. When average demand exceeds capacity, however, the team looks for best ways to refuse or divert business; see the right side of Exhibit 7-3. This may include stretching out deliveries or response times to the point where the customer begins to look elsewhere. The usual marketing imperative—sell, sell, sell—makes no sense in this situation. Every sale is not equal. Some are very good sales, and others are not. Finance needs to be involved to help show total financial impact, and operations needs to be there to articulate capacity alternatives, such as overtime and subcontracting. A marketing contribution is

EXHIBIT 7-3
Role of the Multifunctional Product Strategy Team (MPST)

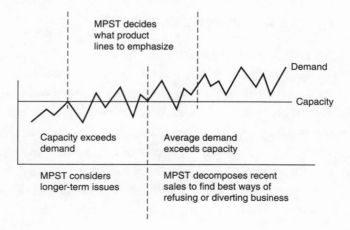

MPST decides
what product
lines to emphasize

Demand

Capacity

Capacity exceeds
demand

Average demand
exceeds capacity

MPST considers
longer-term issues

MPST decomposes recent
sales to find best ways of
refusing or diverting business

to note when it is advantageous to be a full-line producer despite losses on some items. In other words, keep selling a certain product at a loss to a major customer in order to also sell highly profitable items to the same customer.

One company that follows this type of differentiated sales/production strategy is Cincinnati-based Queen City Treating Company.[16] A small, privately owned job shop specializing in heat-treating metal parts, Queen City had been typical of its industry. As President Ed Stenger put it, it was "Be everything to everyone. Compete on price. Quote all comers—regardless of part or process. Promise whatever it takes on delivery. And never tell a customer anything more than he absolutely needs to know." But Stenger had heard a different tune at a meeting on strategy sponsored by the Cincinnati Chamber of Commerce. Consultant William C. Menke, the speaker, stimulated Stenger and some of his young managers to rethink their conventional strategy.[17] They studied their customer base and developed a strategy of targeted growth as opposed to being all things to everyone.

Under the new strategy, Stenger and his management team arranged customers into three tiers. First-tier customers: high volume, common processes; second tier: substantial volume, considerable process commonality (these two tiers are "key accounts"); third tier: low volume, irregular frequency, and little process commonality. A new price and delivery structure strongly favors key-account customers both in dollars and delivery times—at the expense of the third tier.

Stenger explains: "The simple fact is, and always has been, that the lowest-tier customer interrupts our ability to service the upper tiers—those who pay the bills. . . . Which doesn't mean we won't service [the third tier]. It just means they'll pay more and wait longer if they want us to do the work. What we are doing in effect is renting time in our furnaces to our volume customers."

Volume customers are on the mind of James E. Schwarz, Sr., as well. Schwarz is owner of Omni-Circuits, Inc., a small circuit-board assembler in Glenview, Illinois. Omni has trimmed its customer list from two hundred to twenty. Schwarz says, "I can't march to the tune of ten different drummers."[18] In Chapter 2 we learned that Nypro has a similar strategy, cutting its customer base from six hundred small and large to thirty-one big ones. The same for Microelectronics Modules Corporation, Milwaukee, where each Friday morning CEO Kenneth A. Hammer and key lieutenants sit down and decide which customers to accept or decline.[19]

Donald B. Bibeault follows the same modus operandi in his role as a highly successful turnaround artist (a temporary CEO brought in by bankers and creditors to fix a company that has fallen into bankruptcy). He extends the version of Pareto's law that says 20 percent of customers or products generate 80 percent of sales. Bibeault's corollary states that 120 percent of profits come from just 20 percent of products, dealers, or customers. Wait a minute. How can any group earn more than 100 percent of a company's profits? It works out (adds up to 100 percent) because the bottom-tier customers, dealers, or products collectively lose 20 percent.[20]

Capacity Management and New Initiatives

The center zone in Exhibit 7-3 portrays periods when business occasionally exceeds capacity. In this situation the product strategy team has a narrower charge: trying to match sales with capacity excesses or shortages. Production must identify the underused and the overheated processes and related product lines. Sales then shifts its tactics to try to steer customers to the underused and away from the overheated. The results are better service to customers and fuller, more balanced use of capacity. Finance may provide profitability data that make these decisions less than cut-and-dried.

The product strategy team has a more relaxed role when business is slack and capacity is underused—the left side in Exhibit 7-3. It meets less often, and its main agenda is longer-term matters. These might include capacity changes, market initiatives, product development, and major improvement projects. To be sure, some organizations already have cross-functional groups that deal with such issues.

For example, in 1984 I was engaged as advisor to one of 3M Corporation's business units. A sizable cross-functional group of 3M'ers—marketing, production, and others—was involved. Our task was to sift alternatives for upgrading customer service in one major product line.

What emerged was the outline of a plan to shift from a single large production facility in the center of the United States to scattered, small satellite plants. Many would be located next door to a major customer. Large-scale movement of equipment and people would be involved. It was a strategy that required customer-service and distribution inputs from marketing, cost and other financial analyses from finance, capacity and production management information from operations, employment impacts from human resources, plus more inputs from others.

SMOOTHING THE DEMAND TURBULENCE

Today multifunctional product strategy teamwork is beginning to affect whole business sectors. One sign of this, in retailing, is everyday low pricing (EDLP). Wal-Mart Stores, Toys R Us, and most of the megastore retailers are thriving on the strategy. Multifunctional team analysis in these firms reveals the advantages: discounts for high-volume, leveled (rather than spiky) buying; simplified stock management, pricing, advertising, and employee training; and high consumer acceptance.

If, in the same companies, independent departments were to plot strategy and tactics in the usual way—separately—EDLP would not be the result. Instead, the advertising professionals would seek to preserve sizable departments geared toward ever-more arresting ways to do promotions and inform the public about the next sale. Buyers would have their eyes out for discount deals on big shipments—which to other departments are overstocks, but that's their problem. Stock management people would be trumping for larger distribution centers with more automated handling systems. And so on.

Retailers that have not converted to EDLP may have it rammed down their loading docks—by some of their suppliers. Multifunctional analysis in a few prominent supplier companies, such as Procter & Gamble and the "new" Quaker Oats, is turning the tide against promotions, deals, trade loading, and the end-of-period push. The new strategy calls for leveling demand. This more closely matches real customer-use patterns, cuts assorted administrative costs, and produces big capacity-management savings backward through the manufacturing echelons. Quaker's Pennsylvania plant, for example, now makes all nine flavors of instant oatmeal about weekly versus every six weeks under trade loading in the 1980s.

Industrial companies have their own complement to the retailer's everyday low pricing. To level demand, manufacturers employ value pricing, selective on-and-off advertising, and altered sales-bonus and performance-appraisal criteria. Marketing Corporation of America, a consulting firm, found that 75 percent of manufacturers it surveyed have initiated value pricing or are studying it.[21] The rest, presumably, are still separate castles—production planning one way and distribution another.

FORCING THE ACTION

We have seen three ways of bringing crossed strategies into alignment. Manufacturers harness end-user sales data to force collaborative activities back through the supply chain. They jointly plan with key suppliers and customers. Or they get their own divisive functionaries to work out collectively beneficial strategies. Where applied together (e.g., in such leading-edge organizations as Milliken and Wal-Mart), multi-echelon, next-echelon, and internal collaboration are mutually reinforcing.

Of the three types of collaboration, multi-echelon—quick response and related ideas—seems most potent. Quick response was a Western innovation. It probably could not have developed in Japan, given that country's notoriously inefficient distribution system, with layer upon layer of middlemen. QR may go down in history as one of the twentieth century's most important management innovations.

Next-echelon and internal partnerships are perverse, because they depend on middle managers to attack their own towers. Total quality management offers good reason for doing so: alliances in the name of customer service. Nevertheless, the towers resist destruction even in companies advanced in TQM. Perhaps the reason is that internal collaborations produce results slowly and not so visibly. Multi-echelon agreements (quick response and vendor-managed inventory), on the other hand, are company-to-company and are sweeping in scope. Moreover, they take the matter out of the hands of cautious functional managers. They force managers to think and plan outwardly instead of inwardly.

TWO CASTLES IN SERVICES, TOO

Much of this chapter's message applies in human services as well as manufacturing. Only the superfunctions are not production and distribution. Instead, in services one castle houses the planners and the other the frontline service associates expected to execute the plans. Neither participates in the other's activities.

So far, the dominant examples of multi-echelon linkages are among big retail chains and the major manufacturers who supply those retailers. To compete, smaller retailers and manufacturers must do the same, and some are. Supporting service organizations, too, have castle walls to contend with (see box). At the same time, total quality management gets companies' functionaries thinking beyond their fiefdoms—about customers. This approach slowly but surely breaches barriers in both the castle's interior turrets and its outer walls.

Best advice to manufacturers, retailers, or service organizations is to look aggressively for next-echelon and multi-echelon partners and to also continue the TQM drive, with constant reminders that the object is service to customers, not functional glory.

8

Impediments: Bad Plant Design, Mismanagement of Capacity

Principle 15 calls for simple, flexible, movable, low-cost equipment in multiples. One participant enclosed a note explaining why they had scored themselves zero on this principle: They are in chemicals, where plant rigidity is a given.

I phoned him to mildly disagree. I cited a piece in *Target* magazine on Mitsui Toatsu's "pipeless" chemical plant. In that facility in Japan, mixing tanks move on rails along a production line, stopping to hook up three times—for charging, mixing, and discharging.[1] Another example is Milliken's Blacksburg, South Carolina, chemical plant, designed for flexible response. As noted in Chapter 6, instead of the usual single reactor group, the plant has two, a large and a small. One can be processing large batches while the other fills small orders. The plant is laid out for quick changeovers and elimination of non-value-adding drumming, charging, and inspecting.

Still, he's right. Chemical plants cannot score very high on this principle (other participating chemical companies scored themselves low to medium). Even so, the *principle* is correct—for any kind of manufacturing. Other industries and companies besides chemicals have their own problems in following the principle. We consider several of them in this chapter along with issues in managing physical and human capacity.

PRODUCTION LINES: FAILURE DESIGNED IN

"Lean and simple" is a centerpiece of world-class manufacturing. We find plentiful examples of it in almost every industry, with one glaring exception: filling and packing. While other industries were tearing out or shortening conveyors and closing the gaps between processes, the brewers, bottlers, canners, and packagers weren't. As protection against erratic filling and packaging equipment, they did what they had always done: They inserted long, wide conveyors between workstations and stuffed them with buffer stocks. Here and there they added accumulators to hold more stocks. In other words, failures, and allowances for them, are designed in.

The rationale goes something like this: Increasing line speeds, complex packaging equipment, and ever-lighter-weight containers and packaging materials make jam-ups likely—usually many per day. So to avoid full line stoppages, lay more conveyor and load it up. Minor problems—a clogged inserter or a filler out of ingredients—need not halt the whole line. Instead, operators race to the problem for a quick fix while the rest of the equipment keeps chunking. Still, major problems do stop the whole line. Despite the loaded conveyors, so many minor and major things go wrong so many times per day that lines in this business are down 30, 40, or even 50 percent of the time. Corporate headquarters' solution: Make the lines run even faster, which only increases the number of jam-ups.

TOO LONG, TOO WIDE, TOO FAST

Take, for example, a Swanson's frozen-dinner plant in Salisbury, Maryland, in 1985. The conveyor-driven fill-and-pack lines were 600 to 850 feet long. Line speeds—about 270 trays per minute—were a matter of pride for the company's designers and managers. But with light aluminum trays moving that fast past several fill stations, through long and not always straight and level sections of conveyor and into temperamental cartoning and packaging equipment, slight misalignments could result in spectacular jam-ups. Trays and their contents would fly into the air and quickly litter the floor and cover the equipment—and sometimes the operators—with gravy, peas, and apple cobbler. Average down time in the plant was three hours per shift.[2] Plant managers were tuned in to world-class concepts but fought a losing battle against the poor plant design. Campbell Soup, Swanson's parent, shuttered the plant in 1993.

The practice continues.

• A tea plant in England has just a few value-adding processes: teabag filling, boxing, wrapping, and case packing. Yet these processes stretch out along nearly two hundred feet of conveyor. Many hundreds of boxes containing thousands of tea bags separate the processes and put distance between the operators. Operators are not very busy. Yet they cannot tend more than one station, because stations are too far apart.

• A Coca Cola plant in Córdoba, Argentina, is equipped with a brand-new bottling line in a plant addition separate from the older lines. The equipment is the very best, the facility gleams with evidence of good upkeep and cleanliness, and the work force is highly skilled and cross-trained. Still, lengthy conveyors between stations hold many hundreds of bottles or cans.

• At Miller Brewing Company's Trenton, Ohio, works, distances between stations on canning lines are vast. Line associates could not communicate with each other over the din were it not for radio communicators clipped to the shoulders of their uniforms. Between some pairs of stations, several hundred cans occupy the non-value-adding conveyors. Whereas the old glass bottles or steel cans could usually make the circuit upright, today's lightweight, thin-walled aluminum cans sometimes get in trouble. A small imperfection in a conveyor segment, a bearing dry of lubrication, or a jerk in the mechanism can tip one can. At the speeds that modern fill-and-pack lines move, the result is similar to a many-car pileup on a fog-bound Southern California freeway.

Plant design weaknesses notwithstanding, both Coca Cola–Córdoba and Miller-Trenton have achieved high levels of excellence. They've done so through advanced human resource practices. More on Miller-Trenton in Chapter 9.

CONVEYOR REMOVAL

I wish I had a few good examples of well-designed production lines in the fill-and-pack sector. I don't. But there are plenty of examples in other industries. One is Plamex, a maquiladora plant in Tijuana, Mexico, manufacturing Plantonics-brand headsets by the thousands per day. Their headsets are used as hands-free telephone receivers by telemarketing companies, earphones for pilots and air-traffic controllers, and hundreds of other purposes.

In early 1994 assemblers clustered around long, powered conveyor lines. Alejandro Busamante, the plant's new manager, saw to the conveyors' removal, replacing them with thirty-foot by five-foot assembly-bench modules. A row of up to ten such modules is a focused production line, with first modules making components and last ones testing and packing finished units. The dozens of modules in the plant employ simple gravity slides made of wood. An associate completes an assembly step and places the component on a nearby slide, which delivers it to the next assembler, usually on the other side of the bench.

After the long conveyors had been removed, one automated module remained, and its performance was directly comparable with a nonautomated module next to it. Both produced exactly the same headset components. The automated module required eight operators. The nonautomated module had only six—and produced more components per day.

The design of the modules—assemblers on the two sides of the wide assembly benches—keeps Plamex teammates in close contact. Separation of each line into several modules has two beneficial effects: It keeps the teams small, and it allows each module some independence so that a problem in one module does not immediately affect the others. (As Harmon and Peterson noted at Kenmex, also in Tijuana, a single, long line is too hard to balance.)[3] One deficiency: The lines are straight rather than bending around themselves into an arc or U.

ARCS

By now the rationale for U-shaped or serpentine assembly lines and cells is well known. At least in general. But there are subtleties relating to such factors as flexibility, human operation, cycle time, and focus. One is the radius of the arcs. When the arcs are too tight, there is little room to insert more stations, either in the line or as subassembly stems directly feeding the line, as processes change. The other extreme is a straight line with no S's at all. Adding stations can only be done by stemming off the line; and taking out a station creates a gap—the bad solution for which is a conveyor.

Briggs & Stratton's factory in Milwaukee making small gasoline engines has many fine examples of machining cells. The sizable footprint of metal-cutting machines puts distance between each machine in a cell. In these cells short conveyors span those distances. Did I see the conveyors chockablock with inventory (e.g., shafts or gears)? I did not. Briggs follows the dictates of the Toyota production system: Set standard work-in-process quantities for each process, and hold to them. The standard WIP in the cells that I saw was just one or two pieces between machines. Operators and supervisors know those queue limits and see that they are enforced (Principle 6, cut flow distance, flow time, etc.). Without standard WIP, or space denial, keeping to the queue limits may require a "kanban cop," as with Martin Marietta in Denver.[4]

Enforcement is not so hard in machine-intensive manufacturing. Machines do not get upset when slowed down by a downstream problem. Labor-intensive processing is different. In the face of downstream stoppages, people's tendency is to keep right on assembling, filling any handy conveyor or flat surface. The discipline of kanban—formal space limitation—helps people abide by the queue limit, stop, and go to where the problem is to help.

At Briggs-Milwaukee, machining is followed by assembly lines— three of them. As is proper, the lines are S-shaped, not straight. However, they are lazy, wide-radius S's, with a large number of assemblers spaced rather far apart. My suggestion: Expand to about six assembly lines, each focused on fewer models (Principle 1, focus), and each in a more compact space with somewhat smaller arcs. The S's—or U's— still must be wide enough to allow subassembly stems, or even some machining, right off the line. Under the six-line design each assembler has more operations to do than before—a more complete task—but fewer models.

Exhibit 8-1 displays the points just discussed (but does not conform to the actual numbers of assemblers, distances, etc., at the Briggs plant). Part A shows three big S-lines, and Part B, four little S's and two U-lines. Part C demonstrates alternative ways of "flexing" the six small lines to incorporate process improvements.

The connection between line design and human performance bears closer scrutiny. The following examples begin with some seemingly trifling matters in order to arrive at grander issues. (Academically inclined readers may associate this discussion with a body of management thought known as socio-technical systems, which dates back to the work of F. E. Emery and E. L. Trist in the 1960s.)[5]

EXHIBIT 8-1
Assembly-Line Shapes

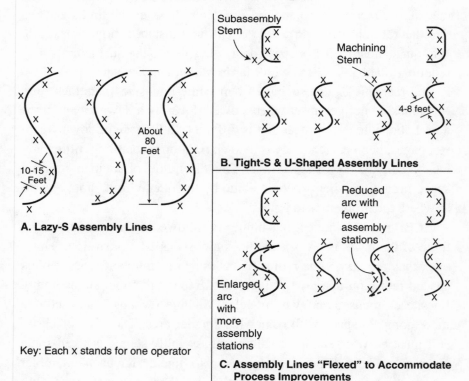

A. Lazy-S Assembly Lines

Key: Each x stands for one operator

B. Tight-S & U-Shaped Assembly Lines

C. Assembly Lines "Flexed" to Accommodate Process Improvements

ASSEMBLY LINES, STATION CYCLE TIMES, AND PEOPLE

An engineer for an assembler of lawn-care products was of two minds: One mind preferred U-lines. The other liked them straight because in a U-line he saw inefficiencies, plus ergonomic problems, for assemblers at corner stations. To pass parts to the next station around the corner, a seated assembler must reach left and also backward. (In light, manual assembly, the rule is to pass from right to left. This assigns to the left hand the simple task of passing the part to the next station, while the more dexterous—for most people—right hand completes another work element.)

The root of the issue, I maintained, was not line shape. It was the very short station cycle time designed into the process. It was about ten seconds. (To the industrial engineer cycle time means the time to do a task at one workstation. In common usage, however, cycle time has come to mean total throughput time through all stations.) Combine, say, six ten-second assembly stations into one, and the new station cycle time becomes a minute. Only one-sixth as many pass-offs from assembler to assembler are one result. Also, this design reduces repetitive motions and related health problems.

Combining several small work elements into a single assembler's task can change the job from sit-down to stand-up, walk-around assembly. At the U's turn point—where the engineer saw parts-passing inefficiencies—walk distance is at its shortest. Thus, combining elements to create longer-cycle jobs resolves the engineer's concerns about U-lines.

Let's look at station cycle times more closely. For examples, we'll revisit Mexico's maquiladora community, plus the cut-and-sew industry. The sheer numbers of maquilas—over two thousand plants (including those not on the U.S.-Mexico border)—along with their similarity of purpose, make them a convenient target for research.

Maquiladoras

A ten-second station cycle time used to be an accepted lower limit within the industrial engineering profession. Today, it should be outlawed. One reason is lost efficiency. We've just seen why. A longer station cycle time reduces the number of times an assembler has to pass parts—a non-value-adding element. Engineers at Sony, troubled by ten-second cycles at Sony's maquiladora assembly plant in Tijuana, Mexico, put the matter to a test. By time-study, they found in each 10-second cycle an average of two seconds lost to parts passing.

But efficiency loss is not the main objection to very short cycles. Nor is the higher incidence of repetitive-motion disorders and higher costs of insurance and medical claims, serious as those are. It is this: Assemblers doing the same task repeatedly twenty-five hundred times a day (which is the effect of a ten-second cycle) cannot think, record data, study, teach, learn, maintain, improve, and otherwise perform as a world-class work force (several principles apply here). It is a mind-numbing kind of work life, which surely contributes to the more than 100 percent employee turnover per year that plagues most maquiladora plants.

Still another objection: Short station cycles put too many associates into each line. Many of Mexico's maquilas have the too-many-people deficiency. When lines have thirty, forty, or fifty assemblers (as is generally true of auto-parts and consumer electronics plants all along the border) teamwork has little likelihood of taking root. Front-end people can't know the tasks, nor the people toward the middle and back end of the line. Then in group meetings people are passive, or they split off into cliques.

Some of the automotive wiring-harness plants in Ciudad Juárez are looking for alternatives. They have been experimenting with small cells in which each assembler takes on the tasks of six to ten narrow-task assemblers. This may require more training and may or may not affect labor productivity. In some companies, any idea that fails to improve productivity or cut head count is a loser. Corporate headquarters too readily turns a blind eye to all other merits—which can be substantial.

Cut and Sew

With few exceptions high-volume apparel plants have short cycle times, plus other deficiencies. Most still lack teams and a product focus (violating Principle 1). Instead, they have separate departments for separate pieces: This one just does collars, that one just left sleeves, and so on. Within departments each sewer is an island, surrounded by bundles of cut pieces and partly completed units.

The main pathway to world-class excellence is to break up the departments, eliminate the islands bunkered by bundles, and reorganize into modules—that industry's term for cells that build complete garments. A few plants have reduced stocks between sewers to a single piece. This can slash total throughput time from, say, ten days to as little as three minutes.[6] However, it doesn't improve productivity, which is the fixation of corporate executives.

Take the manufacture of jeans. Say that an operator is sewing on back pockets. She reaches and grabs a pair of jeans and a pocket, positions them, sews for five seconds, then reaches out to drop off the completed unit near the next sewer. That's a lot of reach and position time. Making this efficient can require putting in simple feeders, positioners, take-away devices, and stackers. The idea is to free the operator from the non-value-adding steps that can take more time than the sewing itself.

One maker of jeans that I visited already had such devices but for operators separated into islands and surrounded by heaps of stock. Some of that company's plants had tried the modular system, but it was generally abandoned. An obstacle was the need to modify all its devices for transfer to and from next stations rather than for unstacking and stacking in place.

While this company dithered, other companies marched, especially VF Corporation, maker of Wrangler and Lee jeans (see box, "Morning Edition"). VF's modular plants are meeting tough demands for quick response from customers like Marks and Spencer in the United Kingdom and Wal-Mart in North America. As a result, VF has taken market share from other famous jeans makers.

Genesis of Modular Sewing and TSS

The next step is to combine tasks so as to lengthen station cycle times. This reduces numbers of associates per module, creating a better climate for teamwork. But lengthening cycle times adds to the numbers of components feeding each workstation, creating congestion. Avoid-

"MORNING EDITION"—ON JEANS MANUFACTURE, YESTERDAY, TODAY, AND TOMORROW*

Yesterday

DAN CHARLES, reporter on "Morning Edition":[7] "Jeff Kernodle is an executive at Wrangler, the jeans company. He says typically nearly a third of the sizes of jeans that should be on the shelf aren't, they're out of stock."

KERNODLE (V.P. of Replenishment Services): "Now, guess which sizes are out of stock? The ones that sell the most. The ones that people never buy you don't get out of stock on because nobody buys them."

Today

CHARLES: "These days when the checkout clerk at your local J. C. Penneys or Kmart runs her laser scanner across the bar code on a pair of Wrangler jeans, the information flashes back across telephone wires to a huge computer center in Greensboro, North Carolina, Wrangler's headquarters. Wrangler keeps track of what's selling and ships just enough jeans to restock the shelves. . . . With this system in place, sales of Wrangler jeans shot up."

Tomorrow

CHARLES: "And now Kernodle is planning to bring small stores into this system, mom-and-pop operations where they may not even have a cash register, just a cigar box under the counter where they keep the cash. In his left hand Jeff Kernodle is holding the technology he hopes will make it possible. It's a combination of bar code scanner and computer, not much bigger than a walkie-talkie. On the front there's a keyboard with numbers, and there's a cord that plugs into any telephone jack. . . . Then, as customers buy their jeans, the store owners rip off the tags and collect them in a basket. At the end of the day they take this little handheld computer and scan the bar code." And the sales totals transmit to Wrangler's Greensboro data center, which triggers stock replenishment.

*© Copyright National Public Radio® 1994. This new series by NPR's Dan Charles was originally broadcast on National Public Radio's "Morning Edition" on December 19–21, 1994, and is used with the permission of National Public Radio. Any unauthorized duplication is strictly prohibited.

ing that—by limiting each sewing machine to just one or two component operations—requires one more step: Getting rid of the chairs and elevating the sewing machines for stand-up, walk-around sewing. These are defining characteristics of what is called TSS, the Toyota sewing system (originated in Toyota's textile business). Under TSS each associate in a module tends more than one machine. If sewer B is temporarily slowed down by a broken thread or other problem, sewers A and C cover more machines, and the work continues. (My first awareness of TSS was at U.S. Shoe Co., which adopted it in the early 1980s, perhaps the first Western company to do so. Lately, apparel manufacturers have been trouping to one of its shoe-manufacturing plants in Kentucky to see the system firsthand.) Until these steps (modular, with longer station cycles, and ideally TSS) are taken, the sewing industry will be stuck with ragged hems: No employee involvement, because no time to record data and ponder it.

The Textile Clothing Technology Corporation in Cary, North Carolina, has been active in promoting modular and TSS derivatives to the apparel industry. Calling itself $(TC)^2$, the corporation is a not-for-profit enterprise with 103 subscriber-members. Apparel companies, plus leading fiber and textile makers and even retailers, make up the member companies. Formed in 1981 through a National Science Foundation grant, $(TC)^2$'s original mission was robotics, automation, and pure research and development. By 1986 or 1987 it was becoming clear to $(TC)^2$ and its members that high-tech solutions were, for the most part, too costly. The main issue, after all, was how to compete with very-low-cost competitors in such countries as Indonesia, India, and China.

The cost factor has brought the textile and apparel industry labor unions into the act. The Crafted with Pride Council, a labor-sponsored organization, has actively promoted QR (quick response), which includes modular assembly methods along with producing to recent point-of-sale data from the retailers. Peter Butenhoff, now president of $(TC)^2$, had been affiliated with the council. $(TC)^2$'s data say that wages are only 10 percent of a garment's cost; 27 percent are the overhead costs (inventory carrying cost being one of them) that fall out under QR as a result of synchronizing the value chain. Unfortunately, says

Butenhoff, too many apparel companies are putting in modular systems for good but narrow reasons: higher quality and productivity, better ergonomics, and lower employee turnover. They tend to be a bit less committed to gaining the quick-response aspects.

(TC)^2 still finds occasional interest in a high-tech assembly method for apparel. It is called the modular production system (MPS), which involves overhead conveyors delivering a full set of cut pieces to individual sewers at individual sewing machines, all controlled by a personal computer. (I first saw an MPS in action in 1987, but was immediately turned off by it. Heavy-duty industrial overhead conveyors carrying lightweight cloth? It looked entirely out of place to me.) Mainly, (TC)^2's subscribers are interested in certain specialty automated devices (e.g., to sew collars) and, especially, a working model of a TSS in (TC)^2's demonstration center.[8]

The idea of elevating the workstations for walk-around operations can have merit in more than just the apparel industry. It gives each assembler a larger, more meaningful work unit, not to mention a healthier work life than in sedentary assembly.

WHOLE PLANTS

Like U-line logic, flexible factory concepts have been well aired. We know about the two ways to create focused factories or plants-in-a-plant: (1) dedicated capacity for high-volume standard products; (2) high-flex cells and flow lines, with movable equipment where possible, for families of diverse low-volume products. Those concepts are incorporated as customer-focused Principle 15.

Other ways to make factories flexible are through information systems. One approach is to harness information technology to plan, schedule, and control factory operations. Another is almost the opposite: Implement processes so simplified, standardized, and reliable that they can be managed visually. This latter approach is what Principle 12 is all about.

We take up a few of the issues in flexible production and production support next.

Flexible Limits

Flexibility has limits. Baldor Electric, producer of specialty electric motors, is a case in point. Its Fort Smith, Arkansas, plant was featured in *Fortune* magazine for having figured out "how to make thousands of models in small quantities—profitably."[9] The plant is a marvel of kanban devices, which limit queues in front of each stage of production: cutoff saw, rough machining, fine machining, coil winding, varnish and bake oven, and so forth. Pictured in the article is a wide assortment of AC motors converging on final assembly in lot sizes of what look like one. We are told that the manufacturing cycle time is a measly five days.

After my own inspection of plant operations, I had one critical question: Are all the motors really that different? The answer was no. About 25 to 35 percent are a single dominant model—the 35-frame—except for a different color, special decals, alternative power cord, or a special bracket to be added on.

My hosts could see what I was driving at. And a few times when I've used the example in guest-lecturing at a university, the students knew, too. The 35-frame model deserves its own plant-in-a-plant. I already knew the plant had multiple pieces of equipment at nearly every process (I'm a machine counter). Therefore, a plant-in-a-plant dedicated to the high-volume models could get by without acquiring more equipment, except that a second bake oven would probably be advisable. With dedicated equipment and team, the throughput time might be cut to two days, or maybe one, with impressive reductions in unit cost.

The issue is not cut and dried. Baldor managers have kicked around these ideas and so far have not made the change. One factor holding them back is seasonality of the 35-frame motor's single-phase versions, whose sales are somewhat farm-equipment related. Sales of that version peak in about June and are off from about September through April. That means the plant-in-a-plant for the 35-frame would be running below capacity for about three quarters of the year. Other models that may peak during that period could make use of some of the 35-frame plant's equipment. (Except for machining of shafts, end bells, and so forth, most of the equipment in a motor plant is quite adaptable.) But that would introduce the inefficiencies of back-and-forth handling.

Baldor has already had such an experience at its Clarksville, Arkansas, plant making treadmill motors. It put in a dedicated line for the star model, and sure enough, it worked well and the team spirit of the dedicated crew was excellent. Still, volumes were somewhat unstable, which created the aforementioned problem of under- and overcapacity usage.[10]

Baldor may yet resolve the issue of unstable demand and its effects on a dedicated plant-in-a-plant. Perhaps the solution will be a combination of equipment and human measures. Some equipment, for example, might be put on casters and simply rolled either to the dedicated or the high-flex sides of the plant as needed. For greater human flexibility, perhaps Baldor could make use of Allen-Bradley's idea: SWAT teams.

In the mid-1980s A-B had implemented cells (to produce electronic factory control devices) all over its impressive seven-story clock-tower building in South Milwaukee. People had been pulled out of their old departments—subassembly, final assembly, test, packing—and thrust together. This process, cell formation, is always upsetting to the people involved. After working together for a time, however, the cell teammates had learned each other's jobs, had developed new social bonds, and could experience newfound fulfillment in being able to produce whole products instead of just doing a narrow job. The problem: When one cell needed to borrow labor from another cell, nobody wanted to go. The solution: Some of the more experienced and able A-B associates became a go-anywhere-and-help volunteer group, called a SWAT team. The SWAT-team concept allows the company to plan staffing in each cell at minimal projected demand levels, then fill in as needed with SWAT team members.[11]

Flexible Automation

Feats of factory flexibility are so much admired, especially in the engineering world, that taking it to excess can be hard to resist. Baldor's capacity is easily changed, moved, or reengineered. But when flexibility is built into an automated plant, refocusing usually entails great cost.

Examples of flexible automation beyond reason are plentiful in Europe, less so in the United States and the United Kingdom. The contrary reason probably is that Europe invests in its factories, whereas money managers in the United States and United Kingdom cough up for capital equipment only reluctantly.

Even Japan, the home of lean and simple, occasionally overdoes it:

• *Nissan's Kyushu "Dream Factory."* The *Wall Street Journal* describes Nissan's Kyushu auto assembly plant as a "convoy of 'intelligent motor-driven dollies,' little yellow platforms that tote cars at variable speeds down the production line, sending out a stream of computer-controlled signals to coach both robots and workers along the way." The lines can handle four models in as many as eight different body types. But the plant's price tag, 100 billion yen ($803.9 million), is nearly twice the cost of a conventional assembly plant.[12] Is it a costly mistake? It may seem so, now that Nissan has grown concerned about its proliferation of models and options (e.g., from Chapter 6, 28 different types of chassis, 87 of steering wheels). It especially seems so in light of Nissan's financial problems: The company is deep in debt— $37 billion worth—and has lost money for three years straight.[13]

• *Mazda.* Mazda's simpler plan for flexible assembly of a variety of models is to surround a half-length "simple base line" by a few subassembly lines. The subassembly lines do much of the irregular work that distinguishes the models, ending up with complete units that go to the base line for final assembly.[14]

• *Toyota-Kyushu.* Toyota's fling with high automation occurred in the 1980s. "Now," according to Toyota CEO Tatsuro Toyoda, "we have returned to more of a simple and very productive people-focused system at our newest plant in Kyushu."[15] There Toyota sliced the "traditional long, monotonous assembly line into eleven short ones. Each is independently operated by a team of twenty to twenty-five workers held responsible for that stage of production quality." The plant has no assembly robots.[16]

• *Mazak USA.* Mazak, a Japanese machine-tool manufacturer justly admired for the excellence of its CNC (programmable) machines, seems oblivious of the Toyota system. Its Florence, Kentucky, plant is a marvel of automation—to a fault. Most everything—tools as well as components—moves automatically. Parts do not, however, go directly from receiving to fabrication, or fab to subassembly, or sub to final assembly. They must first go into one of the many automatic storage and retrieval systems scattered all over the plant. Even if the part is to be used the same day or same hour, it has to trace a conveyorized path to an AS/RS, then be picked, then rattle onward by another conveyor to the point of use. Simplicity, kanban style, is not in evidence. (In partial defense of company management, Mazak *sells* automated machine tools and may derive promotional benefits in showing off high-end automation in its own plant.)

Production Support

Information technology for linking final sales points to manufacturers is just coming into its own. Ultimately, factory machinery may turn itself on and off automatically in concert with sales ups and downs. That image of plants run by data communications and customer activity is futuristic. For now, we have to dispose of the often heavy-handed, dysfunctional information systems that have been used to run our plants for two decades. Being that "ancient," the systems were designed to keep one step ahead of delays, quality problems, poor training, machine stoppages, and so forth.

Now many manufacturers—such as those scoring at the thirty-nine-or-higher (adolescence) level on the principles—have largely worked themselves free of the kinds of problems that their systems could plan around. Now, sometimes, the computer system gets in the way.

3M Company's proofing supplies plant in Weatherford, Oklahoma, is an example. The plant has accelerated its throughput time to where the computer can't keep up. 3M headquarters in St. Paul owns the computer that schedules the plant's orders. But often the plant has already produced and shipped before the computer gets around to issuing the scheduling notice. Late paperwork for the quick shipments fouls up the documentation trail, which is a glitch that would earn demerits under

ISO-9001, on which the plant has been registered. So every day a clerk has to make manual adjustments.

One problem is that old computer systems take on lives of their own. Another is that old definitions of a Class A factory system required turning on a full set of subroutines, such as shop-floor tracking, work-order generation for every part, and labor-hour accumulations for every operation. Class A today should be redefined as simple, simple, simple. Turn off the tedious subroutines, for one class of part numbers at a time. Continue with the really vital subroutines—those needed for outside interfacing tasks, such as ordering materials and filling orders to customers. Industry is in need of a W. Edwards Deming of information systems to step forward and fix things.

One industry requires its own special kind of information system: manufacturers of health-care products. Their requirements for keeping track of product origins go beyond those of other sectors because of needs to find causes of health-care disasters when they occur. One group of companies has formed a consortium to meet this sector's special needs. It is called the *Strategic CIM* (computer-integrated manufacturing) *Alliance.* Members are several pharmaceutical companies— Burroughs-Wellcome, SmithKline, Baxter Healthcare, plus a few information and automation technology companies, such as IBM and Allen-Bradley. A goal is to develop a computer system, usable by all members, that can effectively deal with the special regulatory requirements for good traceback record trails.

Computer simulation is still another popular information technology tool. Simulation helps manufacturers plan new plants or, more often, new production lines in existing plants. The inputs are such factors as machine speeds and labor standards for the intended product lines. The simulation can test different combinations of machines, layout, production rates, shift schedules, buffer storage areas, and so forth. (Along the same lines, graduate engineering students test hypotheses using simulation for their master's and doctoral theses. A few dozen of these have been completed, and more are on the way.)

I am acquainted with the results of a number of these factory simulations. They tend to have the same flaw, discovered when the plant or production line goes into operation: The simulation model calls for more buffer storage than necessary. Plant people keep telling me, "We built an automated storage system, and it's never been more than half full." Caterpillar managers said, about an automated storage system in a new diesel engine plant, "We've only used about one out of six pallet openings."

Why? I suspect the answer is twofold: First, the static simulation models do not allow for continuous improvement, and nearly every kind of improvement reduces needs for inventory to at least some extent. Second, the models do not recognize human flexibility. Buffer stocks go in where there are capacity imbalances among machines, long setup times on certain equipment, occasional demand surges, and other perturbations. In many cases, people can substitute for buffer stock. If a machine changeover takes one person an hour to complete, the economic lot size may work out to be two days' worth of stock, which requires rack space. But it may be possible to assign four people to do the changeover in fifteen minutes, which cuts the economic lot size way down. Or someone might do the changovers off-shift each day, so that the lot sizes are one day's worth instead of two. Many other kinds of human flexibility allow manufacturers to do more than the simulation models account for.

Still, simulation models are nice, especially since computer animation can bring the simulations to life. (TC)² has developed a simulator that apparel plants are using to test different modular or other production plans. Sometimes, however, an older, simpler approach works just fine: paper-doll cutouts. Hamilton Standard, Windsor Locks, Connecticut, is a fan. The Association for Manufacturing Excellence had sponsored several Kaizen Blitz events, one of which was hosted by the Hamilton plant. Three AME kaizen teams spent three days in the plant working out—for one thing—the design of a bulkhead cell. Besides detailed time- and work-flow data, the teams used flat cardboard cutouts with the same footprints as the machines going into the cell. They found an empty building where they could move the cutouts around for the best flow and fit within marked-off cell dimensions. Art Soucy, a Hamilton Standard improvement specialist, said, "Our shop floor is like Monument Valley in Wyoming—full of machines as big as mountains. . . . The paper-doll layout approach let us work out the walk patterns. Even though we must have changed things a half-dozen times in one morning, it's better to do that now than *after* we get the machines in place. I don't care if we have to do this in a parking lot, we are never going to set up a cell again without doing a paper-doll layout first!"[19]

UNCONSTRAINED CAPACITY

Economists and stock analysts have an abiding concern about capacity. So does the Federal Reserve. When industrial production pushes against capacity limits, the Fed leaps in with an interest rate hike. This is meant to snuff out would-be inflation. When production in a certain industrial sector approaches capacity limits, stock analysts see company revenue and profit growth being choked off. This may turn them from bulls into bears.

During the latest long period of economic growth in the United States, a funny thing happened. The Department of Commerce's statistics showed that companies were running out of capacity, but they weren't. Alexander Blanton, an analyst at Ingalls & Snyder specializing in heavy industrial goods, checked with Caterpillar, a company he watches closely. Caterpillar managers gleefully told Blanton that they keep exceeding old capacity limits, producing and selling more and more out of the same plants. I have found the same thing in other companies. Despite years of downsizing the work force, consolidating plants (industry's code words for shuttering one plant and moving its products to another), and in Caterpillar's case, suffering a long strike, production keeps climbing. R. A. Jones, a producer of packaging equipment, is experiencing a similar phenomenon. By engineering manager Paul Grimes's estimate, Jones is producing at about 140 percent of its capacity.

Why is this? Caterpillar knows why, Blanton knows why, Grimes knows why, and so do I: The years of slashing non-value-adding wastes and delays simply unleash more capacity. Continual improvement continues, sometimes as fast as sales grow; for example (from Chapter 1), Caterpillar increases its inventory turnover 8 percent per year on average.

One way that capacity grows continually is through quick-setup activities—and through its close relative, dedicating equipment to a star product so that it doesn't ever have to be set up. Sometimes sheet metal, machining, sheet stock, fill-and-pack equipment, and chemical processing equipment take hours or days to change over, but responsiveness to customers requires running every product often. Changeover time can exceed production time. Therefore, just as every work team should continually be working on improvements in quality and machine capability, so should every team continually be working on quicker machine and line changeovers.

While this wisdom may seem like common sense, there is an unfortunate contrary idea that has been making the rounds in manufacturing. It is the notion that there is no point in improving setup and changeover times on nonbottleneck machines. This is extremely poor advice for the following reasons:

1. Quick-setup expertise is a scarce commodity only if the company fails to train the work force. A training effort worth its salt will teach all operators the simple guidelines for cutting setup times, make copies of the late Shigeo Shingo's *SMED* (single-minute exchange of die) book widely available,[18] give operators access to videotape cameras, and turn them loose. As Shingo has stated, just converting internal setup elements to external (done while the machine is still producing) "can usually cut some 30%–50%" of setup time.[19] Most internal-to-external improvements require no physical modifications. Thus, no engineering or tool-room expertise is needed. Operators can handle this step using trained-in common sense.

Realistically, most companies still are in a fairly primitive state of employee involvement. Quick setup projects are still led by engineers and maintenance technicians, with operators playing second fiddle. So read on.

2. When teams work to reduce process variation or to improve safety, handling, preventive maintenance, or housekeeping, they probably are at the same time cutting setup times. They all involve process improvement—as a piece, not as separate assignments.

3. When setup times decrease, setup labor and startup problems decrease.

4. When setup times decrease, it is economical to run smaller lots, which reduce inventories, scrap, and rework.

5. The habit of continuous improvement must not be discouraged. No operator should be told, Don't improve your setup times, because yours is a nonbottleneck machine.

6. As conditions change, a nonbottleneck can easily become a bottleneck.

Another way to keep capacity unconstrained is to follow the example of Solectron, which analyst Blanton also watches closely. As we learned in Chapter 1, Solectron, the electronic-circuit-board specialist, will go through flaming hoops for its customers. Its customers are high-tech companies like Intel and IBM, whose products ramp up steeply and quickly, then drop off the map suddenly. How do you meet demands like that? Solectron's answer is to deliberately operate at 75 percent to 80 percent of capacity. It wants to be certain the equipment is there when the customer needs it.[20]

Thus, this chapter ends on the same note as it began: We need to transform our factories for quick response—and keep up the transformations continually.

9

Remaking Human Resource Management[1]

Management by principles transforms the firm's human resources. People are finding themselves trained, evaluated, recognized, rewarded, grouped, titled, and managed differently. Sometimes these changes are carefully orchestrated. More often they evolve fitfully. The trouble is, conventional human resource management practices—and theory—are partly at odds with customer-focused principles. Three propositions underlie this chapter's discussion:

- To be fully successful and self-sustaining, management-by-principles requires extensive changes in human resource management (called for in Principles 4, 8, 9, and 11).
- The shifts in HR practices are necessary, interlocking elements of the total package of principles, not independent options.
- Adopting the HR changes should neither precede nor follow implementation of the other principles, but should occur in concert.

Three exhibits in this chapter summarize the many premises and practices in human resource management that must be altered. Exhibit 9-1 is an overview on people and their roles. People in teams (Principle 4) is one of the key role changes. Later in the chapter we take up performance management revisions (Principle 9), including frontline ownership of process data (Principle 11) summarized in Exhibit 9-3. Still later, Exhibit 9-5 deals with how the work force upgrades itself

(Principle 8)—and how the HR department adapts. A summary of one company's impressive achievements on these principles appears near the end of the chapter.

ROLES

We begin with the role changes noted in Exhibit 9-1—pertaining to jobs, teams, titles, managers, and leadership.

The New Owners of Process Improvement

The first item is jobs. Everyone's must include process improvement in the eyes of the customer. Conventionally, managers and specialists hold the process-improvement reins. At best, frontline employees are allowed to make suggestions. But since none receive training in data collection, process analysis, and customer-focused goals, suggestion programs are feeble. Usually, the few good ideas that emerge concern someone's task (good for one point on Principle 4, frontline associates involved in change and strategic planning), not whole processes. For process improvements, it takes a team's breadth of vision (team-based process improvement qualifies for two points on Principle 4).

EXHIBIT 9-1
Shifting Human Resource Premises and Practices:
Jobs, Teams, Titles, Managers, Leaders

- Jobs: Process improvement is part of everyone's job—not left to managers and specialists.
- *Teams*: Multifunctional work-flow teams have high potential; single-function teams, low potential.
- *Organization*: A transition—from solid vertical to project assignments to dashed-line to colocated teams to horizontal with peer review and recognition.
- *Titles*: Associates, not workers.
- *Managers*: Everyone is a manager. The former manager class becomes facilitators.
- *Leadership*: Inspirational leaders are rare; teamsmanship, shaped by the demands of customer-focused principles, fills the void.

High-Potential Teams

Teams, second on the list in Exhibit 9-1, are a centerpiece of process improvement. But not just any kind of team.

At a wholesale food distributor an improvement team got its start on a Saturday morning. My friend—call him Phil—was among the hand-picked group of senior drivers who met with management all day to contribute their ideas. Phil and the others went in excited, proud to be selected and happy to be paid overtime wages for what they thought would be a meaningful experience. They left the meeting thoroughly dejected. Phil said, "It was just a gripe session." He said the drivers griped about dispatchers who devised routes nearly impossible to complete in a single shift, such as over the Cascade Mountains to the east, then back to Seattle, and out to one of the islands in Puget Sound. They beefed about stock pickers and fork-truck drivers who loaded potato chips on the bottom and heavy canned goods on top, maintenance that didn't fix torn sheet-metal facing inside trailers, stores that had nearly unusable docks, and so on. But no dispatchers, pickers, fork-truck drivers, maintenance people, or store representatives were on the team. It was clear to Phil who should have been at the meeting: a multifunctional group.

The distinction is this: A single-function team is severely hemmed in. A multifunctional team, on the other hand, has broad bandwidth powers. Management at the food distributor did not see the difference. The consultants the company hired didn't either.

An ideal kind of multifunctional team is the in-place work-flow team. The product-focused work cell in a factory or office is a potent example. A group of people who do the same thing (e.g., a group of stock pickers in the warehouse) does not qualify. Browse any of the dozens of books on team building. But look in vain for this all-important point: *Organize teams around the flow of work, not around common functions.*

Another type of work-flow team is the project team. People from various functions complete a process improvement project and disband. At the food distributor a project team composed of driver, dispatcher, stock picker, loader, and store representative could tackle several related issues: truck routing to improve on-time delivery, sufficient store personnel on hand to promptly stow perishable dairy products, trailers loaded for right-sequence unloading, and bad dock conditions at stores.

Organization Charts Lose Their Lines

Organization, the third item in Exhibit 9-1, once could be charted in boxes and vertical lines. The transition first puts mixed people, line and staff, onto project teams. (Just doing that qualifies for one point on Principle 1.) If the project form becomes dominant, as in aerospace, a matrix organization arises: vertical lines to functional bosses, horizontal ones to project bosses.

The next phase injects dashed lines. An example is assigning engineers to operating units, represented by dashed lines snaking back to the chief engineer's box. When the organization gets itself refocused on products rather than functions (three, four, or five points on Principle 1), the vertical reporting lines go into meltdown. Instead of reporting to a boss, associates report to and may be appraised by teammates. Organization charts—if still maintained—may become bizarre: upside down triangles, circles within circles, and so one. When the organizational is truly customer-focused, the result is dozens or hundreds of supplier-to-next-process chains. It is difficult, if not impossible, to draw. But that's not bad.

Associates, Facilitators, and Teamsmanship

Titles and revised thinking about managers and leaders are the fourth, fifth, and last items in Exhibit 9-1.

In a flourishing environment of work-flow teams, all involved become process managers.[2] In some companies that are advanced in TQM (e.g., Milliken & Co.), the word *worker* has been abolished. (I regret that "worker" appeared in my initial works, in 1981 and 1982. In all my succeeding books—four trade books and four more editions of a textbook—the word was not used.) In a few even the word *employee* is a no-no. At Electronic Controls Company (ECCO), Boise, Idaho, uttering the dreaded E-word incurs a $1 fine (except they didn't make me pay). Everyone at ECCO, an employee-owned company, is a team member; this includes all managers. In other companies frontline employees are "associates." Bosses and staff professionals become "facilitators." If walk follows talk, line and staff distinctions blur.

Most organizations have a few people—frontline associates, bosses, or staff experts—who are inspirational. By charisma, wit, wisdom, and communication skills they light a fire under whatever initiative is current. These are rare and valuable resources. Regrettably, the great majority of people in positions of influence are not. Typically, they direct rather than inspire. Direction ("Here's what we're going to do"), however, violates the total in TQM, as well as the team concept.

Under principles-based management, frontline associates gather and analyze their own process data and thus have the power of process knowledge. To be effective, supervisors, accountants, buyers, engineers, and the like must interact with and work to enhance process teams. This interactive work environment shapes their behaviors. Leadership becomes less important. (Casting aspersions on leader is not PC—politically correct. Yet I'll not shirk from doing so and will tap Peter Drucker for support: "Leadership," he says, "is all hype. We've had three great leaders in this century—Hitler, Stalin, and Mao—and you see the devastation they left behind." Beyond that, he continues, what passes for leadership is "nothing but hard work and conscientiousness.")[3] Teamsmanship fills the leadership void. Their former modus operandi was based on superior education, expertise, position, perquisites, and so forth. Their new one is based on such factors as willingness to share knowledge, egalitarian communication talents, common sense, consideration, empathy, and kindness.

Knowledge sharing should be systematic, not haphazard. At Miller Brewing Company's Trenton, Ohio, facility, all professionals are teachers. They instruct frontline associates in budgeting, maintenance, purchasing, scheduling, employee selection, inventory management, and so on. The training topics group into five "star points" (see Exhibit 9-2), and every team has one representative on a separate star-point team charged with improving the functions of that point. Within eighteen months of being hired, the frontliner in bottling or in the warehouse

EXHIBIT 9-2
Star System at Miller Brewing, Trenton, Ohio

Star System

Administrative
Budgets & cost   Purchasing
Time & attendance
Overtime coordination/recordkeeping

Personnel   *Quality*
Selection   Training   Process improvement
Employee activities club   Product specifications
Pay-for-skills coordination   Housekeeping/GMP
Plant newsletter   Raw materials   Records
Employee assistance program
Peer review coordination

Productivity/Maintenance   *Safety*
Production schedules   Safety standards/practices
Maintenance schedules   Safety training/education
Spare parts inventory   Emergency action plans
                                         Safety inspections/surveys
                                         Behavior observation/feedback
                                         Accident prevention/investigation

---

knows the business, not just the job. And these are not a malleable, un-tainted crop of young, new recruits. Most had been laid off by a nearby, shut-down General Motors plant. In fact Miller-Trenton's labor union is still the United Auto Workers.

The unionized work force and management have devised ways to provide associates with the needed expertise and make use of it. Though it's a three-shift operation, associates work nine-hour shifts. The first hour is devoted to self-management (scheduling, work assignments, maintenance planning), interaction with previous-shift people, and improvement projects of all kinds. The resulting forty-five-hour week means five hours of overtime pay—a small price to pay for the benefits: The plant produces about twice as much beer per employee as similar plants in the industry.

The inspirational leader, too, must learn teamsmanship. When that happens, companies win quality awards and prosper—for example, Motorola under Robert Galvin, Xerox under David Kearns, Federal Express under Fred Smith, and Milliken and Company under Roger

Milliken (all winners of Macolm Baldrige national quality awards in the United States).

It is instructive to examine the change process in these companies. Their histories segment into two periods. Call them B.C. (before change) and A.D. (after discovery—of TQM). In the B.C. period (prior to about 1980) management was conventional at all four companies. The four CEOs were generally authoritarian. Their inspirational traits were directed at needs other than process improvement, customer requirements, external partnerships, and cross-functional teamwork. In the A.D. period these executives' behaviors changed. They became highly involved, as facilitators, in their companies' TQM training, reengineering (toward cross-functional teams and partnerships), and revising reward and recognition. TQM shaped their behaviors even as they were proselytizing TQM.

Early training in these and other firms notable for TQM emphasized the hard sciences of quality. More recently, companies have often been sidetracked. They have given first emphasis to the softer side: team building, conflict resolution, group dynamics, and related topics. This approach is likely to slow down the implementation effort, simply for lack of the object—Q, for quality. (See box, "TQM Training at Cummins Engine.")

In contract to the success stories of the TQM pioneers is General Motors' decade of decline (the 1980s). GM did not mount a strong TQM effort until the decade was nearly over. By that time it had be-

---

TQM TRAINING AT CUMMINS ENGINE

"At other Caterpillar facilities, we taught people group skills, like interaction and how to run a meeting. Factory teams met regularly, but ended up frustrated. . . . People lacked . . . skills to discover root causes. [In Belgium], we decided to teach techniques first and then follow up later with group skills, if necessary. . . . The problem-solving training has been well-accepted and worked beyond my expectations."

—Don Western, plant manager, Caterpillar Belgium[4]

come clear to many insiders that other companies' quality efforts—notably Ford's—were paying off. Consequently, GM mounted a retraining program for middle and senior managers. That effort, in 1987, was oriented toward communication, team building, general problem solving, and allied topics so that it could prepare the human organization for quality management. The concepts and tools of quality improvement, however, were missing. Finally, in 1990, a new training program addressed the missing ingredients: customers, statistical process control, cross-functional teams, work cells, quick response, and so on. One GM executive, attending one of the 1990 sessions at which I was the presenter, said, "This is the training we should have had in 1987."

MOTIVATION AND REWARD IN THE AGE OF CONTINUOUS IMPROVEMENT

Exhibit 9-3 lists five more changes in human resource management—under the general category of motivation and reward.

Results

The first factor is process data and results. Under TQM frontline teams not only "own" the process data they collect; they also actively track

EXHIBIT 9-3
Shifting Human Resource Premises and Practices:
Results, Recognition, Reinforcement, Pay, and Reward

- *Results and Process Data*: Immediate, visual, and owned by frontline associates—not collected by clerks and periodically analyzed by managers.
- *Recognition and positive reinforcement*: Public and team oriented (private, boss-to-subordinate de-emphasized).
- *Negative to Positive Reinforcement*: Mishaps (not errors, not mistakes) become opportunities—to be documented categorized, controlled, and fail-safed. Negatives become positives.
- *Performance Appraisal*: Subordinate to boss, customer and supplier to team, peer to peer—not just boss to subordinate.
- *Pay and Reward*: An enlarged basket of values—not just pay, benefits, and random, unfocused praise.

their team's improvements, usually on wall charts kept in their own areas. Under the old practices—outside inspectors or clerks collecting data and forwarding results to remote managers for review—pledges about team ownership and empowerment ring hollow. (The power of self-recording has been documented—e.g., the Emery Air Freight studies, cited by Luthans and Kreitner.)[5] Summarizing results in a periodic report loses the motivational benefits of quick reinforcement. Instead, plot the results as they occur—in the workplace.

Special Recognition

Second on the list in Exhibit 9-3 is recognition and reinforcement. While self (team)-recording of results has general reinforcement value, special results deserve special recognition. A generation or more of managers have been taught that it's their job to praise and reinforce fine deeds. But under principles, managers are facilitators, not judges. Praise and recognition had to be reinvented. Leading-edge organizations have fashioned the following key features of recognition:

- *Based on measurable, customer-oriented results (rather than on managerial judgment).* Primary results include reduction of defects, mishaps, returns, complaints, warranty costs, scrap, unsafe incidents, response time, time to market, changeover time, and flow distance. Also relevant are secondary activities—measurable as well—leading to primary results, such as numbers of suggestions, processes certified, suppliers certified, training modules completed to mastery, and uptime on equipment. At Milliken and Company these kinds of data are on display in main traffic ways in every plant, office, lab, or design center. At Gilbarco they are called halls of measures.
- *Systematic (rather than sporadic).* Systematic recognition may include weekly, monthly, quarterly, and yearly awards—for complaint reduction, number of suggestions, and so on. Though award criteria are measurable, comparing one group's measured results with another's is not always straightforward. Some judgment—by a senior official or awards committee—may still enter in. Each year, Motorola brings twenty-odd teams (pared from some three

thousand worldwide) to a fine Chicago-area hotel for its Total Customer Satisfaction Team Competition. Using statistics, scatter and fishbone diagrams, and comedy, the teams present their projects, and top management staffs the scoring tables.[6]

- *Public.* Winners are feted in awards ceremonies, publicized in house organs and sometimes in the local news media, and enshrined in the form of photos and displays on corridor walls. Milliken and Company, Baxter Health Care, and Hewlett-Packard's Malaysia business unit call them walls of fame. At Midland Communications, Inc., they're halls of quality; and at Timken, walls of recognition.

- *A bias toward teams (rather than individuals).* Certain of the awards— perhaps specified as a percentage—may go only to teams. General Motors' Antilock Brake Systems division in Toledo has such a policy for suggestions: 95 percent of savings from suggestions must go to teams; only 5 percent may go to individual suggestors.

Negatives to Positives

We have been talking about positive reinforcement (third item listed in Exhibit 9-3), which as we all know, is good; negative reinforcement is not so good. It seems to go against human nature, however, to bite one's lip and not react to negatives, which are always plentiful. And when we are the perpetrators, we become defensive. If no one is looking, we may hide the error, or attempt to shift the blame. How can performance improve when, out of fear of criticism, people are inclined to hide mishaps?

The quandary partially resolves itself. A concept called fail-safing turns negatives into positives. Fail-safing means embedding in the process a device or procedure that will never again allow a nonconformity to occur or to go forward.[7] Via training, associates become imbued with this way of thinking. Then whenever problems surface, their response is to form study teams to isolate root causes and fail-safe the process so the problem is stamped out forever (see box).

A few successes at fail-safing alter behaviors and mindsets: Instead of sweeping mishaps under the rug, team members cheer! They wel-

---

FAIL-SAFING AT MICROSOFT-IRELAND

At Microsoft's Dublin, Ireland, software plant, associates devised a simple fail-safe solution. The device went into all the plant's disk-duplicating machines. The problem was that, once in a great while, an operator failed to notice that the last disk in a set got stuck sideways in the take-up hopper. The rest of the set then got packed, and the shipment went out short one disk. The next set included an extra one—probably in the wrong language, since the Dublin plant serves all of Europe.

Engineers proposed several high-tech solutions. An improvement team of frontline associates, however, found a simple root cause. The equipment was painted black and the disks are black, too. Their solution: A team member bought a can of white paint and a brush and painted the insides of the hoppers white. Since it is virtually impossible not to notice a black disk against a white background, the process is effectively fail-safed.

---

come each chance to expose and attack another problem, thereby reducing exposure to criticism, real or imagined. Defensiveness about negative happenings ebbs. The fail-safing idea is neatly summed up by Murphy's Antithesis: *Anything that can't go wrong, won't go wrong.*

Careful choice of words helps shape the positive, fail-safing response. Trainers, facilitators, and associates: Don't say error, mistake, or defect. People take those words personally and get their dander up. Call them problems, malfunctions, or, as is the rule in one of Kodak's production units, mishaps. George Heuring, the outside trainer-consultant for this unit, told the Kodak teams to "document 100 mishaps before my next visit. We'll tackle those 100, and then go for 100 more." The Kodak people did so. Had Heuring asked them to find a hundred errors or mistakes, the reaction would not have been the same.

Performance Appraisal

At performance-appraisal time (fourth item in Exhibit 9-3), both positive and negative reinforcement are at work. The usual way is for supervisors to rate their subordinates. Under customer-focused principles, however, it makes as much sense for lower-level people to give feedback to their facilitators (bosses and supporting professionals) as the reverse. Thus, performance appraisal is multidirectional, including outside suppliers and customers. At Harley-Davidson, five colleagues critique each salaried employee's work. Jostens Diplomas, Red Wing, Minnesota, is now 100 percent on peer appraisal. Part of the Jostens pay package is merit and team based—and tied to the peer appraisals. Each year Jostens corporate sets forth weighted criteria on which associates are to judge their peers. One year, for example, the weighting factor for teamwork might be highest, with scrap and rework second; the next year's weightings might be reversed. Other manufacturers using peer review include Northern Telecom, Morrisville, North Carolina; Harris Corporation's Farinon Division, San Antonio, and Square D's Raleigh, North Carolina plant (by lottery); and General Electric (for managers).[8]

Quid Pro Quo

Fifth in Exhibit 9-3 is pay and reward. People who add value to products and services should receive commensurate rewards. Back in the days when equity theory was first articulated,[9] there wasn't much to it. Frontliners had little to contribute—they just did their narrowly defined jobs. And they received minimal rewards in return: base pay, plus the usual benefits package (and sporadic praise).

Today's superior organizations receive a broad range of contributions from their people. Associates own and continually improve their own processes and master multiple skills, as well as make products or provide services. Since they contribute in many ways, the rewards they receive should be of many kinds.

Actually, reward is not quite the proper term. Reward implies things bestowed by the organization or its managers. The associate may value those things greatly or not much. The key is creating an environment from which the employee derives values rather than the company just meting out rewards. Since no two employees value exactly the same thing, the available set of values must be broad. An attendee at one of my seminars was perceptive. He said, "Oh, I see. What you are talking about is a basket of values." Well put. Exhibit 9-4 graphically displays

EXHIBIT 9-4
Basket of Values

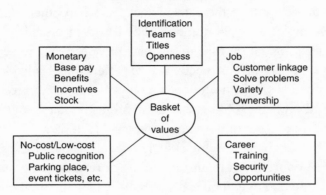

key values that need to be in the basket. (I have used a textual version of this in my seminars for several years. The schematic presentation in the exhibit was inspired by a similar graphic in an article by Elizabeth Hawk and Christian Ellis.)[10]

How is the employee identified? That is the issue of the topmost block in the exhibit. This is no small matter. In the new era of the virtual corporation, which some say is already upon us, loyalty to the company fades. Employee alienation can arise and do no end of harm. Combating this requires that the employee identify with teammates and fellow associates and that two-way communication channels extend from the bottom to the top of the organization.

One's job is the concern in the upper-right-most block in the exhibit. It is hard to derive high value from a job with no customer or product visibility. It is easier when the job is linked with one's customer; better yet, a chain of customers with whole-process sightlines. The well-rounded job also entails use of mental acuity in improving processes, and frequent job rotation provides the spice of variety. Associates who are linked into the customer chain, who solve problems and experience job variety, develop feelings of process ownership.

The career block in Exhibit 9-4 includes a highly esteemed value: training. While yesterday's employees had job security on their minds, recent years of endless downsizing have changed that. People today are likely to be more concerned with long-run work-life security than job security. Training in and use of multiple skills, including process improvement skills, provide more lines on a résumé, should one be needed.

Opportunities, last in the career block, relate to other items in the basket. Examples are opportunities to be a part of organizational and team goal setting, go on trips to evaluate prospective new equipment, visit key suppliers or customers, use experience and wisdom in improving processes, join professionals on projects, make presentations of proposed problem solutions, rate as well as be rated, and wear the same uniform and eat in the same company cafeteria as senior executives. Still others include being associated with whole processes, gaining satisfaction from self (team)-recording of results, being recognized in awards ceremonies and on walls of fame, and being promoted.

The basket also includes simple, low-cost or nonmonetary values— lower left in Exhibit 9-4. These include a best parking place, dinner at a fine restaurant, and tickets to an entertainment event. Craig Sue, a Hewlett-Packard manager in San José, California, passes out lottery tickets as awards. Meaningful as well are team, site, and company celebrations (picnic, beer, and pizza) for launching a product, completing a project, meeting a stringent quality target, achieving zero customer returns, and so on. When it comes to selecting people for recognition and rewards and handing them out, peer-to-peer can be more effective than top-down. For this approach (complementary to peer appraisal) to be fair and effective, it should be carefully planned, including training of associates in criteria and tools for judging people's contribution. Gene Milas suggests that peer-to-peer avoids antimanagement cynicism, solidifies employee cooperation, and promotes the internal-customer side of continuous improvement.[11]

On the monetary side (upper left in the exhibit) are base pay, bonuses, company stock or stock options, profit sharing, gain sharing, merit pay, pay for suggestions, and pay for skills or knowledge.[12] These payment options may be individual or group oriented.

The old system—base pay and benefits—recognizes performance only in gross terms. Another old system, incentive payments for output, output, output may seem more discriminating, but actually buries bad performance in the semblance of good. Until the 1990s the Jostens diploma plant in Red Wing, Minnesota, was on output pay incentives.

Output was counted. Then inspectors culled out all the rejects and sent them back to operators for rework that was counted as output again! That system was eliminated over a two-year buyout period. Its replacement is partly team-based merit and partly skill based.[13] In the textile industry Milliken was one of the first major manufacturers to totally eliminate its output incentive system.

In augmenting a system that is too narrow, some might say, one or two supplementary values or rewards—not a whole basket—are sufficient. A profit-sharing advocate, for example, might argue that a share of profit provides appropriate motivation and equity. But profit is time biased. Last year's record earnings—before TQM and reengineering kicked off—may be owed to a booming economy. Next year, after improvement teams have raised quality and cut wastes by orders of magnitude, poor economic conditions may produce a loss. So no bonus. And the following year's high profit might be largely the work of key people no longer with the company. They did great work but got no bonus and left. The president of Toyota says that company managers "are not rewarded on outcomes because the company does not want to reward people for being lucky."[14]

Bonuses and gain sharing involve another kind of bias. Everyone in the bonus group gets the same fixed or percentage share. Persons or teams that perform exceptionally feel poorly rewarded, and laggards overrewarded. Pay for knowledge (or multiple skills) has still another, obvious kind of bias. It says nothing about performance. Rewards are only for potential or expected performance, which will not necessarily obtain. Pay based on performance appraisal is so problematic that some in the quality movement (the late W. Edwards Deming, for one) call for its abolition.[15]

When the basket of values contains slim pickings, performance rating inequities loom large. However, when appraisal is just one of several avenues to value, arguments against it lose some of their punch. When taken alone, each of the values in the basket is weak. Collectively, they provide enough kinds of rewards that most people will feel well treated. A member of a high-performing team says, "We didn't get profit sharing this period, but we got a bonus," or "We didn't get profit sharing or a bonus, but at least the company invested in us—eighty hours of training in job skills and process improvement techniques." Those who garner new skills certificates may receive a pay increase—plus the perception of greater work-life security. And those who feel unfairly appraised may not stew about it long if they receive other kinds of values.

THE WORK FORCE UPGRADES—AND HR ADAPTS

The human resource department is not necessarily inclined to lead or subscribe to the necessary changes in HR concepts and practices. As elsewhere, changes in the HR function can be upsetting. Those listed in Exhibit 9-5 are mostly related to Principle 8 and how it affects the HR department.

Role and Size

First on the list in Exhibit 9-5 is upgrading the department's role and reducing its size. The latter is a stumbling block since size traditionally bestows power and pay. Nevertheless, enlightened HR professionals see expanded opportunities to play a vital part. Role importance and average staff pay may rise, even as department size and payroll shrink. At an

EXHIBIT 9-5
Shifting Human Resource Premises and Practices:
Human Resource Department Adaptation to
Work-Force Upgrading

- *HR department's role importance increases, size reduces.* More emphasis on employee selection and development, facilitator of training; less on wage and classification, employee relations.
- *Training—to certification*: For everyone, not just staff professionals and managers; process-improvement methodology, not just job skills; and train-do, train-do, not all-at-once training overload.
- *Line involvement.* Everyone involved in human resource management.
- *Labor relations*: Partnership for improvement, not adversarial or grievance oriented.
- *Job classifications*: Few (e.g., three).

annual conference of the human resource directors for the Pharmaceutical Manufacturers' Association, attendees understood the need for change. The moderator, Jonathan Griggs, HR director at Park Davis, commented on the evolving concept of labor-force management:

> "In the 1960s, it was 'beat 'em and cheat 'em.'
> "In the 1970s, . . . 'cheat 'em but make 'em feel good.'
> "In the 1980s, . . . 'allow them a voice but retain control.'
> "In the 1990s, it's employee ownership."

The other HR directors gave him a hand.

Important targets for change are employee selection, development, and training. The trend is toward much higher standards in selection. Examples are hiring people with aptitude for working in teams or who have been trained in statistical process control. Also, the wheels are in motion in the United States for national skills standards, initially in twelve industries.[16]

Training—to Certification

Training (item 2 in the exhibit) is for all employees—not just the professional staff. We saw in Chapter 2 that earning two points on the training principle (number 8) required use of the train-do, train-do, just-in-time training method. Scoring five points calls for 80 percent of associates to be certified as multiskilled and most also certified as trainers. Hewlett-Packard's Penang, Malaysia, components facility, has the right idea: three levels of certification: Weekend training classes aim at upgrading operators, step by step up the ladder of expertise. First attainment, after the probationary period, is operator. Next step is certified production specialist; then technician/associate engineer; and finally, for the best and the brightest—who take company-subsidized college classes—engineer. The accompanying photo is of the certification stepladder, which is displayed as a banner hanging in the cafeteria, a constant reminder to the work force. Other banners display the same thing elsewhere in the plant.

These upgrades in employee training do not call for an enlarged staff of trainers. Rather, they require a few professionals to benchmark best train-

Steps to personal fulfillment, a banner in the cafeteria at Hewlett-Packard, Penang, Malaysia.

ing practices, collect training materials, contract with local community colleges, and bring in experts to help launch train-the-trainer. The subject matter must include not only job skills but also process improvement.

For example, in 1987 Seagate Associates (then a division of Control Data) near Oklahoma City set up within-plant facilities for trainers. Seagate brought in seven full-time instructors from El Reno Junior College, who trained the work force in SPC, calibration, safety, maintenance, and other topics—even budgeting. At the same time, the plant developed a strong train-the-trainer program in which eighty-five production associates provided various kinds of training (e.g., for new employees).

Line Involvement in HR

Human resource responsibilities are not the sole purview of HR professionals. Line people should be taking on quite a few of them (item 3 in Exhibit 9-5). The HR people at Hewlett-Packard's San José operation have made it easy. They've set up self-service centers with personnel action forms, desk space, a phone, and advice on whom to call for further help. In some companies, frontliners interview job applicants, and at General Motors' Saturn division, frontline teams make the hiring decision.

Labor Relations

Training and development have uplifting effects that can improve attitudes of the work force. This lessens the unpleasant side of employee relations: dealing with substandard performance, grievances, absenteeism, and other dysfunctions (fourth item in the exhibit).

Job Classifications

The multiskilling objective carries with it a need to dismantle much of the job classification system. A reasonable goal is three or fewer classifications for production associates (last item in Exhibit 9-5).

Historically, management created narrow classifications and lots of them. This had the effect of dumbing down the work, which permitted hiring warm bodies off the street at minimum wage to do the jobs. The theory dates back to Adam Smith and his famous pin-manufacturing example, which "proved" that division of labor leads to higher efficiency. In application, management's not-so-hidden agenda included avoiding the expense of training and careful employee selection. Unfortunately, multiple narrow classifications evolve into work rules, which can embed themselves in labor-management contracts. Later, in blatant irony, management blames the labor union for restrictive work rules.

How bad can it get? By one estimate Boeing has well over 1,000 separate classifications. An even worse example, since the organization's size is a fraction of Boeing's, is the hospital in Indiana that had 598 job classifications, most with only one incumbent.[17]

TRW's steering and suspension systems plant in Sterling Heights, Michigan, is among the many manufacturers that have slashed job classifications. Management and the United Auto Workers agreed to a plan in which classifications in their first work cell, organized in 1986, collapsed from sixty-eight to one. Many of the absorbed skills, such as quality and machine setup, were formerly performed by overhead people. Numerous training modules and additional pay for additional skills are part of the agreement.[18]

Cross-careering is the same idea but applied to managers, professionals, and technicians. Companies tend to stick these talented people into a career track and keep them there for life (except for the few fast-trackers being groomed for senior management). After twenty-five or thirty years the lifer's pay is high and outlook is narrow. This partly explains why so many companies want to early-retire their senior people at age fifty-five. Such human resource policies are guilty of the sin of failing to develop human resources.

Mars Inc., the multibillion-dollar, multinational candy and food company, has long avoided this sin. Mars has only six pay levels. It also pays all vice-presidents about the same salary regardless of function. These practices make it easy for Mars to transfer people from function to function and business unit to business unit. Managers come to learn the business well, which leads to a consistency in operations and culture worldwide, with minimal rules and procedures.[19]

Medical-devices maker Becton-Dickinson has coined a term—horizontal promotion—that suggests another approach.[20] No, it's not a contradictory term. As companies flatten their organizations, vertical promotion paths disappear. Horizontal promotion has people make a lateral, cross-career move and be paid more for it—even though the individual is sure to be a poor performer for some time in the new position. The logic of this is clear. Take two buyers, one who has been a buyer for twenty-five years and the other who has been both a buyer and an accounts payable clerk. The first knows only a function, whereas the second knows a process: how the company buys things—and pays for them. The second employee has high potential for solving process problems, the first, low potential. The second employee also has good potential to be effective on multifunctional teams, in that she can relate to and communicate with either accounting people or purchasing people; the first relates and communicates well only with other purchasing staff. Alas, at Becton-Dickinson horizontal promotion is open only to fast-trackers, not to a mere buyer or accounts payable clerk.[21]

As noted, training, cross-training, cross-careering, and reducing job classifications are the stuff of customer-focused principle number 8.

Results from the principles-based research show bottom tier (eyes-open) and middle tier (childhood) participants scoring slightly better than their average scores on this principle. Top-tier participants (adolescence range), on the other hand, scored way above their average on the principle: an average score of 3.5 versus an average of 2.9 for all sixteen principles. This stands to reason: Narrowly trained associates who are stuck in a narrow job classification can do little but keep their noses to the grindstone. Multifunctional skilling—no work rules—provides freedom to reach out to next-process customers. That drives up scores on most of the other principles.

AN EXAMPLE

Quickie Designs Inc., one of the eighteen companies featured in the "improvement pathways" discussion in Chapter 4, is a subsidiary of Sunrise Medical, producing manual and power wheelchairs. Quickie's main facility, producing custom wheelchairs and employing about five hundred associates, is in Fresno, California. An Avon Lake, Ohio, plant employing about eighty-five people, makes standard lightweight wheelchairs; and a new acquisition, Jay Medical, Boulder, Colorado, is a small plant producing chair cushions. Quickie scored well overall on the sixteen principles, especially on those relating to human resource management (4, 8, 9, and 11). The Sunrise Pursuit of Excellence program, crafted largely by CEO Richard Chandler over the past five or six years, has matured at Quickie Designs. Dave Lauger, vice president of human resources, explains the program's facets:

• Project Exceed. Any of Quickie's nearly six hundred associates who catches someone else doing something special writes it up on an Exceed-O-Gram, using E-mail. Those without E-mail access get their boss to write it up. All funnel through the HR office—some five hundred in a year, or two per day. Customers (health-care-supply retailers) even contribute some of the Exceed-O-Grams. To publicize the good deeds, Exceed-O-Grams are posted on the walls; typically, fifty or sixty are posted.

• Teaming. Some thirty-five teams serve Quickie Designs. The factories are well along in this, and reasonably good progress has been made in the support offices: a credit team, an accounts payable team, and a few others.

• Sunrise Olympics. Bronze, silver, and gold lumens are the awards in the Sunrise Olympics. (Scientifically, a lumen is a measure of light, which relates to the Sunrise name and its logo, a torch.) Teams and individuals earn lumens in a variety of ways. These include kaizen projects, submission of OFI's (opportunity for improvement), Quickie volunteer work in the community. In 1994, 869 OFI's and 655 kaizens were submitted at the company's principal site. Every third contribution wins a bronze lumen, every fifth a silver. Also, the top monthly contribution receives a silver lumen, and the top quarterly a gold lumen.

• Celebration and prizes. The company shuts down monthly for all-employee-sharing rallies. Recognition goes to best ideas of the month, and ten cash prizes are awarded. Both teams and individuals receive awards. The quarterly rallies are bigger events. Still bigger are the yearly rallies, led by President Tom O'Donnell, which include the usual recognition of years of service and a slide presentation on the state of the business. The culminating event is a drawing. For every lumen that has been awarded during the year, one chit with the person's name on it goes into the bowl. In 1994 there were twenty-two hundred chits. For the last three years, the first name drawn has won a new car. As was noted in Chapter 3, the winner in 1992 was a temporary employee. Having earned fifty-seven lumens, the temp had the odds in his favor—and was among the most deserving of the award, a 1992 Saturn. Second prize is $2,500 and a paid one-week vacation.

• Training and cross-training. Every employee receives at least forty hours of education and training yearly. Topics include statistical process control, conflict resolution, teaming, and so on, plus company support for outside schooling. The forty hours are in addition to job-related cross-training.

• Participation in Earnings (PIE). All Quickie associates get a piece of the PIE, up to 10 percent of their regular pay, based on company profitability. One component, amounting to up to 4 percent, is a cash bonus dispersed every fall. The remaining 6 percent is in the form of tax-sheltered pension.

INTERCONNECTIONS

Many of the changes in human resource management listed in Exhibits 9–1, 9–3, and 9–5 are individually beneficial. They might enhance any organization, even one without a trace of customer thinking. We've noted, however, that they are a meshed set—a building block in the framework of continuous, customer-focused improvement.

When the set's elements are treated sequentially rather than interactively, nothing much happens. An example is spending initial months solely on "preparing the human organization." That is, kicking off the change process with employee surveys; training in team building, general problem solving, conflict resolution, leadership, communication, listening, and presentation skills; and altering the pay and benefits package. All these are valuable but lead nowhere if not closely connected to the science of process improvement and the objects—customers.

Thus, the first phase must bring in the customer focus (including next-process-as-customer), multifunctional teams, and tools of statistical process control (data collection, measurement, and analysis). Each early success prods more changes:

- An improvement team commits to same-day response to customer inquiries. To do so, frontline associates see the need for cross-training—so an overloaded (or absent) specialist will not cause a delay.
- The need for cross-training induces HR managers to do an about-face. They actively work toward dismantling the job classification structure their people had spent years erecting. The new goal is as low as one, two, or three classifications—everyone cross-trained and able to go to where the work is.
- A production team—good at measurement, analysis, and innovation, but poor at conveying its ideas—requests training in how to make presentations.
- A key process, improved 50 percent, resists further improvement. The multifunctional project team concludes that department walls

and geographic distance are the obstacles, and it launches reengineering to create several work cells, each having responsibility for a different family of products.

- Mishaps plunge tenfold, but then the improvement rate stalls as associates see the rewards going to senior managers. A cross-functional team is persuasive in fattening the thin reward package and relating its expanded values to contributions of all employees.
- As frontliners progressively take ownership of processes and their improvement, managers drop divisive terminology and practices. Words like *associates* and *facilitators* take root, along with 360-degree performance appraisal.
- Senior executives become aware—through associations with other companies and other outside sources—that every good organization seems to be taking about the same path, whereas in the past all sought unique strategies. Management by principles begins to replace management by sifting, weighing, and reckoning.

False starts and backsliding are inevitable, and many manufacturers will respond too late to the competitive need for fast-paced improvement. Organizations that survive and thrive, however, will do so through extensive, continuing, and interlinked changes in the management of their human resources.

10

Quality:
Picture a Miracle

There is no need to retell the familiar stories about quality. Instead, I'll aim at less-told or underappreciated matters. The main theme in this chapter is making quality and process improvement simple, visual, positive, and cohesive—when sometimes it is the opposite. This slant on quality subdivides into three topics, each separately addressed:

1. The power of numbers transformed into pictures.
2. The need to improve in forward gear (miraculous new ideas) as well as back-looking (depressing process failures).
3. Maintaining stability—for qualitative reasons—even as organizations "go virtual."

The first two topics, taken up next, require only brief discussion. The third constitutes the latter half of the chapter.

PICTURES

Daniel Sloan is a cerebral kind of guy. His impressive works on quality in health care are liberally sprinkled with references to David Hume, Emmanuel Kant, Albert Einstein, C. I. Lewis, and Ludwig von Bertalanffy.[1]

On the other hand, when it comes to application, Sloan believes in simplicity: His favorite advice: "Count, measure, and draw pictures." The phrase crops up repeatedly in his new book, in which several of his hospital-based clients relate success stories punctuated with examples of the power of charts and graphs.[2]

Sloan isn't alone. Michel Greif of Proconseil, a consulting firm based in Paris, France, gives us a book full of examples from French and North American plants in *The Visual Factory*.[3] Greif's subtitle, *Building Participation Through Shared Information,* makes a subtle but profound point: When it's visual and out in the open, everyone shares. On the other hand, teamwork is an uphill battle when plans, schedules, procedures, results, and recognition are hidden, personal, private, or obscure.

More visual examples are in *JIT Factory Revolution: A Pictorial Guide to Factory Design of the Future*.[4] The book saves "a thousand words" by showing numerous photos of JIT-related applications from Japanese plants. Topics captured in pictures include the five S's, cellular layout, standard operations, multiprocess handling, rate-based scheduling, quick changeover, kanban, total preventive maintenance, and others. As Robert Hall puts it, "Visibility is communication from anyone to *everyone*."[5]

René Simons appreciates the power of pictures. McDonnell-Douglas Helicopters in Mesa, Arizona (a participant in the management-by-principles research), had brought Simons in from another aerospace company as supervisor of the wire shop. She held once-a-week, thirty-minute meetings with her sixteen employees. The meetings were supposed to be for safety and company announcements, but Simons began to squeeze in training in the tools of process analysis. Then the group went to work. Exhibit 10-1 is one of their pictures, a Pareto diagram. It charts (pictures) the team's count of causes of defects: eleven cases of "solder not per PS," nine of "loose backshell tie-wrap," and so forth. (The product is wiring harnesses, which on completion were shipped to another McDonnell-Douglas facility producing the F-18 military fighter aircraft.)

Seeing the counts visually had an eye-opening effect on the team. The typical reaction was, "Now we know what's wrong." Without the need for further study, they also knew what to do about it. One month later, the team had reduced the defect causes down to the lower shaded parts of the bars.

EXHIBIT 10-1
Picturing the Problems

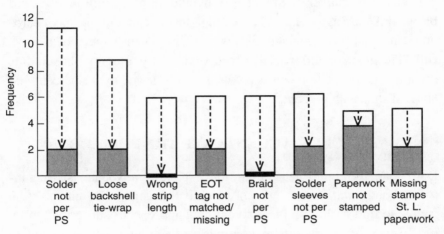

Causes of wiring-harness defects

"Measure the problem. Measure it simply. Post it for all to see." This is the persistent advice of Leonard Bertain and fellow trainer-consultants at the Productivity Connection in Oakland, California. Bertain's favorite version of measure-simply-and-post is a yes-no chart: Yes, the desired outcome did occur. Or no, it didn't. Bertain cites an example from a client having no success shipping on time. Associates in the shipping area learned the concept from Bertain and put up a yes-no chart. Every day for the next four days, a mark went up beside the "no" on the chart. By the fifth day the shipping team had enough bugs worked out of the system to be able to post their first yes. Breaking through the string of noes had an uplifting effect. "From then on," says Bertain, "to every-one's satisfaction, yeses appeared on the chart with regularity."[6]

Sometimes an outsider gets ideas from a wall chart. Lemco Miller, a precision metal stamper in Danvers, Massachusetts, displayed the status of work-in-process on a "pull board." A customer, Bob Fulford, purchasing and supply-base manager at Varian Ion Implant Systems, Gloucester, Massachusetts, paid a visit. In studying the pull board, Fulford spotted a machine with excess capacity, and he was able to send Lemco Miller some extra work just for that machine.[7]

Visual management is an underachiever when it's visual in miniature. Office stationery-sized displays are too inconspicuous. The example cited in Chapter 8 of paper-doll cutouts at Hamilton Standard brings this message home. The visiting kaizen team cut pieces of cardboard to match machine footprints in planning the layout of a work cell. The team could visualize the options by moving the cutouts around. The ultimate result was to slash floor space by 75 percent and travel distance 85 percent.[8]

MIRACLES (ACCENTUATE THE POSITIVE)

Dan Sloan, the count-measure-and-draw-pictures advocate, is also a fanatic about *management by fact,* which is four-square Deming. Yet he is able to find fault with the conventional approaches subscribed to by nearly everyone in the quality community, Deming and Juran included. The fault: The approaches focus on negatives—defectives and nonconformities. Sloan believes, also, that the approach is too slow. By following his nose for new ideas, Sloan has found and made use of an alternative approach from the field of counseling. It calls for "doing something different" or "creating a miracle," which are elemental in Steve deShazer's *brief therapy* method.[9]

In Sloan's use of the method, his role is that of facilitator or consultant (in counseling it would be a therapist). First step is identifying a problem, usually based on complaints. Next are highly focused interviews, one at a time with everyone associated with the process. The facilitator asks, "If a miracle could happen around here, what would it be?" and "Describe how it would be when the miracle happened. How would you know it happened?" These interviews are confidential, which encourages people to open up, get creative, and not worry about someone else's feelings—or turf.

Sloan sometimes includes three other questions in the interviews. The first one employs compliments: "Given your expertise and knowledge and experience, what improvement leadership role might you be willing to accept?" The second recognizes that what people are willing to do on the job must relate somehow to their greater life plans: "Where do you want to be in five years?" The questions so far build rapport for the third question: "Anything else you would like to share?" Sloan says that this is when some interviewees bring out lists of additional miracles.

The miracles technique, while a known commodity in counseling, still is experimental for quality improvement in a business setting. It catches one's fancy for three main reasons.

• First, the miracle idea puts a positive tilt to the matter of quality improvement. As noted in Chapter 9, so does fail-safing—though in a more roundabout way.

• Second, create-a-miracle has a breakthrough flavor to it. Some people simply have a low tolerance for continual, incremental improvement. Moreover, until TQM came along, incremental improvement scarcely existed. It was just occasional big-change events. For managers and professionals steeped in the old ways, the little-miracles approach may have appeal. Big miracles are too infrequent and too upsetting to be relied upon solely (and too often the big-bang project explodes, and disastrous aftershocks wipe out what had been working reasonably well).

• Third, it's fast, it's therapeutic, and it offers a way for consultants or facilitators to play a more positive role.

VIRTUAL STABILITY

As everybody knows, employee loyalty is a thing of the past. Nobody wants to be a lifer, staying with the same employer. People have itchy feet. Everyone really is a temp.

In the United States those in-the-vogue views may not fully stand the test of data. An industrial relations expert studied employee longevity using eight Census Bureau reports spanning the years from 1973 to 1993. He found that 20 percent of the American workforce, in the 45-to-54 age group, say they have worked more than twenty years for the same employer. That proportion has been stable since 1973. Forty-five percent of this group have stuck with one employer for at least ten years; the figure is 30 percent for the work force between ages thirty-five to forty-four.[10]

On the other hand, the virtual corporation's time has arrived. It's like the virtual home: Hire someone to do the yard, someone else for your taxes, caterers for a big event, and so on. They are the experts, and we don't have to have them as full-time, fixed-cost employees. The trick is to gain the advantages of outside expertise and cost savings but still have loyalty and stability. In other words, virtual stability.

In the remainder of the chapter, we take a hard look at going outside the firm for help, along with stability issues.

Keeping the Core and Hiring Out

Alfred Chandler, the great business historian, has called Ford Motor Company in the 1920s the greatest single business mistake in United States history. Huh? Everyone else thinks it was brilliant. I myself have cited the amazing just-in-time feat of this vertically integrated mass-production marvel: four days from the mining of the iron ore to the vehicle driven off the end of the assembly line.[11]

Chandler explains that automobiles are simply too complicated for any single company to control all their elements. He says an automaker should find and keep good suppliers for many of those components and concentrate on the finished car, not producing the glass, steel, and plastic.[12]

Gaining outside expertise has several sides to it besides where the parts come from:

- Companies can contract out for high-impact functions like product development.
- They may bring in outsiders for ancillary work such as janitorial and food service.
- They may turn over their computing, payroll, or equipment maintenance to outside specialists.
- Resellers and supplier reps might occupy space alongside one's own work force.
- Project work pulls people in from other functions, other sites, other companies, and temporary employment agencies (e.g., contract computer programmers).
- Increasingly, companies rely on casual labor (temporaries) to handle upticks in demand.

These diverse sources and uses of expertise introduce new management challenges. Each source requires different planning approaches, policies, training, and pay practices, and different regulations and laws may govern each. The more sources, the higher the costs to administer them. It was easier in the old days when nearly every job was staffed by regular, full-time employees. We suffer the costs and inconveniences, because it pays to stick to your knitting—the core competencies—and look for other, nontraditional sources of expertise for the rest.

Outsourcing has even become a branch of consulting,[13] and *Fortune* magazine has included advertising specials on the topic.[14] Outsourcing of computer and data communications services is the main thrust of this consulting and of the advertising specials. So far, according to one report, this outsourcing has had its successes—and its misconnects. On the misconnect side are IBM and EDS, two of the biggest players in this kind of outsourcing. While each surely has plenty of satisfied customers, Southern Pacific Rail Corporation is decidedly unsatisfied with IBM's computer management, and Blue Shield of California has little good to say about EDS's management of its information systems.[15]

Outsourcing computer services has a big impact. Collectively, outsourcing various small-potatoes functions can add up to big impact. Bob May, head of material management for Physio Control (a participant in the principles research) got assigned as outsourcing coordinator for his company. He has studied everything on the subject that he can get his hands on and has attended outsourcing conferences. In one conference he was prepared to doze off as a speaker talked about his company's specialty: running other companies' mail rooms. Mail rooms? Yes, and the speaker proceeded to explain about new mail-room technologies, ways of uplifting the jobs of lowly mail-room assignees, and ten steps to improving mail rooms. Part way through, May perked up and madly began taking notes because a valuable message of things May had never thought of was being conveyed.

May and his associates took it upon themselves to look even at lowly functions like mail rooms. They found that about three-quarters of the things Physio presently does probably should be outsourced, but probably just one-fourth will be outsourced. In most cases, the outsourcing will be painful, political, disruptive, and costly (e.g., for employee buyouts). One outsourcing move was not painful at all— quite the opposite: the technical writing function. The writers in Physio's tech writing department were ignored, had the crummiest of- fices, and no semblance of a career track. They were dead-ended and backwatered. The outsourcing company that ultimately took over the function explained the many reasons why they could do the job better than Physio could. They explained, as well, how they could offer the technical writers promotion and career opportunities and professional pride. May said the reaction of the Physio tech writers was immediate: "Get me out of here!"—and onto the payroll of the technical writing company. A good deal for Physio, for the outsource, and for the peo- ple involved.[16]

Hard-nosed, cost-based decisions on going outside need to be coun- terbalanced by concerns about stability. We've always admired stable relationships, from romantic and marital to intra- and intercompany to politics and diplomacy. A central theme of Tom Peters's *Thriving on Chaos* is that "Nothing is predictable. . . . We don't know from day to day the price of energy or money. . . . We don't know who our competi- tors will be, or where they will come from."[17] And so on. This is all the more reason to seek at least some stability. Where outsourcing is the choice, stability may be gained by sticking with the same supplier for the long haul and by requiring that the supplier dedicate certain people to your account.

Peters also has said, "I never worked with the same people in my seven years at McKinsey."[18] Too bad for Tom. Too bad for McKinsey. Too bad for the clients, who had to pay for two or three weeks of Tom and his new team shaking hands and getting to know one another in order to get several more weeks of good work out of them.

Actually, that statement from one of Peters's columns reaches into his remote past. It says nothing about his current situation, which relies on a competent, loyal staff plus, undoubtedly, outside service entities whose talents he appreciates, has grown used to, and will continue doing business with. His syndicated column, which appeared for years in my local newspaper (Peters has since bowed out of it), involved a strong support network. Virtual stability.

The Organization: Bulwark of Stability and Effectiveness

The traditional and strongest support network is the organization. Peter Drucker is in favor of it, even in this age of the knowledge associate: "Knowledge workers are of necessity specialists [who need to] work as members of an organization. Only the organization can provide the basic continuity that knowledge workers need in order to be effective. Only the organization can convert the specialized knowledge of the knowledge worker into performance."[19]

The bashings and thrashings of organizations that have taken place in the era of downsizing and reengineering cannot be, on the whole, good. Countercurrents of good sense advocate suppliers for life, customer retention, employee and work-group stability, and project team intactness.

Customer (and Supplier) Stability

In the discussion of strategic linkages in Chapter 7, the point was made: Every sales dollar (or deutsche mark or pound) is not the same as every other one. There are good sales, mediocre sales, and downright harmful sales—at least when business is brisk. Companies like Nypro and Queen City Treating are building their dynasties by serving higher-volume customers and striving for long-standing relationships with them. The same is true in the other direction: Find good suppliers and stick with them. While supplier stability has become standard, good-business practice (a core element of just-in-time and total quality management), customer retention is still mostly talk.

A Bain & Company graph, Exhibit 10-2, details the value of loyal customers. In year zero, there is cost—no profit—in gaining a new customer. Profits begin the next year and grow each year thereafter. The graph shows the contributors to increasing profit: greater sales volume, lower costs, referrals, and price premiums (e.g., the customer may pay more for the ease of dealing with the same supplier and staying on the learning curve together).[20]

Even in high tech there is a place for customer stability. A reporter interviewed George Fisher, CEO of Eastman Kodak, on the subject of

EXHIBIT 10-2
Why Loyal Customers Are More Profitable

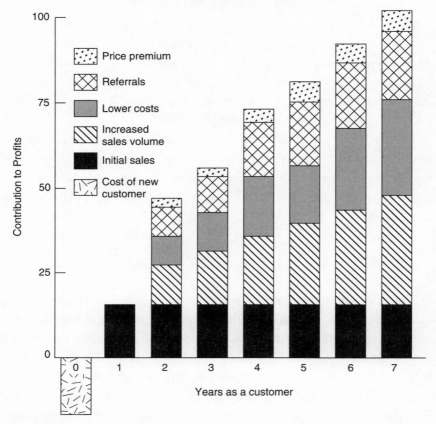

Source: Adapted from Rahul Jacob, "Why Some Customers Are More Equal Than Others," *Fortune* (September 19, 1994), pp. 215–224. Reprinted by permission of *Fortune* and Bain & Co.; © 1994 Time Inc. All rights reserved.

the technology paradox, which is this: Given how fast prices for new electronic and other technologies plummet, how can the firm afford to develop and exploit new technologies—and make a profit? The key to the quandary, says Fisher, is expanding sales faster than the decline of prices. From Fisher's and others' comments emerges this conclusion: "Value," the reporter writes, "will be in establishing a long-term relationship with a customer—even if it means giving the first generation of a product away." The profits come from selling upgrades, services, or—for Kodak up to now—camera film.[21]

Barrie Dempster, manufacturing manager at Davey Products in Australia (an Improvement Pathways respondent in Chapter 4) comments on how to establish strong relationships with customers. In the remarks block on his scoring sheet, Dempster writes, "There should be some gauge of establishing social links, particularly the level of trust that is established." His point is valid. As Drucker maintains, in a supplier-customer partnership there is no room for the command style that characterizes conventional management. These are marketing relationships and call for marketing questions: Not "What do we want to do?" he says, but "What do *they* want to do? What are their objectives? Their values? Their ways of doing things?"[22]

If there were space for more words on the scoring sheets in the principles research, social linkages would be mentioned. As it stands, the first principle awards points when suppliers get customer/client representatives onto their teams. Being on the team is a strong (though incomplete) step toward establishing social, trust-based bonds. And companies are doing this:

• At Kodak's Optomechatronic/Mechanical Systems unit an assembly team set forth a new policy: Each team member will visit a customer site within three months of starting training within an assembly cell. Since each cell is focused on its own customer, the policy is that much easier to carry out.[23]

• Amtico, a division of Courtaulds, making specialty floor tile in Coventry, England, sent a team of four operators across the English Channel to a supplier in Calais. The small French supplier provided polyvinyl chloride to Amtico, but its PVC was arriving with black spots in it. This wouldn't do for the white tile Amtico was making. The French had expected high-level managers from Amtico and had arranged a fine luncheon in the best Calais restaurant. The four operators loved it. When the meal was over and the parties got down to business, the operators presented the problem—and the threat that Amtico was considering another supplier. The French supplier went to work and fixed the problem. And now factory operatives at both ends have ongoing communications with each other.

A supplier-customer trend that began in the eighties, and that needs another decade to be realized, is portrayed in Exhibit 10-3 (the exhibit first appeared in my seminars in 1985).[24] The norm in the past was for each customer to seek large numbers of suppliers, most delivering in low, sporadic volumes. Each supplier, in turn, sought as many customers as possible, even if most of them only bought in trickles. The network of relationships looks like a map of the cosmos but with transport lines between the big and little planets and stars.

The next decade must include evolution to the pattern in the lower half of the exhibit: every supplier with fewer customers, every customer with fewer suppliers, and larger, steadier flow volumes between each pair. In industries where shipping weight is a concern, the new

EXHIBIT 10–3
Customer/Supplier Networks

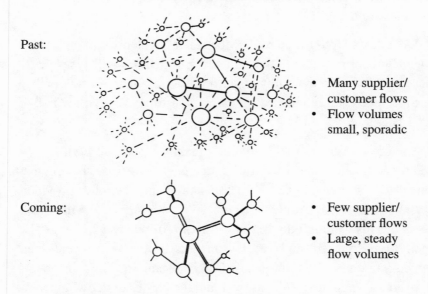

Past:

- Many supplier/
  customer flows
- Flow volumes
  small, sporadic

Coming:

- Few supplier/
  customer flows
- Large, steady
  flow volumes

Key: Circles are companies: Big circle, big company. Little circle, little company.
   Lines are flows of purchased materials: Double lines are large-quantity flows with more or less
   continuous deliveries. Heavy lines, light lines, dashed heavy, and dashed light signify progressively lighter flow volumes, and more sporadic deliveries.

pattern includes geographic proximity: customers and suppliers located closer together. Nypro, the injection molder, tries to build its plants next door to its shrunken number of customers, no matter where they are in the world.

Employee Stability

The Kodak team's visitation policy would be for little gain if the team split up. Likewise, the shop-floor-level communications between Amtico and its Calais supplier require a certain amount of employee stability to come to anything. Frederick Reichheld, who heads the "loyalty/retention" practice at Bain & Company, estimates that employees become about three times more productive after ten years with the same employer than when they started work. These employees' knowledge is key to keeping customers—whose longevity is the source of repeat sales and referrals.[25]

But a number of firms are not even paying heed to the trappings of employee retention. According to one report, the following companies have cut out or cut down on simply saying thanks, with a small gift, for years of service: IBM, Scott Paper, Merck, and American Express. Scott Paper abolished its entire service-award program in 1994 as part of a cost-cutting move. Timken Company eliminated some of the lower-year awards in 1993, thinking that few people would care. A barrage of letters from employees proved that assumption wrong. Timken reinstated the full package of service awards.[26]

A current trend, especially in the United States, is toward greater use of casual labor. This can be good practice in that temps can ease the firm through seasonal peaks and sporadic ups and downs. Steps need to be taken, however, to avoid degradation of work-force cohesiveness. Hewlett-Packard's Marysville, Washington, business unit developed its own cadre of fully trained temps, called flex force. These are people H-P can call upon on short notice and who plan to be available to H-P for some years. Flex-force sources may include recent retirees, a spouse, college students, or a parent willing to be away from the kids only part-time. In practice, each cell team at H-P calls back the same flex-force people each time, so that the temps come to feel like real teammates.[27]

More typically, companies are turning the job over to temporary employment agencies. Some managers tell me that their agency is willing and eager to work with them. Where that is so, the company and the agency should try to do as H-P did: Develop a more permanent pool of temps dedicated to the same customer. For the temp agency to just send "somebody good" to the firm invites insider-outsider culture clashes.

Some manufacturers employ another way of gaining loyalty and longevity among their temps: Provide them benefits equal to their time contributions. One company in the fast-food and hospitality industry even does so: Starbuck's, the fast-growing premier coffeehouse company.

Quality Individuals Versus Teams

The Real Heroes of Business, we are told by the authors of a book by that title,[28] are exceptional individuals that make all customers feel like kings. The authors got several hundred nominations from *Fortune*'s top five hundred service companies and winnowed them down to fourteen employees, each of whom gets a full chapter in their book. And yes indeed, it was an immense pleasure to be met by Phil Adelman, doorman at Marriott's Cambridge, Massachusetts, hotel. (I've conducted seminars there a few times.) Phil is Chapter 1, which lauds him in every which way and summarizes thus: "The talent and charm of Phil Adelman's performance is that he does these small favors for people without the slightest suggestion that they are favors, and with a graciousness and assurance that leave the hotel's customer with a feeling of well-being. . . . More than this, Phil never hangs around, waiting expectantly for a tip." Moreover, and especially to the point of this chapter on quality, Phil submitted sixty-three suggestions one January and commonly comes up with ten in a week.

I would also like very much to be waited on by Ruby Doricchi at Ruby Tuesday restaurant number 24 in Greenville, South Carolina, but I won't go into the glowing report of her special relationships with customers detailed in Chapter 2 of *Real Heroes.*

I only want to make the point that individual heroes cannot be the stuff of business success. There simply are not enough of them. Business success must revolve around heroic *teams,* or even nonheroic ones. We cannot tell from *Real Heroes* whether the fourteen individuals cited are or are not team players. Probably some of them would function well in a team environment (except that most of their employers don't have a team mind-set), and some wouldn't. A team structure does things to people that change their behaviors even without team-oriented training. Then, by giving them the training, plus the hard-science tools of quality improvement, the result is a good deal more noteworthy than the excellence of the fourteen heroes.

This is not to say that companies must rely only on teams, not individuals. Most real work—of a nonheroic variety—still gets done by individuals. Personal excellence therefore makes an enormous difference. Harry Roberts and Bernard Sergesketter, in their book *Quality Is Personal,* describe how individuals can enhance their own contribution and value to their company.[29] The user of the method simply makes a list of chronic personal failures and mishaps. Then the person makes a check mark beside the listed item every time he or she does the incorrect thing. This is another variation on the checksheet, or Bertain's yes-no chart. Roberts, Sergesketter, and their colleagues have found that self-recording raises one's sensitivity to the personal failing and almost immediately reduces their frequency—often by a factor of ten.

Among numerous problem solving and self-help devices that we are invited to use, the personal quality checksheet has distinct advantages. A basic tool that all teams ought to use, it prepares individuals for the time when team processes kick in. Usually, that takes a long time, and people become frustrated by the delay. If individuals use checksheets themselves first, it should be quicker and easier to get teams to use it. In the meantime, improving one's self provides frustration relief and a sense of personal satisfaction.

Team Stability and Cohesiveness

A natural way to gain labor stability and cohesiveness is through natural teams. Two of the people interviewed for the Improvement Pathways case studies in Chapter 4 used this term, "natural teams." Both made it clear that they were not talking about people in the same function. A natural team is composed of people in a process flow-path relationship. This is an outcome of full-scale reengineering. The process flow becomes a cell or plant-in-a-plant fully staffed cross-functionally to make a complete product or perform a full service. (Doing so in the plant meets the criterion for 3 points on Principle 1). If the organization has not been reengineered, we may turn for help in smoothing over the interface problems to a somewhat less than natural team: a project, staffed by people drawn from the departments along the flow path. These sentences touch on three degrees of stability and cohesiveness:

1. Minimal. When associates reside in functional shops and departments, work-flow relationships are department to department, not person to person. If I were an assembler, and if I cared at all, I might wonder, Which of the eight packers in shipping will pack this assembly? And which of the ten stock pickers in the warehouse pulled the parts that I am working on? The flow pattern and people involved change every time. This introduces continual operator-to-operator and machine-to-machine sources of variation and difficulties in pinning down root causes of problems.

2. Medium. Collaborative teams bring people together on a project. They pitch in in twos, threes, fives, maybe tens to develop a plan, design an aircraft, transport passengers, conduct surgery, build a house, or improve a process. Work does not pass from person to person on the team; instead, all are at work on the same assignment in different ways at once. If done well, interactions among the specialists take place all the time. This works best when team members are colocated. E-mail interactions are less effective but can do reasonably well if the group meets face-to-face now and then in between E-mailings.

The enormously successful animated film side of Walt Disney Company attests to the advantages of the collaborative team structure. Company Chairman Michael Eisner and Disney Studios Chairman Jeffrey Katzenberg reorganized films shortly after their arrival at Disney in 1984. A key step was detonating the functional structure of the animation unit and rebuilding it so that associates work in teams focusing on one movie.[30]

A movie is easy compared to an airplane. Boeing's remarkable—for the airplane industry—team development of the 777 commercial airplane employed a hierarchy of teams: over two hundred cross-functional teams in three layers. At the top was a single oversight team of five or six managers. Next layer consisted of twenty-five to thirty two-person leader teams, each with one person from operations and the other from engineering. They oversaw some two hundred work teams having responsibility for specific parts of the plane, such as flap and tail. These groups were cross-functional, usually with five to fifteen associates.

After this structure had functioned for a while, problems surfaced. Information wasn't flowing well horizontally team to team. The solution was to add a fourth layer of five airplane integration teams, each with twelve to fifteen associates drawn from the work teams. A typical problem in airplane design comes when two different design groups go after the same small space in the plane. In one case, one Boeing team had put the passengers' oxygen system in a space that another team had dibs on for the gasper, a nozzle that blows air at the passenger. A team member called in the integration team, which initiated a joint attack on the problem. Within three hours the three teams had worked out a solution—a special clamp that holds both systems. In the old days such conflicts usually weren't seen until assemblers tried to build the plane.[31]

Boeing's multilayered approach, with integrative features, touches all the bases. Too many companies, on the other hand, practice teaming at one level and not at others—with predictably poor results. Greyhound, the bus company, came out of Chapter 11 bankruptcy protection in 1991 only to go on a spending spree that included management perks and ill-advised teaming ventures. "Breakthrough" seminars at off-site motels involved hundreds of employees and several days of role-playing games. One was Circle of Truth, in which small groups of managers revealed their perceptions of each other. Meanwhile, experienced rank-and-file employees, and bus terminal managers as well, were being sacked right and left and replaced by part-timers and low-paid "customer-service associates" who had little or no chance for pay raises. Reasoned Greyhound's vice president for customer satisfaction, "if people stayed around too long, they would get too sour and cynical."[32] So much for teamwork and strong working relationships. So much, too, for customer service and customer satisfaction.

3. Maximal. Work-flow teams, cells, and plants-in-a-plant form out of the broken pieces of the functional (castle-tower) organization. The aforementioned person-to-person and machine-to-machine sources of variation shrink or disappear. This brings about magnitude-level possibilities for isolating and fixing root causes.

It is possible to create a work-flow team or cell without colocating all its members. The result is what is called a logical cell (as opposed to a physical one) or, we could say, a virtual cell. A semiconductor assembly plant in Penang, Malaysia, is moving in this direction (on the advice of consultant Thomas Billesbach and myself). Their equipment is grouped together in the usual way: some two dozen die-attach machines in one clean room, which is a supplier to two dozen die-bonding machines in the next clean room, and so on. For certain technical reasons (e.g., different clean-room requirements) breaking up the departments and regrouping into cells (e.g., a die-attach and die-bonding pair) was not clearly the best way to proceed. Experiments on the effectiveness of cells would take some time. For immediate improvement the simple, no-cost action is to designate a specific die-bonding machine as a customer of a certain die-attach machine. Do this for as many machines as possible. This eliminates the machine-to-machine sources of variation mentioned earlier.

Kodak's black-and-white film business did the same thing. For many years, the process had been split up in buildings scattered about Rochester, New York's mammoth Kodak Park. Master rolls of film were produced here, paper backing there, film coating elsewhere, sensitizing in still another location—all this taking place for rolls a mile long and as wide as a living room. Later, in still other buildings, the slitters, cutters, winders, boxers, and other equipment go to work making the little yellow rolls of film. A full-length book on black-and-white's resurrection as a viable Kodak product describes how *Team Zebra* (the title of the book: "zebra" for black and white) evaluated the options:

> A bit of thought was given briefly to splitting the flows physically across the Park—transporting equipment to different buildings. But the expense would have been prohibitive and the chaos and downtime catastrophic. Instead, the planning group wound up creating "virtual flows"—no equipment was actually moved. . . .[33]

Given the low esteem that "ancient" B&W film products had at Kodak—in a Kodak era of severe cost cutting—it is easy to see why the team quickly rejected trying to get budgetary approval to move the equipment into physical cells. This should be considered temporary, however. As the company's cost cutting begins to generate retained earnings, some of those earnings should be plowed into moving the machines. Not doing so impedes team socialization, knowledge sharing, and real teamwork. It also perpetuates certain non-value-adding wastes, especially the costs of shop-floor control and related coordination and synchronization software and hardware—which are easily done away with when physical cells become a reality. My observation, based on several firsthand visits, is that some of Kodak's most serious quality and cost problems have to do with physical process separation, plus retention—and growth—of costly systems to coordinate the separated entities.

Project Cohesiveness and Stability

We've considered natural and virtual teams. Project teams, which more and more people spend more and more of their work lives on, are a special problem. The trouble with project teams is that they are unnatural. People are pulled out of other jobs, are thrust together with a charter or challenge, fumble around trying to attack the matter efficiently, and disband just about the time when project teammates are working cohesively. Projects are an imposition to an orderly organization chart. Weird-looking charts of the matrix variety attempt to show who does what for whom.

Bob Kantor, consultant at the Lotus Institute, Lotus Development Corporation, has an opinion that is especially applicable to project teams. He says "the wiring together of talented professionals is necessary but not sufficient" to gain the full advantages of teams. "Teams," he says, "are a higher form of organism than mere groups of individuals sharing information and tasks." He believes that true teams must demonstrate a common commitment and must reach consensus on roles, responsibilities, and processes.[34]

Okay. But how? Where is the book on world-class project management? As far as I know, it hasn't been written yet. However, I can glean some answers from my own research and experience (also, see the box

"Projects to Win Projects," which supports these points for a special kind of project):

1. Apply TQM to the process of project management. I've discussed this in depth with a software engineer at Microsoft. "Oh, yeah," he said. "We make the same mistakes over and over, project after project." And no, they don't document these mistakes (at least not on the projects he had been assigned to). The reasons why TQM is so slow to be applied to project management is that projects are always a rush—get it to market fast. And they are nearly always late and overbudget. The team, and the company, feel they can't take time for anything but the project itself. This is clearly just passing the same problems from project to project "forever."

The documentation methods of SPC are ideal for the purpose of finding and fixing chronic project management problems. Most applicable is the simple checksheet. Documentation of mishaps is the first step leading to elimination of their root causes. The improved methods then become the new, standard way to run a project. And the improvement process repeats. All of this must begin by making improvement of the process of project management one factor on which every project team is evaluated.

2. Keep project teams somewhat intact. This is the approach of Florida-based Harris Corporation's government systems business. The unit has established four teams, each for a different series of its high-tech electronic products. Each team has a project manager, a project specialist, a material planner (transitional), a buyer, and a production team. The project manager and project specialist have complementary skills, one usually being an electrical engineer and the other a mechanical engineer. As one government contract winds down, the team gets started on the next contract.[35]

3. Share information. Members of a project team can do little without information. However, sharing it goes against the grain of most people in Western cultures. The common individualistic attitude is, "My expertise, my experience, and my information are my competitive advantage, and I'll keep them for myself."

PROJECTS TO WIN PROJECTS

The aerospace and defense (A&D) industry's lifeblood is government contracts. Some A&D contractors are very good at winning lucrative contracts. Others win less often, and get the dregs. A three-year benchmarking study probing the methods of twenty-four A&D divisions neatly defines what the more successful contractors do (and that the less successful do not do):

1. *Pursue only a limited number of contracts* (the queue limitation, or kanban, idea). They probe the customer's funding, which is sometimes shaky, as well as competitors' strengths. They get to know the views of the project and the competition held by the customer's technical people and key decision makers. They turn down the dubious projects. (Poorer performers focus their planning on financial analysis, with little effort to understand competitive responses.)

2. *Form a capture team two years in advance of the award.* The capture team gets close to customer's decision makers to learn their real wants, develops a solution, presells it to the customer, notes the reaction, and revises the solution to correct perceived weaknesses. As an award reaches the proposal stage, the capture team joins forces with proposal specialists and other functional specialists. (Poorer performers throw a proposal team together of whoever is available and rarely provide proposal training.)

3. *Maintain a core multifunctional staff of proposal specialists.* They train other members of the proposal team in proposal methodology. The methodology focuses on the requirements, technical concerns, and communication of the win strategy to the proposal writers on the team. (Poorer performers disband each proposal team and start over with new people who have to learn or relearn the proposal process.)

4. *Monitor and improve the process.* Management reviews are frequent and thorough. The core staff conducts postproposal debriefings, seeking ways to improve the whole proposal process. (Poorer performers hold management reviews late in the process, often resulting in substantial proposal rewrites.)

Source: Research conducted by Price Waterhouse and twenty-four A&D contractors, reported in Michael O'Guin, "Aerospace and Defense Contractors Learn How to Make Their Businesses Soar," *Quality Progress* (June 1995), pp. 35–42.

While no one wants to snuff out the Western spirit of individual-ism—a valued source of innovation—neither do we want team members to withhold information from other team members. Information is power, and project teams with wide access to information, including each other's, are powerful and effective.

But what is the mechanism for pulling knowledge out of people's heads, personal files, desk drawers, and other hiding places? Here, we need to go to the Far East, where the culture is group oriented rather than individualistic. Jeffrey Funk, now a professor at Penn State University, details systematic procedures for information sharing at Mitsubishi Electric Company in Japan. He learned the Mitsubishi system while on a two-year project-engineering assignment arranged by Westinghouse, his employer at the time. At Mitsubishi, engineers insert into file cabinets, fully cross-referenced, every scrap of information gleaned from visits to libraries, customers, trade shows, conferences, committee meetings, and so forth. Newly hired engineers spend a good deal of their orientation period getting to know the filing system and the rules for its use.[36] Any engineer who is lax about following this system is not a team player, for a clear, known measure of teamness is willingness to share information.

Mitsubishi engineers used ordinary filing cabinets, an unmodern way to store information. Technologically advanced companies use electronic memory and link up their engineers with Lotus's Notes. Still, experience shows that Notes won't work well without somehow creating the incentive to share information. Johnson & Higgins and Anderson Consulting include as a performance appraisal item how effectively its users of Notes share information. Hewlett-Packard's personal computer division has altered the compensation system of its Notes-using sales force to reward working in teams.[37]

Oticon, the Danish manufacturer of hearing aids, achieves information sharing in a different way. The firm had fallen back in the pack in technology and market share when Lars Kolind took over as CEO. After going through a round of heavy cost cutting and other forms of rejuvenation, Kolind still was dissatisfied. As Thomas Vollmann describes it, Kolind created an office without walls, with no permanent desks or offices, where everyone only has a small caddie to carry around paper so that paper is largely absent, work stations supported by computers where teams form and work through problems as they come up, and an organization with very few control mechanisms. . . .

No one at Oticon has a title—even a business card. People were encouraged to learn at least three different jobs [and] had to define their own jobs. This encouraged a maximum of learning—and it also clearly identified the need for a new type of information repository. Knowledge could not be hoarded or kept in particular places. A new computer system where everyone had access to virtually any piece of information and where information was not kept in other places was a necessary supporting element in the enterprise transformation infrastructure.[38]

We must understand that the Oticon and Mitsubishi systems are *managed in*. Culture only explains why a Japanese company, not a Western one, developed the Mitsubishi system of information sharing. Management alone explains Kolind's creation at Oticon. These systems would not happen of their own accord. Any company can do the same thing. Management is universal.

11

A Ten-Year Plan

The essentials of a ten-year plan for industry—and for your industrial company—were presented in Chapter 2. They are

1. Shift the organization's mind-set forward toward management by principles—beyond edicts, procedures, and policies.
2. Ensure that the principles are customer focused, driven by all employees, and based on factual data. For this purpose, use the sixteen principles presented in Exhibit 2-2 (or your own adaptation of them). Weigh plans and proposals against the principles. If any are violated, reconsider.
3. Keep score on your progress against the principles. (You get what you measure). Use the five-step scoring criteria to disclose blind spots and weaknesses.
4. Improve step by step across all the principles.
5. Don't expect ever to score all fives. As your products, processes, and people evolve and as your competitors react, you will fall back and will need to rise again.

Industry's plan for the next decade must avoid getting sidetracked. It must deal with assorted obstacles, including habits, mind-sets, and plain old resistance to change, but especially misunderstandings. Part of the job of clearing up the misunderstandings and removing the obstacles belongs to the consultants, book authors, journal publishers, and professional societies. Where they won't do it, the company must do so on its own for its own people. This chapter targets some of the misunderstanding and related obstacles. Specific issues include upgrading from cost to value, pushing the goal setting downward and unmonetarized, pursuing multiple improvement sets at the same time, and keeping everyone sensitized to the continuing evolution of new ideas in manufacturing management.

FROM COST TO VALUE

None of the customer-focused principles directly addresses cost. Customers don't care about cost. They want cost's richer relation, *value,* which is named in Principles 3 and 13.

Value is still a fuzzy concept. It's like pornography, or like what quality was fifteen years ago. It's "I know it when I see it." But value has gained status as one of the business world's top concerns: value shopping, value pricing, value-addedness, non-value-adding waste, and so on. Harmon suggests that value has even gained higher stature than quality:

> Most of this country's companies are working to improve the *quality* of their service and products, when what they really need is to focus on *value.* Value, simply stated, is the customer's perception of a product's worth vis-à-vis its price. In Japan, department stores are filled with far more European products than products from the United States. The reason is clear to the perceptive consumer, who notices a distinct difference between these European products and the American-made products commonly found in department stores in the United States. While the prices of the European products are usually higher, the value is almost always markedly superior.[1]

Harmon's definition of value—perception of worth for price—is a good start. It is like defining quality as fitness for use—a simple definition (a Juran contribution) that gets things started. Next step in the quality progression was breaking the simple definition of quality into its multiple dimensions, as customers see it. Garvin offered eight dimensions: conformance, performance, features, reliability, durability, serviceability, aesthetics, and perceived.[2] We could add to those eight four more: quick response, readiness, humanity, and safety. Then to manage these dimensions, we needed to state them in terms that allowed measurement—which has been done. For example, common measures of conformance are parts per million, or percentages defective. Finally, use of those measures becomes a part of every employee's job.

Now, this pattern—definition, multiple dimensions, measures, and use—must repeat itself—for value. This must be an early task in industry's, or your company's, ten-year plan. Measures are needed to activate, energize, and sustain continuous improvement.

Some measures are process-specific (e.g., a process-control chart for a mold-press, or changeover time on a certain production line). They stay with the operator, cell, machine, or production line. Other measures monitor not by process but by business unit. Scorekeeping by business unit is a separate issue, full of hazards and ripe for change.

SCOREKEEPING

The customer-focused principles detailed in Exhibit 2-2 tell what to do, and the zero-to-five point scoring scale tracks the results. Some companies may prefer their own version or variation. Famous examples of alternative scoring schemes are Japan's Deming Prize, the U.S. Baldrige Award, and the Shingo Prize. Criteria for those awards have been widely publicized. Less known are the homegrown and industry-specific scoring methods.[3] An example of each follows:

• *Homegrown.* AlliedSignal has developed a self-scoring methodology for rating its businesses. Called Total Quality Maturity Path, the scoring scale ranges from one point (lowest) to four points (world-class). Units score themselves in six areas: (1) leadership, including employee participation and management by fact; (2) organization, including cross-functional teamwork, supplier participation, and internal and external customers; (3) measurement and recognition (including many of the criteria for customer-focused Principles 8 and 9); (4) development activities, including cost targets, design simplification, and value for customers; (5) work processes, including process flexibility, inventory turnover, cycle time, and setup/changeovers; (6) quality of results, including rejects, scrap, rework, and process variability.[4] We see, from all the words, that these categories capture most of the content of the sixteen principles. They provide AlliedSignal a firm foundation for its next decade.

• *Industry-specific.* AlliedSignal's defense businesses could also score themselves using DoD 5000.51G, "Guide to Assess Status of TQM Implementation." That Department of Defense directive provides a one-to-five point scoring scale across eight TQM categories. The eight delve into quality in some detail and encompass about five of the sixteen customer-focused principles.

Can these kinds of first-order metrics coexist with the higher-order, highly aggregated derivatives that seem to capture most of the attention of senior executives? Fallacies of managing by the typical "financials" were addressed in earlier chapters. Here we'll consider some newer largely financially oriented measures: the balanced scorecard, cost of quality, zero working capital. For good measure we'll also include throughput and stretch goals.

Balanced Scorecard

Most CEOs know that revenue, market share, and earnings are insufficient indicators of company strength and value. In 1990 the KPMG Peat Marwick consulting firm organized a research group that included a number of senior executives and an academician to develop a mix of financial and nonfinancial measures of business performance. They called their creation the balanced scorecard,[5] which a number of companies have adopted in some form.

One anonymous adopter is "a major corporation involved in the voice-messaging business." The company's CEO heard about the balanced scorecard, became an ardent enthusiast, and took his seven senior officers off-site for a week to hammer out a customized version. They came up with five key performance areas. They are customer satisfaction, product quality, shareholder value, human resources, and business process improvement (for which twenty-five lower-level managers developed performance measures).[6] Whatever the merits of these five areas, they do not make a balanced scorecard. Product quality, customer satisfaction, and perhaps human resources are first-order results (as defined in Exhibit 5-1). Business process improvement might also be first order, depending on how it is specified. Shareholder value, however, is at the other end of the spectrum, a last-order result. Companies that pay heavy heed to shareholder value tend to have the tampering problem (the disease also known as short-termitis). They cut and chop in ways that often adversely affect product quality, customer satisfaction, and human resources—less training, for example. These negatives will show up a couple of years later as retarded share prices.

From the discussion in Chapter 5, scorecard management itself is an oxymoron. We can watch the score but can effectively manage only the basics, the causes, the processes. This is not to say that there is no value in the so-called balanced scorecard, as its adherents are using it. At 3COM Corporation, a scorecard user since 1993, the operating committee members appear to get "a better handle on the . . . business processes outside their functional areas."[7] Strictly financial measures do not have this look-past-your-own-area effect. The *unbalanced* scorecard, therefore, is better than conventional by-the-financials management. The KPMG-sponsored development may serve a transitional purpose, helping to wean executives off an overly financial focus.

Cost of Quality

In some companies, even quality has a financial focus—in the form of cost-of-quality reporting. Retaining quality costing (well beyond its time) is non-value-adding waste. First uses, at TI, IBM, Xerox, Motorola, and others, were vital milestones in the total quality progression. Money-minded executives needed to see that quality losses were so large—10 and 20 percent of revenue—that they had to make quality improvement a key strategic initiative. They did. Everybody else did, too. Few managers today still hold the opinion that quality costs too much money.

The quality community has done a wondrous job of getting people to believe in statistical process control—and that lot sampling is, in comparison, a poor way to get quality. These days, leading quality journals hardly mention lot sampling, and textbook chapters on quality methodologies sometimes reduce the lot-sampling topic to a paragraph or two.[8] (Likewise, economic lot sizing has lost esteem in the inventory management community.) A similar fate should befall quality costs. Yet a recent issue of *On Q,* the journal of record for the American Society for Quality Control, listed ten references on quality costing.[9] Let's bury quality costs, which Japan never has had a use for since the success of quality-driven companies was its own proof.

Renaming Things

Also symptomatic of the financial fixation is the zero-working-capital scheme. For most manufacturers, working capital is a double-digit percentage of revenue. It ranges from 12 to 14 percent for Whirlpool and Campbell Soup to 27 to 29 percent for GE and McDonnell-Douglas— an apparent mother lode waiting to be mined. One component of working capital is that invested in inventory, which really is a mother lode. More on that in a minute.

The other element—usually at least as large as the inventory component—is the cash tied up in billing. Achieving zero money tied to billing, however, does dirt to supplier-partners and valued customers. The method is to slow down payments on supplier invoices and cajole customers to pay immediately—or in advance! Companies with the clout to do these things are simply shifting the working capital burden to their external partners. The supplier must raise prices to compensate, so no one benefits. The customer must raise prices, which cuts sales, which cuts purchases. Again, no benefits. Of course, companies in a cash crisis must resort to such extreme measures to stay afloat. Otherwise, good sense recommends fair treatment of external partners on billing matters.

A number of examples of companies striving for zero working capital were included in a *Fortune* magazine feature story. The article discusses how they cut cycle time and setup time, eliminated trade loading and adopted quick response, converted to daily production of every model, and installed work cells. Not a word about the billing component of working capital.[10] In other words, this article is simply a rewrite of *Fortune*'s many stories over the years on cellular production, just-in-time, time-based management, and quick response. This is putting a financial spin on measures that in their own right are vital because they relate directly to customers' primary needs (quality, speed, flexibility, value). Boiling everything down to a single metric, money, has a certain elegance to it. But doing so diverts minds from root causes and customer concerns and demeans the efforts of frontline associates.

In partial defense of *Fortune,* probably the story writer was following a lead. Continually parading out new management initiatives—many of them renamed existing ones—is how management staff people hang on to their jobs. The same goes for the management consulting profession. The same for business magazines.

Throughput

Synonyms also can get us into trouble. An example is speed (a basic customer concern), a.k.a. cycle time, lead time, flow time, or throughput time. The last of these synonyms, throughput time, takes on a very different meaning when the second word, "time," is dropped. Throughput is quantity pushed through the plant, which is output. Increasing output (throughput) is not serving customers. A hard lesson of the past is that an output emphasis drags down quality—and more.

Sometimes "throughput" is intended to mean all the way through to collection of payment from a customer. That has a somewhat better ring to it than just "how much can we make?" Still, the quest for revenue is fallacy laden as well—as other chapters have noted (especially Chapters 5 and 7). The direct goal of the firm is not to produce revenue or make money. It is to serve customers. Making money is derivative.

When I hear manufacturing people talk about throughput, I'm never sure whether they really mean cycle time. I always hope so.

Stretch Goals

To reiterate this chapter's purpose, it is to provide a ten-year plan for adopting principles-based management and remove obstacles in the way. One more obstacle is executive-level numeric goal setting, even including stretch goals. The new executive role (articulated in Chapter 9, on remaking HR management) is that of facilitator and calls for teamsmanship. More specifically, executives have the massive job of visibly promoting, facilitating, and inculcating the management-by-principles mind-set into the membership. This might involve having a diagonal slice of the organization work out the firm's general, nonnumeric goals and letting every team, department, and person set their own course, possibly including numeric goals charted weekly and monthly. This is precisely the approach of Baldrige prizewinner Zytec in its five-year strategic planning process.[11]

How can senior executives reasonably put the numbers to the goals? They are too distant from machines, materials, suppliers, customers, products under development, and root causes to do it well. When lower-level doers set their own numeric goals, they sometimes turn out to be tougher than their superiors would have set. More importantly, when we set our own goals, we own them. Owners treat their possessions with more respect and conscientiousness than do those who rent.

But most of today's senior executives got where they are by projecting a strong-leader (much different than effective-facilitator) image. Setting tough goals conveys that patina of toughness. Executives see stretch goals as presenting themselves as visionary to boot, and vision may be held, currently, in even higher esteem than toughness.

We hear about stretch goals when they are launched and about those that emerge successful (companies usually keep mum about those that don't). Best known (and perhaps the father of stretch-goaling) was that of then–Hewlett-Packard president John Young, who called for a tenfold reduction in hardware failure rate in ten years. The goal was met and nearly on schedule.[12]

General Electric has aired some of its stretch goals in its annual reports. One, pronounced in 1991, was to double its inventory turns, achieving ten by the end of 1995. GE's 1994 annual report says, "Well, 1995 is upon us, and ten turns may be just beyond our reach, but by year's end we'll be over *nine*." The report neglects to mention that GE (and some other companies) had been calculating inventory turnover by a nonstandard method: *sales revenue* divided by average inventory. The standard way is *cost of goods sold* divided by average inventory.

For trend-watching, it makes little or no difference. (The French companies' trends cited in Chapter 1 are based on sales, whereas the U.S. companies' trends are on cost of sales. But the trends are comparable.) Otherwise it does make a difference. By GE's method its 1994 turns were 7.9, while the standard method yields only 5.9. GE is stretching the metric as well as the goal. (Standard accounting practice uses cost of sales because it provides more stable results. Sales revenue—and inventory turns based on it—may be jerked this way and that by competitors' plays and ploys.)

In using sales in the calculation, GE gets a better-looking result. Also relevant is GE's overarching emphasis on market share (be number one or number two in every business), which pumps sales revenue, sometimes at the expense of cost of sales. Furthermore, a story making the rounds has it that GE began using sales in the calculation because its manufacturing units could too easily fudge the numbers on cost of sales (e.g., count inventory at just the right time). Sales revenue numbers are toted up outside of manufacturing.

All of these points about scorekeeping and goal setting entail a shift in mind-sets: We need to think more about states and less about flows. Management-science scholars will understand this. A system may be characterized by things that are in place—states—and things that flow. In a manufacturing company in-place factors are its capabilities, capacities, ways of doing business, and values. Its flows are product volumes, sales revenues, profits, and so on. We spend too much energy on the flows, which are fleeting. The underlying strength and power of an organization show up as states. But neither states nor flows make much headway without effective follow-through, our next topic.

FOLLOW-THROUGH

In any sport that requires propelling an object up and away, a strong follow-through gets the distance and the accuracy. The ten-year plan requires an equally strong follow-through.

One of the most persistent hindrances to a firm follow-through is the restrictive view that a company cannot pursue multidimensional strategies—such as all sixteen principles at the same time. This viewpoint is still often found in books on strategy and articles in our most prestigious business journals.

For example, we are told how in only three years Komatsu raised its quality level from half that of Caterpillar to winning Japan's Deming Prize. In so doing, Komatsu "focused almost exclusively on quality until it had achieved world standards. Then, and only then, did it turn successively to value engineering, manufacturing rationalization, product-development speed, and the attainment of variety at low cost."[13] What this says is that, during its three-year quality campaign, Komatsu did not encourage its design engineers to use value engineering, which simplifies products, which makes them easier to build with high quality as well as lower costs. Nor did the company encourage its manufacturing engineers and frontline associates to rationalize by wringing non-value-adding wastes out of the processes, wastes which always carry with them bad practices that degrade quality. Nor did the company want its design engineers to work closely with its production engineers, which speeds up product development and at the same time makes products easier to produce without error. And so on.

If this is really true of Komatsu, shame on its management. The many stories on how the Toyota family of companies successfully intertwine quality, speed, flexibility, and value and make it all hum like a 4-cam, 32-valve, 300-HP, V-8 engine were well known when Komatsu began its climb to world prominence. Actually, if Komatsu really did hold back its people on matters other than pure quality, that strategy would at least have been superior to the very weak strategies common in other companies at the time. As Mintzberg notes in *The Rise and Fall of Strategic Planning,* companies have had a pronounced tendency "to favor cost leadership strategies . . . over product leadership strategies."[14] A cost emphasis (not at all the same as attacking non-value-adding wastes) often actually harms quality, speed, flexibility, and value, as well as product development. In contrast, a single-minded quality emphasis has some spillover benefits in speed, flexibility, and value.

But to return to the point, world-class manufacturing in the next decade must be a strategy of wholeness and linkages. It rejects the old one-dimensional, fractionated business school view of one thing at a time. It is good to be demanding—but across the dimensions of customer sensitivity, not on just sales this year and flexibility next.

IMPLEMENTATION TENDENCIES AND NECESSITIES

Chapter 4 gives us the diverse improvement pathways taken by eighteen high-scoring manufacturers. All relied on several different sources of help, wisdom, and inspiration. No company relied on just one source, such as outside consultants, or books and tapes.

Consultants, Advisors, and Trainers

Using consultants and attending seminars were mentioned the most often, though by fewer than half of the eighteen manufacturers. If I had probed how the consultants operated or how the seminars were run or their contents, I surely would have gotten a wide range of answers. The most famous seminars were those of the late Dr. W. Edwards Deming. His four-day marathons covered his own fourteen points, which perhaps could have had about the same title as my sixteen principles: customer-focused, employee-driven, data-based management. The content, however, differs. In particular, the Deming approach hits quality harder but speed, flexibility, and value softer than my own sixteen principles. Deming kept his programs on a rather high, generic level, not the approach of a consultant.

Pure consultants (no training) are at the other extreme from Dr. Deming. Most consultants start by conducting a thorough assessment of the client company's strengths and weaknesses. Sifting those data, the consultant arrives at a prioritized, time-phased implementation plan, which usually employs the consultant, intermittently or sometimes continuously, for a number of months. An alternative approach, which I think is more effective, is for the consultant to focus much of the initial assessment on finding paths of least resistance. That is, look for pockets of prior knowledge and enthusiasm, and target those for earliest improvement projects. (Which things to do first, second, third, etc., is less important.) Internal train-the-trainer efforts can then work on bringing the unknowledgeable and the fervent resisters up to speed and into the improvement community. A good tactic for handling resistance is to find and address reasons for resistance and not single out the resistors, just as a quality improvement team finds and addresses root causes of mishaps rather than mete out blame.

Kaizens

Somewhere in between the high-level Deming brand of assistance and pure hands-on consulting are people who run seminars and workshops drawn primarily from many real-company experiences. A nice blend of training and hands-on action is the kaizen workshop, a live improvement blitz hosted by a manufacturer hoping for a quick, effective learning experience and sponsored by an outside organization. "Kaizen" is a Japanese word that translates roughly as "continuous improvement." Some manufacturers have made kaizen a mainstream element of work life. For example, over a three-year period Wiremold has run several hundred weeklong kaizens involving the full-time efforts of small teams of employees.[15] The kaizen workshops, however, are different. They are one-time, quick-hit indoctrination efforts. They aim at convincing the participants that (1) big improvement opportunities are everywhere, (2) getting results doesn't take much time or money, and (3) you're a fool if you don't exploit these opportunities—continuously.

As they have evolved, mostly in the United States, these kaizens are usually two, three, or four days of intensive improvement work sponsored by an institution such as Productivity, Inc., or the Association for Manufacturing Excellence (AME). The host is usually a small company that either has little prior experience with continuous improvement or is in need of a restart. AME kaizens have taken place in Farmington (September 21–23, 1994) and Hartford, Connecticut (May 17–19, 1995), and Norristown (April 7–8, 1994) and Philadelphia, Pennsylvania (May 17–19, 1995). At each host manufacturer, kaizen teams define and attack set problems. A team consists of a facilitator from outside the company, a team leader from inside or outside, and a few people from both the host company and other companies who are there to participate and learn. At the AME events the facilitators have been kaizen veterans who learned the method in their own companies. The first facilitators came from big companies (including Black & Decker, Pratt & Whitney, Hamilton Standard, and Criticon) that had previous experience with kaizen via the hiring of a Japanese consulting firm, Shinijutsu, specialists in kaizen methods. Those big companies donate the time of their facilitators, typically because the host company is a supplier whom they care about.

Kaizen workshops might spread to other regions with the help of the Manufacturing Extension Partnership (MEP), sponsored by the National Bureau of Standards and Technology, U.S. Department of Commerce. Following the example of the AME workshops, one MEP site, the Delaware Valley Industrial Resource Center (DVIRC) is conducting two kaizen workshops per month in its region. DVIRC, one of the forty-four manufacturing extension centers in the United States, has a staff of seventeen, including nine outreach people, in a region that takes in some five thousand manufacturing companies.

One DVIRC kaizen was hosted by Powell Electronics, a one hundred-employee manufacturer and distributor of electrical connector components in Philadelphia. In two days the kaizen team achieved the following: Production cycle time fell from 7 minutes to 2 minutes, work in process from 500 units to 2 units, and production space from 312 to 180 square feet. Productivity per shift improved about 25 percent, and savings added up to $105,000.

Other extension centers are sending observers to these kaizens, which suggests that the method will spread. This is good news for small manufacturers, which usually lack the resources (and money) to learn what's necessary to survive and thrive in a world of fast-paced, never-ending improvement.

Application Seminars

Another way to convey continuous improvement messages is the application-oriented seminar. A number of people (myself included) run public and in-company seminars that blend high Deming-style theory and tools with examples of nitty-gritty manufacturing issues. On-site seminars may be partly customized for the given company—based on preparatory plant visits and other advance information. (Usually I am able even to customize invited talks. For example, prior to giving a speech at a conference for a paint association and another for an optical laboratories group, I badgered the program committee and headquarters people to line up plant tours for me and provide names of people I could talk to in order to understand the industry and its problems.) Some seminar presenters follow on with consulting visits. Since local ownership is part of the definition of TQM and WCM, follow-on consulting is most effective when directed toward train-the-trainer. (My own approach involves little follow-on consulting since there are plenty of good consulting companies around that are well-versed in world-class concepts.)

For the in-house seminars and workshops my preferred audience is a diagonal slice through the company. There is no good reason why a few opinion leaders from the shop floor and key staff departments cannot sit in the same audience with the department heads and senior executives. The message is not nuclear physics. The emphasis is, after all, on seamless through-the-company flows, and integration of tactics for getting there.

Points of Light

Whether the catalyst comes from consultants, kaizens, seminars, or otherwise, the hope is for a thousand points of light (to borrow from a U.S. presidential campaign a few years back). A hundred, or five hundred, or seven hundred, may flicker from time to time—such as when business is booming. But substantial numbers of lights still burn on. The company's improvement processes do not die out even if its top management structure turns over or has its attention seized by a regulatory issue or an outrageously hot new market opportunity.

Two of the seventeen companies featured in Chapter 4 (Improvement Pathways) mentioned experiencing setbacks related to sales surges. Pierre L. Tanguay, who coordinated Wheelabrator's participation in the principles research, enclosed a letter with his company's scores. He pointed to Wheelabrator's "dramatic improvements in performance" and cited the company's current enjoyment of "increased market share and business levels which have not been seen since the mid-1970s." The price, however, is "a slowdown in process improvement and focus to continuous improvement." He ends his letter by asking if I might refer him to similar companies who need to "re-focus [their] improvement efforts in the midst of 'more work than we can handle.'"

My best answer is that improvement efforts that come unglued are strong symptoms of uneven commitment. Japan's best are not immune. Leading edges of the waves of Japanese improvement have coincided with oil shocks and currency shocks. Prior to each new shock, the Japanese companies lost some of their keen drive to improve and change.

Complacency spores are in every company's genes. Companies fail to keep those spores in check when they spend their training and learning budgets too selectively. What is most important is to broaden, not deepen, the commitment. Too many companies send a select few people on benchmarking trips, to trade shows, and to multiple seminars to learn about the next breakthroughs. This deepens their own level of expertise but only increases organizational learning—and commitment—in small ways.

Along with broadened training, the company needs to build in systematic improvement—make data collection, analysis, and improvement a part of everyone's daily work life. Occasional improvement projects are not enough. On the measurement side, the critical need is to ensure that internal measures are consistent with external ones—meaning what the customer wants and is delighted by. Alcatel (twelfth example in Chapter 4) validates its internal metrics through periodic customer satisfaction surveys and report cards.

LEARNING AND TRAINING

In January 1994 I temporarily assigned myself to the Phoenix, Arizona, area, where I hand-carried the management-by-principles research to several manufacturers. I housed myself in Scottsdale, where I had the privilege—yes, privilege—of dealing with the employees of the Postal Service branch on Via de Ventura. For attentiveness, empathy, warmth, and overall customer service, those postal associates put nearly all other retail, hospitality, and airline employees that I deal with to shame. I hand over a parcel to be weighed, and the man behind the counter quickly notices the name on the return address. While doing the weighing and stamping, he maintains his smile, looks me in the eye, and inquires about my stay in Scottsdale, "Mr. Schonberger." A brief but pleasant conversation continues as he and I complete the business at hand. The experience had been equally pleasant with the woman at the other end of the counter the day before. The inviting, nicely appointed waiting area, complete with chairs and a take-a-number queuing system, made waiting for my turn at the counter that much more agreeable.

Two months later, my wife and I were wrestling with some inquiries about our payroll-related tax deposits with the Internal Revenue Service. The letter said to phone a number at the IRS's Ogden, Utah, center. We talked with tax specialist Joy Hawkins, whose friendly and patient resolution of the inquiry was pleasant on a par with the Scottsdale Post Office.

What's going on here? Post offices and tax authorities have always been among the most brusque and unpleasant to deal with. In the case of the IRS, I know what's going on: total quality management, which, among other things, focuses on training everyone to treat clients as customers. For several years the quality journals have singled out the IRS as being among the more advanced government entities in TQM.[16] I did not check to see if the explanation is the same for the Scottsdale Post Office. I don't need to. When you get caring, attentive service from several employees of the same organization, you know that training is the explanation. As noted in Chapter 10, the fourteen stellar service employees in *The Real Heroes of Business* could be whole companies if only their employers would provide the necessary training.

Peter Drucker credits Frederick W. Taylor as the father of training. Taylor was a pioneer in documenting work elements so that people could be trained to do the work efficiently without process variation. Without well-documented work, skills training cannot proceed. (So let's quit bashing Taylorism.)

Drucker states that Hitler was confident the United States would be unable to play a serious role in World War II. Hitler knew that on sea, in the air, and on land, warmaking depended heavily on optics for precision targeting. He compared Germany's large force of highly skilled optical technicians with America's lack of them. But, Drucker says, U.S. industry had—as a legacy of Taylor—a compensating response. With amazing speed massive training in optical technology provided industry with the necessary technical skills. High-precision war-making equipment soon poured forth.[17]

Today the world knows the secrets of training. There no longer is a corner on knowledge and expertise—at least not for long. It makes the world a more exciting place for commerce. Your ten-year plan for success must include carefully watching and reacting to what is happening beyond your own limited industry, market, technology, and space. Looking outward and learning is the hard part, because we are unused to it. Training and implementation are easier because we do them all the time. Moreover, constant training and education are keys to better guesses about the future.

GUESSING THE FUTURE

As a kid following the war (World War II, that is) I couldn't understand how an enemy bridge could withstand an Allied bombing attack. I didn't appreciate the strength of bridges or the relative weakness of those bombs. These days a civilian can concoct a witch's brew that will blow down large segments of the downtown of an Oklahoma city. Terrible new plagues and mutations of old ones are another world risk, as are natural calamities and as is nuclear war, perhaps started by a despotic leader of a less developed nation. Other kinds of risk sure to stay with us are economic and political. Exchange-rate shifts or political coups can put a business out of business in a hurry.

These risks are all the more reason to grow but not in place. Expanding in place usually creates unfocused monuments, antithetical to Principle 1. Instead, expand by adding manufacturing sites—not just warehouses and distributors—in multiple markets. Nypro and Solectron have the right idea. So does Dana, only a handful of whose 120 automotive-related plants employ more than 200 people. "Plant managers should know the name and personal circumstances of everyone," says Dana's Chairman Southwood J. Morcott.[18]

Aggressive pursuit of the sixteen principles can pave the way for expansion: More attractive products, more reliable quality, quicker response, and close touch with external partners widen and deepen potential markets. Cash flow from inventory, space, overhead, and other reductions help provide the financial wherewithal for expansion. A Scandinavian manufacturer, for example, has followed a tactic of buying up poor-performing foundries in high-rent districts of various European cities. The company president uses an early version of the world-class manufacturing concepts, all captured in a thick training manual, to get the newly acquired foundry's work force turned on to driving out wastes. On average, factory space is soon halved. Selling off the extra space provides *all* the necessary cash to buy the next foundry.[19]

Arthur P. Byrne, president and CEO of Wiremold Company, headquartered in West Hartford, Connecticut, pursues a similar approach: "We have been able to free up enough cash from increasing inventory turns to acquire five companies in the past year. And we've moved quickly to carry the message to the acquired plants." Byrne explains how he gets people's attention after an acquisition:

Shortly after we acquired Walker Systems, Inc., I was touring the operation with some of the plant management. We walked through a huge WIP storage area known as the ICA (inventory control area). Racks were filled to the ceiling with parts. All I could see was the massive amount of money tied up in that inventory.

So, later on, I went back to the area and posted a handwritten sign on one of the racks that read: "Parts Hotel Closing: This Rack Goes Away 2/15/94." At first, the management thought it was a joke—until they saw I had posted similar signs on all the other racks: "This Rack Goes Away 3/15/94"; "This Rack Goes Away 4/15/94"; and so on. I told them I expected my sign back every time a rack went away.

They got the message. About two weeks later, I received my first sign, along with a poem entitled "Ode to Art" from Barbara Looney, who was manager of the ICA department. I responded with my own poem about "The Parts Hotel" and off we went. Every month, a new rack came down and two more poems were written.[20]

As important as expansion and growth, per se, is growth of competencies. It's simply too risky in a turbulent world to depend again and again on the same resources, products, and skills. As Hayes and Pisano put it, "If a company cannot predict whether future customers will emphasize high performance or low cost, an option that would allow either one as the situation evolves has a very high value." And instead of adding an identical production line, why not "invest in a[n] R&D effort directed at improving productivity, [which] provides an opportunity to gain a deeper understanding of the production process." The new knowledge might open the door to still more opportunities, such as designs for better production equipment or substitute materials.[21]

Being quick to pounce on new products and processes is one element of success in the next decade. The company must be equally adept at capturing important new manufacturing management concepts. It seems likely that the next decade will unearth and unleash another five or ten such innovations (as well as numerous renamed old ones). Regions that have not done so in the past will be among the contributors. It is to be a global decade. At this point, predictions as to the content of the new ideas would be specious. No one could have predicted the outpouring of ideas in Japan's decade of the 1970s nor the United States' decade of 1985–95. What is important is not to be able to guess the future—but to be among the first to know.

The company that has all of its sensory organs functioning is the one most likely to be among the first to know—and quickest to leave behind the familiar and outmoded and venture forth. High commitment to education and training (Principle 8), broad-based teaming (Principle 1), and outreach activities (Principle 2) get the senses firing. This is to say that it is fine for managers to trump for innovative changes, but in the old-style organization nothing much will come of it. The employee-driven organization, uplifted by the principles and abreast of the latest lore, will not be satisfied with the status quo.

Appendix:
Scoring Against the Principles

This appendix has two purposes:

1. To explain the methodology behind the customer-focused research project.
2. To offer the methodology to companies for their own uses. Manufacturers may see fit to develop baseline scores against the principles and to plan and monitor their continuing progress up the scale toward maturity.

METHODOLOGY

First steps were to draft the research documents and select an initial group of manufacturers on which to pilot-test them. The document set includes one page describing the research, one page on how to interpret the scoring criteria, two pages containing the sixteen principles and scoring criteria, and a single scoring sheet. The sixteen principles and scoring criteria were included in Chapter 2. The other three pages in the set of research documents are found in Exhibit A-1.

For the pilot testing, I chose companies I knew to be advanced in world-class concepts. These are former client companies, nonclient plants I had visited, and manufacturers whose accomplishments I had heard about one way or another. Phone calls set up the first in-person visits. I explained over the phone who from the company should do the scoring. I recommended managers who had a breadth of knowledge of the organization. This might include, for example, heads of operations, engineering, human resources, finance, and marketing—or a smaller group whose knowledge covers the functions.

In each case, I hand-carried the documents, explained the principles idea and the scoring criteria, and suggested a few ways the participants might do the scoring. First pilot tests, in September 1994, involved companies in my home area of Seattle and western Washington. Fourteen organizations in the area participated. The research moved on to the Phoenix, Arizona, area, where I spent some time in early 1995. I hand-carried the research to six Phoenix-area participants. I sat in on

EXHIBIT A-1
Principles of Customer-Focused Management

The 5-step assessment tool is useful in sizing up your organization's progress in moving toward principles-based management, which may become the major thrust in management in the 21st century. A goal is competitive advantage. An ultimate goal is to build a dynasty.

The principles are quite specific and action oriented (not just slogans, such as "striving for excellence"). All are customer-focused and employee driven. In contrast, conventional (pre-1980s) manufacturing management focused on internal goals, not those of customers, and did not involve frontline employees.

The principles apply to a company, business unit, or product line (not to a function, department, or process). The criteria for earning points are arranged in steps. First step is generally easiest to do, next step a bit harder, and so on. Sometimes, however, a company does not take the easiest path. Thus, on a certain principle a company may score a point at the second step without having scored at the first step. (Each box in the scoring matrix is worth one point.)

The scoring scale is tough. Few manufacturers will average more than one, two, or three points under the 16 principles. Manufacturers just beginning to adopt a world-class agenda probably will get close to zero points. Those who have been at it for a few years usually will score well on a few principles but score zero or one on others. The top score of 80 points is probably unattainable, for the simple reason that standards of excellence continually rise; managing by principles is a journey, not an attainment.

If your own rating is in the eleven to twenty-five ("early learning") range, be pleased. Your company is among the vanguard that understand the idea that what's good for customers and employees is good for the company and all its stakeholders. You've chosen the right path, which is the hard part. The formula for success is staying on the path and improving step by step.

INTERPRETING THE PRINCIPLES—
A FEW COMMENTS FOR MANUFACTURING COMPANIES

You may not be familiar with all of the concepts and terms embedded in the compressed descriptions. The following may help avoid some of the more likely misunderstandings:

- Consider all departments and functions, not just production. And think in terms of internal as well as external customers.
- Progress may not be linear against the scale. For example, on Principle 1, you may have cross-functional projects (1-point level) and focused cells for key products (3-point level), but no customer reps on projects (2-point level). Give yourself 2.0, not the full 3 points.
- Principles apply to all organizations. Banks, hospitals, government, etc., are taking part in other segments of this research. Hence, no manufacturing terms. Example, Principle 6: Instead of *kanban,* the term is *queue limitation.* Reason: Limiting the queue of work before any process is the essence of kanban; it applies to documents in offices or customers in waiting lines, as well as widgets waiting for production.
- On improvement metrics, use your best judgment as to time interval—except where *yearly* improvement is stated.
- Principles 3 and 13 refer to four customer "wants": All internal and external customers want these factors to improve. (One of the four, *value,* improves by attacking non-value-adding wastes/overheads). Aside from those universals, customers want specific products, which the organization finds out about via other principles, especially 2.
- Product cost accuracy—vital for good product-line management—is not directly stated as a principle. Rather, by eliminating complexities—through product focus (Principle 1), cutting non-value-adding-wastes (Principle 3), simplified designs (Principle 5), etc.—accuracy in product costing becomes easy (e.g., via direct costing or activity-based cost audits).
- Principle 8, two-point level, refers to just-in-time training. It means train in a concept/method, then go do it; return for another training session, then do it; and so forth. Compressing all the concepts into a single training course is more common—but less effective.
- Principle 9: Associates must contribute in many more ways than just production itself. That requires many more ways to reward, recognize, and celebrate the added contributions. Too few ways, and too few people will "buy in." Cross-careering means moving a professional to a new career path for at least three years; new-hire orientations, such as moving engineers or MBAs through several departments in just a few years, do not qualify.
- On counting suggestions, Principle 11: "You get what you measure."
- Principle 12: Most internal transactions arise from something that goes wrong or varies too much. Control causes, and transactions should decrease (become non-value-adding waste).
- Principle 13: We can't manage profit, sales, market share, survival; they are results of what can be and should be managed: root causes of improvement in what all customers want.

continued

EXHIBIT A-1 (Continued)

TOWARD MANAGEMENT BY PRINCIPLES
Five-Step Assessment Tool

Principles of Customer-Focused, Employee-Driven, Data-Based Performance

Steps	1	2	3	4	5	6	7	8	9	10	11	12	13	14	15	16
5																
4																
3																
2																
1																
0																

Assessment (one point for each step, each principle):
11–24 points—Eyes open, first steps, early learning
25–38 points—Childhood: trial and error
39–52 points—Adolescence: checklists and guidelines
53–66 points—Adulthood: policies
67–80 points—Maturity: principles

Total points:_____   Date: _____

Name of company, business unit, or plant: _____

Address: _____

_____

_____

Number of employees: _____

Product line: _____

Names and titles of persons doing this assessment: _____

_____

_____

Remarks: _____   *Please send to:*
_____   Richard J. Schonberger
_____   Schonberger & Associates, Inc.
_____   P.O. Box 66948
_____   Seattle, WA 98166
Phone: 206-433-8066

scoring sessions at several of the companies and was asked to lead the discussion in one case. My presence did not seem to inhibit anyone. Debates were lively. For example, someone would say, "I give us three points on number 5." Another manager would argue, "Three? I give us zero!" Debate ensues, and the consensus score may end up anywhere from zero to three—often about halfway between. In other cases, the managers did the scoring later, sometimes because they wanted to be able to include certain missing people.

During that time and based on feedback from some of the first twenty participants, I made a few small changes in the wording of the scoring criteria and the interpretation sheet. The changes were minor enough that the pilot-test data could be merged with later research results without serious bias. At that point, the project shifted from hand-carrying to phone calls, mail, and faxes. One hundred fourteen organizations participated in this way. Raúl Quiñones and Isidoro Herrera of Quiñones Consultores, Juárez, Mexico, were helpful in coordinating with most of the Mexican participants. Kevin Nestadt of Nestadt Consulting in Melbourne coordinated responses from most of the Australian manufacturers.

Meanwhile, beginning in September, I was having attendees at my public seminars (in Ireland, South Africa, and three sites in the United States) score their companies as seminar projects. World Class International (WCI), a U.K.-based training and consulting firm, sponsored the seminar in Ireland. WCI and the IEC subsidiary of the IIR Consulting Group were the sponsors in South Africa. Some of the scoring sheets were incomplete or otherwise not usable. The rest of the seminar-obtained results were kept separated from scores obtained through direct contact with company executives. By March 1995, when the companies participating exceeded one hundred, I was able to compare the seminar data with the other data. There were no significant differences in average scores and distribution of scores. Thus, I made the decision to combine the seminar data with the rest. (Those attending the seminars were not always the ideal people to score their companies. On the other hand, their attendance provided an excellent venue to fully learn about customer-focused principles, which may have raised the validity of their scores.)

Of the twenty "hand-carry" Seattle and Phoenix-area participants, two are service organizations and two are manufacturers that did not meet my expectation of being advanced in world-class concepts. That leaves sixteen "good" ones. Three more very low-scoring manufacturers turned up in the mail part of the research. The three service companies, plus the four unenlightened manufacturers, serve as control groups—useful for comparison and contrast with the main body of participants. Their scores, however, were not included in the final research results.

I encountered a high degree of cooperation and interest in the research. Only ten companies formally declined to participate, although a number of others who said they would respond never did get around to it. By the middle of May 1995, I had received well over the original one hundred responses that I was shooting for. So I quit pestering the laggards.

Exhibit A-2 lists the 127 manufacturers scoring above ten points in the research in three groups: the 16 to whom I hand-carried the project are in part A; 34 participating via the seminars, part B; and 77 that participated through the mail or by fax, part C.

EXHIBIT A-2
Manufacturers Participating in the Research

A. Personal Visits to Present the Research

AlliedSignal fluid systems, Tempe, AZ (starters, valves, actuators)
American Steel Service Center, Kent, WA (steel distribution)
ATL, Bothell (medical ultrasound equipment)
Boeing Door Center, Renton, WA
Boeing Welded Duct plant, Auburn, WA
Eaton Corp., Everett, WA (optical control devices)
Fluke Corp., Everett, WA (electronic test instruments)
Genie Industries, Redmond, WA (industrial lifts)
Honeywell Industrial Automation Systems, Phoenix (process, field, & production
    control sys.)
Intel, Fab 6, Chandler, AZ (semiconductors)
K2 Corp., Vashon Island, WA (skis, in-line skates)
McDonnell-Douglas Helicopter, Mesa, AZ
Milgard Manufacturing Co., Tacoma, WA (doors)
Physio Control, Redmond, WA (defibrillators)
Precor, Bothell, WA (aerobic exercise equipment)
Solectron Washington (electronic manufacturing services)

EXHIBIT A-2 (Continued)

B. Manufacturers Participating Through Seminars

Arrow Group Industries, Breese, IL (metal storage bins)
Arrow Group–Whole company (metal storage bins)
C. Lee Cook, Louisville, KY (sealing devices)
Cook Airtomic, Louisville, KY (piston rings)
Dow Corning, Midland, MI (silicon intermediates & finished products)
Dow Corning, Hemlock, MI (silicone elastomer, tubing, misc. fluids)
Hill-Rom, Batesville, IN (medical headwall systems)
Lincoln Industrial, St. Louis (lubrication equipment & pumps)
Pilot Chemical Corp., Red Bank, NJ (detergents)
Servend International, Sellersburg, IN (ice machines, drink/ice dispensers)
Vectron Labs, Norwalk, CT (crystal oscillators)
FMC Corp., Cork, Ireland (pharmaceutical & food ingredients)
Killeen Corr Products, Dublin, Ireland (paper)
Telemecanique-Ireland, Cophridge, Ireland (contactors)
Waterford Crystal, Kilbarry, Ireland (crystal glasses)
Herdmans Ltd., County Tyrone, Northern Ireland (linen yarn)
Interlux Louvre Manufacturing, Milton Keynes, U.K. (louvre controls for lighting)
Munster Simms Eng. Ltd., Bangor, Northern Ireland (water systems for rec. vehicles)
Adcock Ingram Critical Care, South Africa (critical health care products)
Adcock Ingram Pharmaceuticals, South Africa (pharmaceutical)
Amalgamated Beverage Canneries, South Africa (carbonated soft drinks)
Autoflug South Africa (safety restraints for motor vehicles)
Beier Albany & Co., South Africa (high-tech textiles, e.g., for filtration, etc.)
Cullinan Refractories, South Africa (refractory products)
Eddels South Africa (footwear manufacture)
Illovo Sugar Ltd., South Africa (sugar)
Lever Brothers, South Africa (detergents)
Mercedes Benz of South Africa (passenger cars & commercial vehicles)
MG Glass, Durban, South Africa (beverage containers)
Power Engineers, South Africa (distribution transformers)
Rhomberg Bräsler Manufacturing, South Africa (industrial electronics)
SAD Saf Medication (EL), South Africa (self medication & personal care products)
South African Nylon Spinners (synthetic fibers & polyester polymers)
Toyota Auto. Co., South Africa (exhausts, fuel tanks, seats, chassis, box bodies,
    fabrication)

C. Manufacturers Participating by Mail and Facsimile Machine

3M Printing & Publishing, Weatherford, OK (proofing film)
Albany International, Albany, NY (paper machine press felts)
Alcatel Network Systems, Richardson, TX (telecommunication equipment)
Baldor Electric, Fort Smith, AR (industrial electric motors)

continued

EXHIBIT A-2 (Continued)

Baxter Healthcare, Marion, NC (intravenous solutions)
Bio Clinic, Ontario, CA (health-care pressure reduction products)
BPI, Kent, WA (office furniture)
Charles Machine, Perry, OK (underground construction equipment)
Chief Automotive Systems Inc., Grand Island, NE (collision repair equipment)
Copeland, Sidney, OH (air conditioning & refrigeration compressors)
Dana Corp., Minneapolis (hydraulic control valves)
Digital Systems International, Redmond, WA (call management systems/services)
Dover Elevator, Horn Lake, MS (hydraulic power units, jacks, car slings, platforms)
Dover Elevator Systems, Walnut, MS (elevator controllers)
Dover Elevator Systems, Middleton, TN (cabs, entrances, signals)
Du Pont Furnishings, Camden, SC (nylon carpet yarn)
Ennis Automotive, Ennis, TX (remanufacture of armatures, copper motor windings,
    stators)
Exxon Baytown, Baytown, TX (chemicals)
Four Seasons, Coppell, TX (remanufacture of auto A/C compressors, etc.)
Gates Rubber, Denver, CO (industrial belts & hoses)
Gleason Works, Rochester, NY (machine tools)
Hewlett-Packard, San José (opto-couplers, fiber optics, etc.)
Honeywell Home & Building Control, Golden Valley, MN (HVAC controls)
Joerns Healthcare, Stevens Point, WI (nursing home beds, furniture)
Johnson Controls, Milwaukee (valves, screw machine parts)
Jostens, Denton, TX (class rings)
Jostens Cap and Gown, Laurens, SC (graduation apparel)
Jostens Diplomas, Red Wing, MN (diplomas)
Kawasaki, Maryville, MO (small gasoline engines)
Linfinity Microelectronics, Garden Grove, CA (integrated circuits)
Midland Communications Packaging Inc., Louisville (custom loose-leaf binders, etc.)
Milliken, Business A (textiles)
Milliken, Business B (textiles)
Milliken, Business C (textiles)
Milliken, Business D (chemicals)
Mine Safety Appliance Co., Safety Products Div., Murraysville, PA (safety equipment)
Mine Safety Appliances, Murraysville plant, Murraysville, PA (safety equipment)
OPW Fueling Components, Cincinnati (dispensing products)
Peerless Chain, Winona, MN (chain and wireform products)
Quickie Designs, Inc., Fresno, CA (manual & power wheelchairs)
Raychem Corp., Palo Alto, CA (cross-linked polymer products)
R.A. Jones, Covington, KY (packaging machines)
Reliance Electric, Flowery Branch, GA (electric motors)
Rosemount Measurement, Chanhassen, MN (pressure products)
Rotary Lift, Madison, IN (automotive lifts, alignment racks)
Sentrol Inc., Hickory, NC (security equipment)

EXHIBIT A-2 (Continued)

Tri-Tronics, Inc., Tucson, AZ (electronic dog-training equipment)
United Electric Controls, Watertown, MA (temperature & pressure controls, sensors, recorders)
Varian Associates, Palo Alto, CA (nuclear magnetic resonance instruments)
Wheelabrator, LaGrange, GA (shot-blasting machines)
Whirlpool Corp., Clyde, Ohio (clothes washers)
Wilson Sporting Goods Co., Humboldt, TN (golf balls)
Johnson Controls, Inc., Juárez, Mexico (pressure/temperature electromech. devices)
Levical division of Leviton, Tecate, Mexico (electrical products)
Metalsa S.A., Apodaca, Nuevo León, Mexico (fuel tanks & pickup frames)
Pedsa plant of EWD Co., Juárez, Mexico (auto wiring harnesses)
Philips Component Group, Juárez, Mexico (transformers)
Philips Consumer Electronics, El Paso/Juárez, Mexico (TVs, etc.)
Philips Modular Systems Plant #4, Juárez, Mexico (remote control, PC boards)
Philips Plant #5, TV plant, Juárez, Mexico (TVs)
United Technologies Automotive, Juárez, Mexico (wiring harnesses)
Dover Elevator, Mississauga, Ontario, Canada (elevators)
Ford Electronics, Markham, Ontario (automotive electronics)
Inglis Ltd., Cambridge, Ontario (clothes dryers, trash compactors)
Northern Telecom, Calgary, Alberta (telephones)
Bonlac Foods, Melbourne, Australia (cheese, milk powder, dairy products)
All Head Services, Braeside, Australia (vehicle cylinder head reconditioning)
Davey Products, Huntingdale, Victoria, Australia (pumps)
Dulux Australia, Victoria, Australia (surface coatings and paint)
National Dairies, Muray Bridge, Australia (dairy dessert/cheeses)
National Dairies, Tiaree, Australia (yogurt, yogo, desserts, powder)
Olex Cables, Tottenham, Victoria, Australia (cables)
Aritech Europe, Dusermond, Netherlands (security equipment)
Honeywell Scottish Opns., Motherwell, Lamarkshire (heating/cooling/micro-switches)
Microsoft, Dublin, Ireland (software manufacturing)
Multibras, Rio Claro Plant, Brazil (clothes washers)
Whirlpool Europe, Amiens, France (clothes washers, dryers)

Notes

Preface

1. Tito Conti, *Building Total Quality: A Guide for Management* (London: Chapman & Hall, 1993); pp. 150–167; originally, *Costruire la Qualitá Totale* (Milan: Sperling & Kupfer Editori, 1992).

Chapter 1. Industrial Decline and Ascendancy

1. John Naisbitt, *Megatrends* (New York: Warner Books, 1982).
2. Max Holland, *When the Machine Stopped: A Cautionary Tale from Industrial America* (Boston: Harvard Business School Press, 1987), cited by H. Thomas Johnson, *Relevance Regained: From Top-Down Control to Bottom-Up Empowerment* (New York: Free Press, 1992), p. 29.
3. "Zone Autonome de Production: Valeo Thermique, LaSuze, France," *Target* (Spring 1989), pp. 10–12.
4. Doug Ekings, Dino Kalaharios, Pete Pandry, and Lea Tonkin, "Second Wind," *Target* (Fall 1990), pp. 20–25.
5. Gary S. Vasilash, "The Five Hottest Manufacturers in Silicon Valley: Customer Obsession at Solectron," *Production* (May 1995), pp. 56–58.
6. Jon Brecka, "The American Customer Satisfaction Index," *Quality Progress* (October 1994), pp. 41–44.
7. Ronald E. Yates, "New Way to Gauge Economy," *Chicago Tribune* (September 18, 1994), pp. 1ff.
8. Data sources: Standard & Poor's and Moody's.
9. Roger Lowenstein, "The '20% Club' No Longer Is Exclusive," *Wall Street Journal* (May 4, 1995), p. C1.
10. Richard J. Schonberger, *Japanese Manufacturing Techniques: Nine Hidden Lessons in Simplicity* (New York: Free Press), 1982, pp. 214–217.

Chapter 2. Building Strength Through Customer-Focused Principles

1. Judith H. Dobrzynski, "Rethinking IBM," cover story, *Business Week* (October 4, 1993), pp. 86–97.
2. Steven Covey, *First Things First: A Principle-Centered Approach to Time and Life Management* (New York: S&S Trade, 1994).
3. William C. Symonds and Eric Frey, "Frank Stronach's Secret: Call It Empower Steering," *Business Week* (May 1, 1995), pp. 63–65.

4. Richard J. Schonberger, *Building a Chain of Customers: Linking Business Functions to Create the World-Class Company* (New York: Free Press, 1990), p. 231.

5. Robert C. Camp, *Benchmarking: The Search for Industry Best Practices That Lead to Superior Performance* (Milwaukee: ASQC Press, 1989).

6. Personal visitation to the plant (June 26, 1990).

7. "Industry News," *Manufacturing Engineering* (July 1992), p. 24.

8. Kiyoshi Suzaki, "Work-in-Process Management: An Illustrated Guide to Productivity Improvement," *Production and Inventory Management* (Third quarter 1985), pp. 101–111.

9. Karen Bemowski, "Three Electronics Firms Win 1991 Baldrige Award," *Quality Progress* (November 1991), pp. 39–41.

10. Geoffrey Boothroyd and Peter Dewhurst, *Product Design for Assembly* (Wakefield, R.I.: Boothroyd-Dewhurst, Inc., 1987).

11. Schonberger, *Building a Chain of Customers, p. 221.*

12. Hallmark is a case study (without the detail on the Shoebox experience) in Michael Hammer and James Champy, *Reengineering the Corporation: A Manifesto for Business Revolution* (New York: HarperBusiness, 1993), pp. 159–170.

13. Thomas J. Billesbach and Marc Schniederjans, "Applicability of Just-in-Time Techniques in the Administrative Area," *Production and Inventory Management* (Third quarter 1989), pp. 40–44.

14. Edward M. Knod, Jr., working notes (April 1993) for "Irwin Operations Management Series," a videotape (Burr Ridge, Ill.: Richard D. Irwin).

15. Leonard Bertain, *The New Turnaround: A Breakthrough for People, Profits, and Change* (Croton-on-Hudson, N.Y.: North River Press, 1993).

16. Leslie Gabriele, Robert McInturff, and Michael Pervier, "Nypro's Team Efforts Put the Customer First," *Target* (November-December 1993), pp. 45–48.

17. Jim Pearson, "Nypro's People Deliver Effective Process Control with Seasoned C_{pk} 2 Measures," *Target* (Spring 1991), pp. 51–53.

18. Ronald Henkoff, "Keeping Motorola on a Roll," *Fortune* (April 18, 1994), pp. 67–78.

19. Willard I. Zangwill, "Ten Mistakes CEOs Make About Quality," *Quality Progress* (June 1994), pp. 43–48.

20. "Lego Systems Builds U.S. Market with New Distribution Pieces," advertising supplement, *Industry Week* (1994).

21. Gabriele, McInturff, and Pervier, "Nypro's Team Efforts."

Chapter 3. Best Manufacturers: How They Rate

1. Tupper Cawsey, "The Sarnia Polymers Department: Esso Chemical Canada," Case Studies in Accountability, vol. 1 (Hamilton, Ont.: Society of Management Accountants of Canada, 1991), pp. 53–60.

2. Conversation with Robert Anderson, April 28, 1995.

3. Conversation with Jim Prettyman, Du Pont manager, April 28, 1995.

4. Weak science easily makes it into print, along with strong science. If one specious statement makes it into print, it becomes fact. That opens the floodgates. The phenomenon has been called the "best-source-yet rule: The most credible party to date to recite or publish the [statement] becomes the [new source]": Barry O'Neill, "The Trouble with Kids," *Seattle Post-Intelligencer* (March 13, 1994), pp. E1 and E3.

5. John E. Ettlie, "Join the Top 10%," *Production* (December 1994), p. 12.

Chapter 4. Improvement Pathways

1. Conversation with Robert D. Miller, vice president, productivity and quality, May 10, 1995.
2. Conversation with John McDougall, director of manufacturing, May 12, 1995.
3. Conversation with John Martino, industrial engineering manager, May 4, 1995.
4. Conversation with Barrie Dempster, manufacturing manager, May 15, 1995.
5. Conversation with Bob Null, vice president of manufacturing, May 9, 1995.
6. Conversation with Douglas W. Fletcher, resident manager, May 10, 1995.
7. Conversation with Carl Campbell, manager, May 11, 1995.
8. Roy L. Harmon, *Reinventing the Factory: Productivity Breakthroughs in Manufacturing Today* (New York: Free Press, 1990).
9. See Philip R. Thomas, *Getting Competitive: Middle Managers and the Cycle Time Ethic* (New York: McGraw-Hill, 1991).
10. Conversation with Johnny R. Abdon, May 11, 1995.
11. Conversation with Dave Lauger, vice president, human resources, Quickie Designs Inc., May 5, 1995.
12. Conversation with Ray Floyd, site manager, May 12, 1995.
13. Conversation with Gary Jow, manager, May 4, 1995.
14. Conversation with Ron Wagner, vice president of operations, May 4, 1995.
15. Conversation with David Lowry, product team manager, May 8, 1995.
16. Conversation with Kelly Hoffman, manager, May 15, 1995.
17. Richard T. Lubben, *Just-in-Time Manufacturing: An Aggressive Manufacturing Strategy* (New York: McGraw-Hill, 1988); Masaaki Imai, *Kaizen: The Key to Japan's Competitive Success* (New York: Random House, 1986); Seiichi Nakajima, *TPM: Introduction to TPM, Total Productive Maintenance* (Portland, Ore.: Productivity Press, 1984); pp. 54–58; Hiroyuki Hirano, *Five Pillars of the Visual Workplace: The Sourcebook of the 5S Implementation* (Productivity Press, 1994).
18. Conversation with Ray Bracy, manufacturing business unit manager, May 24, 1995.
19. Conversation with Ross Matthews, director of advanced manufacturing technology, May 4, 1995.
20. Conversation with Wayne Canfield, manager, U.S. manufacturing, May 23, 1995.
21. Conversation with Gerald W. Bidder, managing director, June 6, 1995; Brian H. Maskell, *Performance Management for WCM* (Portland, Ore.: Productivity Press, 1991).

Chapter 5. Value and Valuation

1. Parts of this chapter are adapted from Richard J. Schonberger, "Product Costing as a Rare Event," *Target* (November/December 1994), pp. 8–16.
2. This is consistent with what Hall says of Deming's philosophy: "It shifts the primary focus of organizations from results (what will we gain) to processes (how do things *really* work and what will happen):" Robert Hall, *The Soul of the Enterprise* (New York: Harper Business, 1993), p. 75.
3. Peter F. Drucker, "The Emerging Theory of Manufacturing," *Harvard Business Review* (May-June 1990), pp. 94–102.
4. Yutaka Kato, Germain Boër, and Chee W. Chow, "Target Costing: An Integrative Management Process," *Target* (Spring 1995), pp. 39–51. Cited in the same source are

the two surveys on use of target costing in Japan: M. Sakurai, *Environmental Change and Its Influence on Management Accounting* (in Japanese) (Tokyo: Dobunkan, 1991); T. Tani, H. Okano, N. Shimizu, Y. Iwabuchi, J. Fukuda, S. Cooray, T. Kobayashi, and Y. Kato, "Genka Kikaku in Japanese Firms: Current State of the Art (Kobe, Japan: Working paper, School of Business Administration, Kobe University, 1992).

5. Tim Smart and Zachary Schiller, "Just Imagine If Times Were Good," *Business Week* (April 17, 1995), pp. 78–80.

6. Prevailing price structures, however, can drive the decision the other way. In Harris Corporation's electronic systems sector, ABC data showed common logic and memory chips to be money losers because of highly competitive prices. Harris shifted toward a less competitive, higher margin business: specialty chips for automotive and medical equipment industries. Martha Brannigan, "Harris Finally Digests Big Semiconductor Acquisition," *Wall Street Journal* (October 10, 1992).

7. H. Thomas Johnson, *Relevance Regained: From Top-Down Control to Bottom-Up Empowerment* (New York: Free Press, 1992), p. 71.

8. Bill C. Bradford, "From the Editors," *Journal of Cost Management* (Spring 1992), p. 3.

9. "Most manufacturing organizations . . . can make reasonable estimates of the magnitude of overhead activities if allowed to do so. . . . These estimates are *better* than the estimates usually used for pricing decisions following accounting overhead allocation procedures." J. E. Ashton and N. Holmlund, "Relevant Managerial Accounting in the Job Shop Environment," *Manufacturing Review* 1, no. 4 (December 1988), pp. 230–235.

10. As H. Thomas Johnson put it, controlling causes is "unlike the distant, often distorted financial echoes of those causes that appear in traditional cost and performance reports"; "Managing Costs: An Outmoded Philosophy," *Manufacturing Engineering* (May 1989), pp. 42–46.

11. The three items, which come from a single source, are representative of similar items in numerous other articles; Michael C. O'Guin, "Activity-Based Costing: Unlocking Our Competitive Edge," *Manufacturing Systems* (December 1990), pp. 35–43.

12. Stacey J. Adams, "Inequity in Social Exchange," in L. Berrowitz, ed., *Advances in Experimental Social Psychology* (New York: Academic Press, 1965).

13. Conversation with Jim Prettyman, Du Pont manager.

14. Carl G. Thor, "Beyond Benchmarking: Directions for Future Research," keynote speech reported by William A. Ruch, *Operations Management Review* 10, no. 1 (1993), pp. 20–26.

15. Malcolm Smith, "Improving Management Accounting Reporting Practice: A 'Total Quality Management Approach' (Part 2)," *Journal of Cost Management* (Spring 1994), pp. 49–56.

16. Robin Cooper and Peter B. B. Turney, "Zytec Corporation (C)," Harvard Business School, No. 9-190-066 (April 18, 1990).

17. Elios Pascual, "Mack Learns the Error of False Pride," *Wall Street Journal* (July 11, 1994), p. A14.

18. Johnson, *Relevance Regained,* p. viii.

19. Personal communication.

20. Karl Geffken, "Activity-Based Costing at Hewlett-Packard's Andover Surface Mount Center," *Target* (March-April 1992), pp. 15–19.

21. Discussion of Robin Cooper and Peter B. B. Turney, "Case Study: Hewlett-Packard: Roseville Networks Division," Harvard Business School, 1989 in Richard J. Schonberger, *Building a Chain of Customers* (New York: Free Press, 1990), p. 180.

Chapter 6. The New Mastery of Mass Production—and Its Close Cousins

1. The term "mass customization" was coined by Stanley M. Davis in *Future Perfect* (Reading, Mass.: Addison-Wesley, 1987), pp. 138–190. It was popularized by B. Joseph Pine II in *Mass Customization: The New Frontier in Business Competition* (Cambridge, Mass.: Harvard Business School Press, 1993). Fine's book presents the vision and the concept, but does not get much into manufacturing nor how to make the mass side of mass production fit with the tail-end custom side of it.

2. Charles R. Day, Jr., "The Ecstacy Is Worth the Agony," *Industry Week* (November 15, 1993), pp. 20–22.

3. Ibid.

4. Shawn Tully, "You'll Never Guess Who Really Makes . . . ," *Fortune* (October 3, 1994), pp. 124–127.

5. Alex Taylor III, "GM's $11,000,000,000 Turnaround," *Fortune* (October 17, 1994), pp. 54–74.

6. John Teresco, "Ingersoll Milling Machine Co.," *Industry Week* (December 20, 1993), pp. 32–33.

7. Geoffrey Boothroyd and Peter Dewhurst, *Product Design for Assembly* (Wakefield, R.I.: Boothroyd-Dewhurst, Inc., 1987).

8. In an earlier book I generalized the concepts, calling them "design for operations (DFO)," and provided three lists of the guidelines—one for piece-goods makers, one for the process industry, and the third for services; Richard J. Schonberger, *Building a Chain of Customers: Linking Business Functions to Create the World Class Company* (New York: Free Press, 1990), p. 220.

9. "IBM Discovers a Simple Pleasure," *Fortune* (May 21, 1990), p. 64.

10. To avoid the bias of widely varying board sizes and complexities, the unit of measure in the study was component placement on PC boards. Craig Divino and Raj Nooyi, "Using Benchmarking to Improve PCBA Operations," *Insight* (newsletter of PRTM) vol. 5, no. 2 (1994), pp. 6–7.

11. Teri Agins, "Apparel Makers Are Refashioning Their Operations," *Wall Street Journal* (January 13, 1994), p. B4B.

12. Clay Chandler and Michael Williams, "Strategic Shift: A Slump in Car Sales Forces Nissan to Start Cutting Swollen Costs: Its Wild Growth in Variations of Models and Designs Is Now Being Reversed," *Wall Street Journal* (March 3, 1993), pp. A1, A6.

13. "Nissan Will Reduce Varieties of Chassis in Cost-Cutting Bid," *Wall Street Journal* (March 3, 1994), p. A10.

14. Chandler and Williams, "Strategic Shift."

15. Brian S. Moskal, "Japan Still Rules the *Lean* World," *Industry Week* (April 3, 1995), pp. 56–58.

16. Willard I. Zangwill tells this story in his masterful work, *Lightning Strategies for Innovation: How the World's Best Firms Create New Products* (New York: Lexington Books, 1993), p. 7.

17. Ibid., p. 213.

18. William Echikson, "Inventing Eurocleaning," *Fortune* (Autumn/Winter 1993), pp. 30–31.

19. Jacob M. Schlesinger, Clay Chandler, and John Bussey, "About Face: Era of Slower Growth Brings a Strange Sight: Japan Restructuring," *Wall Street Journal* (December 8, 1992), pp. A1 & A14.

20. Conversation with Ray Floyd, May 12, 1995.

21. Richard J. Schonberger, *World Class Manufacturing: The Lessons of Simplicity Applied* (New York: Free Press, 1986), chapter 5.
22. James P. Womack, Daniel T. Jones, and Daniel Roos, *The Machine That Changed the World* (New York: Rawson Associates, 1990).
23. Gary S. Vasilash, "How to Avoid Extinction," *Production* (October 1989), pp. 61–65.
24. "New Wave Auto Assembly," *Manufacturing Engineering* (July 1992), pp. 40–41.
25. Alex Taylor III, "The Auto Industry Meets the New Economy," *Fortune* (September 5, 1994), pp. 52–60.
26. Kiyoshi Suzaki, *The New Shop Floor Management: Empowering People for Continuous Improvement* (New York: Free Press, 1993), pp. 87–115.
27. Robert W. Hall, *Attaining Manufacturing Excellence* (Burr Ridge, Ill.: Dow Jones-Irwin, 1987), pp. 77–79.
28. Roy L. Harmon, *Reinventing the Warehouse: World Class Distribution Logistics* (New York: Free Press, 1993), p. 328.
29. Development of agile manufacturing concepts has been spearheaded by the Agile Manufacturing Enterprise forum, Bethlehem, Pa., in affiliation with the Iacocca Institute at Lehigh University. The industry-led effort was originally supported by a $5 million grant from the U.S. Department of Defense.
30. Susan Moffat, "Japan's New Personalized Production," *Fortune* (October 22, 1990), pp. 132–135.
31. Andy Rooney ends *60 Minutes,* the popular U.S. investigative journalism TV show, with his own humorous investigation of quirky social phenomena.
32. Robert W. Hall, "AME's Vision of Total Enterprise Manufacturing," *Target* (November-December 1994), pp. 33–38.
33. Teresko, "Ingersoll Milling Machine Co."
34. John Teresko, "Buyer Turns Seller," *Industry Week* (October 3, 1994), pp. 50–52.

Chapter 7. Strategic Linkages

1. Consultant Phil Ensor coined the term *silo;* Phil S. Ensor, "The Functional Silo Syndrome," *Target* (Spring 1988), p. 16.
2. Kevin Kelly, "Burned by Busy Signals: Why Motorola Ramped Up Production Way Past Demand," *Business Week* (March 6, 1995), p. 36.
3. Shawn Tully, "Raiding a Company's Hidden Cash," *Fortune* (August 22, 1994), pp. 82–87.
4. For a discussion of trade loading, see Patricia Sellers, "The Dumbest Marketing Ploy," *Fortune* (October 5, 1992), pp. 88–92. For an extreme example of channel stuffing, see Andy Zipser, "How Pressure to Raise Sales Led MiniScribe to Falsify Numbers," *Wall Street Journal* (September 11, 1989), pp. 1ff.
5. Extensive factory reengineering took place in the 1980s (and continues today). An appendix in a 1986 book listed 84 "honor roll" plants or companies. To qualify, the organization had to have achieved a five-, ten-, or twentyfold reduction in production lead time. In most cases, realignment of shops into work cells or plants-in-a-plant was a key to the achievement. Richard J. Schonberger, *World Class Manufacturing: The Lessons of Simplicity Applied* (New York: Free Press, 1986), pp. 229–236.
6. For example, in 1986 Nashua Corporation brought people from scattered departments (e.g., sales, accounting for credit check, materials, engineering, master scheduling, and detail scheduling) together to form order-entry cells, which cut order-entry time from eight days to two hours. Thomas J. Billesbach and Marc Schniederjans, "Applic-

ability of Just-in-Time Techniques in the Administrative Area," *Production and Inventory Management Journal* 30, No. 3 (Third quarter 1989), pp. 40–44.

7. "Automatic Data Collection," promotional brochure for the automatic identification industry providing technology for quick-response partners (n.p., n.d, ca. 1993).

8. Myron Magnet, "Meet the New Revolutionaries," *Fortune* (February 24, 1992), pp. 94–101.

9. "Quick Response Extends the Concept," special advertising supplement, *Manufacturing Systems* (June 1992), pp. IM6 & IM10.

10. Tom Wallace, "ECR for Retailers and Their Suppliers," *APICS—The Performance Advantage* (October 1994), pp. 98–103.

11. Alex Taylor III, "GM: Some Gain, Much Pain," *Fortune* (May 29, 1995), pp. 78–84.

12. Rahul Jacob, "Why Some Customers Are More Equal than Others," *Fortune* (September 19, 1994), pp. 215–224.

13. Jeremy Main, "Betting on the 21st Century Jet," *Fortune* (April 20, 1992), pp. 102–117. In a feature story, a Seattle newspaper proclaimed that the Boeing 777 is the first passenger airline to be "designed by customers," *Seattle Post-Intelligencer* (May 3, 1993), p. 1.

14. July 8, 1992.

15. J. Douglas Blocher, Charles W. Lackey, and Vincent A. Mabert, "From JIT Purchasing to Supplier Partnerships at Xerox," *Target* (May/June 1993), pp. 12–18.

16. Information on Queen City based on personal conversations with President Ed Stenger; also, see Robin Yale Bergstrom, "Changing Ahead of the Curve," *Production* (August 94), pp. 46–49.

17. Conversation with Ed Stenger, August 1994; conversation with William Menke, June 9, 1995. Menke is a Cincinnati-based independent consultant who often teams up with Kenneth Wantuck, one of the well-known pioneers of JIT in the United States.

18. Jim Treece, "Get a Competitive Edge by Being a Better Customer," *Production* (April 1995), pp. 16–17.

19. Jim Treece, "The Supplier Is Sometimes Right," *Production* (May 1995), p. 16.

20. Transcript of talk given by Dr. Donald B. Bibeault at a conference, "The High Performance Work Organization (HPWO)," San Francisco, March 29, 1995.

21. "'Value Pricing' Pays Off," *Business Week* (November 1, 1993), pp. 32–33.

Chapter 8. Impediments: Bad Plant Design, Mismanagement of Capacity

1. Tetsu Shimatani, Osamu Okuda, and Go Suzuki, "Keeping Old Plants Continuously New," *Target* (May-June, 1994), pp. 8–17.

2. Example is elaborated upon in "Case Study: Swanbank Frozen Foods," in Richard J. Schonberger and Edward M. Knod, Jr., *Operations Management: Continuous Improvement,* 5th ed. (Burr Ridge, Ill.: Richard D. Irwin), 1994, pp. 578–581.

3. Roy L. Harmon and Leroy D. Peterson, *Reinventing the Factory: Productivity Breakthroughs in Manufacturing Today* (New York: Free Press, 1990), p. 91.

4. Leo Ferras, "Continuous Improvements in Electronics Manufacturing," *Production and Inventory Management Journal* (Second quarter, 1994), pp. 1–4.

5. F. E. Emery and E. L. Trist, "Socio-Technical Systems," in C. W. Churchman and M. Verhulst, eds. *Management Science, Models, and Techniques,* vol. 2 (Pergamon, 1960), pp. 83–97. Socio-technical systems (STS), studied in my own systems courses in the 1970s, are now in a new, wider phase of popularity. However, I think that much of what passes for STS is forced-fit—little real, meaningful blending of technical and human factors.

6. Kyle Marshall, "Labor Chief Checks Out High-Tech Changes in Textile Industry," Raleigh (N.C.) *News & Observer* (March 28, 1995), pp. 1D–2D.
7. National Public Radio broadcast on Monday, December 19, 1994; and conversation with parties at Wrangler's Greensboro, N.C., data center, May 8, 1995.
8. Conversation with Peter N. Butenhoff, May 9, 1995.
9. Alan Farnham, "Baldor's Success: Made in the U.S.A.," *Fortune* (July 17, 1989), pp. 101–104.
10. Conversation with Robert Null, Group Production Manager, May 9, 1995.
11. Visit to Allen-Bradley, April 21, 1989.
12. Clay Chandler, "It's Hello Dollies at Nissan's New 'Dream Factory,'" *Wall Street Journal* (July 7, 1992), pp. 13–14.
13. Valerie Reitman and Angelo B. Henderson, "Nissan, Bowed by Debt, Struggles to Regain Lost Glory," *Wall Street Journal* (April 20, 1995).
14. "Notes from the Conferences," *Production* (November 1993), pp. 48–50.
15. Micheline Maynard, "Toyota Dodging 'Big Company Disease,'" *USA Today* (May 23, 1994), p. 7B.
16. Nobuko Hara, "A People Plant: Toyota Leaves Robots Behind and Comes Out Ahead," *Chicago Tribune* (December 5, 1993).
17. Gwendolyn D. Galsworth and Lea A. P. Tonkin, "Invasion of the Kaizen Blitzers," *Target* (March/April 1995), pp. 30–36.
18. Shigeo Shingo, *A Revolution in Manufacturing: The SMED System* (Portland, Ore.: Productivity Press, 1983).
19. Ibid., p. 29.
20. Gary S. Vasilash, "The Five Hottest Manufacturers in Silicon Valley: Customer Obsession at Solectron," *Production* (May 1995), pp. 56–58.

Chapter 9. Remaking Human Resource Management

1. Parts of this chapter are adapted from Richard J. Schonberger, "Human Resource Lessons from a Decade of Total Quality Management and Reengineering," *California Management Review* (Summer 1994), pp. 109–123.
2. M. Scott Myers makes this point in *Every Employee a Manager,* 3d ed. (San Diego: University Associates, 1991; 1st ed., New York: McGraw-Hill, 1970).
3. John Huey, "The Leadership Industry," *Fortune* (February 21, 1994), pp. 54–56.
4. Kay Falk, "If You're Going to Play the Game . . . Master the Fundamentals—Production, People, and Product—with the Customer in Mind," *OEM Off-Highway* (January 1993), pp. 8–9.
5. Fred Luthans and Robert Kreitner, *Organizational Behavior Modification and Beyond* (Grandview, Ill.: Scott Foresman, 1985), p. 81.
6. *Chicago Tribune* (January 26, 1992).
7. See Shigeo Shingo, *Zero Quality Control: Source Inspection and the Poka-yoke System* (Cambridge, Mass.: Productivity Press, 1985). The Japanese word *pokayoke* translates as "fail-safe."
8. Karen Bemowski, "A Pat on the Back Is Worth a Thousand Words," *Quality Progress* (March 1994), pp. 51–54; Lea A. P. Tonkin, "Patience, Please: Self-Directed Work Teams, *Target* (Fall 1994), pp. 32–38; Lea Tonkin, "Self-Directed Work Teams Power Northern Telecom Service," *Target* (Fall 1990), pp. 30–33; GE 1993 Annual Report, p. 3.
9. J. Stacy Adams, "Inequity in Social Exchange," in L. Berrowitz, ed., *Advances in Experimental Social Psychology* (New York: Academic Press, 1965).

10. Elizabeth J. Hawk and Christian M. Ellis, "A Recipe for Success: Redesigning Rewards in Organizations with Mature Teams," *Target* (July/August 1994), pp. 19–27.

11. Gene H. Milas, "How to Develop a Meaningful Employee Recognition Program," *Quality Progress* (May 1995), pp. 139–142.

12. See Myers's discussion of nonmonetary and monetary rewards in *Every Employee a Manager,* pp. 15–46; also, Jay R. Shuster and Patricia K. Zingheim, *The New Pay: Linking Employee and Organizational Performance* (New York: Lexington Books, 1992).

13. Conversation with Doug Fletcher, May 10, 1995.

14. James Benneyan, "Letters," *Quality Progress* (January 1995), pp. 12–13.

15. See, e.g., Peter Scholtes, *An Elaboration on Deming's Teachings on Performance Appraisal* (Madison, Wis.: Joiner Associates, 1987), p. 1. Tennessee Eastman has eliminated appraisals for over 90 percent of its employees; their system provides for rating only the exceptional people.

16. William H. Miller, "Skill Standards on the Way," *Industry Week* (April 5, 1993), p. 72.

17. Tom Peters, "The 'Patient-Focused Hospital' Is a Stunning Innovation" (syndicated column), *Seattle Post-Intelligencer* (August 5, 1991), p. B5.

18. Bill Ginnodo, "Teaching an Old Plant New Tricks," *Commitment Plus* (newsletter) (July 1987), pp. 2–4.

19. Craig J. Cantoni, "Quality Control from Mars," *Wall Street Journal* (January 27, 1992).

20. Brian Dumaine, "The Bureaucracy Busters," *Fortune* (June 17, 1991), pp. 36–50.

21. Conversation with a Becton-Dickinson officer, May 24, 1995.

Chapter 10. Quality: Picture a Miracle

1. M. Daniel Sloan and Michael Chmel, *The Quality Revolution and Health Care: A Primer for Purchasers and Providers* (Milwaukee: ASQC Press, 1991).

2. M. Daniel Sloan, *How to Lower Health Care Costs by Improving Health Care Quality: Results-Based Continuous Quality Improvement* (Milwaukee: ASQC Quality Press, 1994).

3. Michel Greif, *The Visual Factory: Building Participation Through Shared Information* (Portland, Ore.: Productivity Press), 1991.

4. Hiroyuku Hirano, ed. (J. T. Black, ed., English edition), *JIT Factory Revolution: A Pictorial Guide to Factory Design of the Future* (Portland, Ore.: Productivity Press), 1988.

5. Robert Hall, *The Soul of the Enterprise* (New York: HarperBusiness, 1993), p. 128.

6. This example appeared in "Dr. Elbie's Corner," *Focus on Business* (Oakland: Chamber of Commerce) (December 1993). A longer version is contained in Leonard Bertain, *The New Turnaround: A Breakthrough for People, Profits and Change* (Croton-on-Hudson, N.Y.: North River Press, 1993).

7. Sherry R. Gordon, "Changing the Structure of Business," *APICS—The Performance Advantage* (May 1995), pp. 36–39.

8. Gwendolyn D. Galsworth and Lea A. P. Tonkin, "Invasion of the Kaizen Blitzers," *Target* (March/April 1995), pp. 30–36.

9. M. Daniel Sloan and Jodi B. Torpey, *Lowering Health Care Costs by Improving Health Care Quality: Success Stories and Results-Based Continuous Quality Improvement Theory Applications,* preliminary manuscript (Milwaukee: ASQC Quality Press, 1995). One of their sources is Steve deShazer, *Clues: Investigating Solutions in Brief Therapy* (New York: W. W. Norton, 1988).

10. G. Pascal Zachary, "Data About Job Instability May Be Shaky," *Wall Street Journal* (March 31, 1995), p. A2.
11. Charles E. Sorensen, *My Forty Years with Ford* (New York: W. W. Norton, 1956), p. 174.
12. Cited by John M. Staudenmaier, Jr., "Henry Ford's Big Flaw," *Invention & Technology* (Fall 1994), pp. 34–44.
13. The Outsourcing Institute is headquartered in New York City.
14. "Industry Leaders in the Outsourcing Revolution" (December 12, 1994) and "Outsourcing: Redefining the Corporation of the Future" (October 16, 1995), both in *Fortune*.
15. Louise Lee, "Rent-a-Techs: Hiring Outside Firms to Run Computers Isn't Always a Bargain," *Wall Street Journal* (May 18, 1995), pp. A1 and A13.
16. Presentation by Bob May as a panelist at a meeting of the World Class Manufacturing Interest Group of the Puget Sound chapter of the Institute of Industrial Engineers (May 25, 1995).
17. Tom Peters, *Thriving on Chaos: Handbook for a Management Revolution* (New York: Knopf, 1987), p. 9.
18. Tom Peters, "Redefining Employment Security," *Seattle Post-Intelligencer* (August 22, 1994), p. B3.
19. Peter F. Drucker, "The Age of Social Transformation," *Atlantic Monthly* (November 1994), pp. 53–80.
20. Rahul Jacob, "Why Some Customers Are More Equal Than Others," *Fortune* (September 19, 1994), pp. 215–224.
21. "The Technology Paradox: How Companies Can Thrive As Prices Dive," *Business Week* (March 6, 1995), pp. 76–83.
22. Peter F. Drucker, "The Network Society," *Wall Street Journal* (March 19, 1995).
23. Lea A. P. Tonkin, "Teamwork: Are We There Yet?" *Target* (March/April 1995), pp. 42–46.
24. The exhibit is also found in tape 10 of the Schonberger videotape series, *The World Class Manufacturing Company* (Loveland, Colo.: Management Research Corp.) Roy L. Harmon makes a similar point in *Reinventing the Warehouse: World Class Distribution Logistics* (New York: Free Press, 1993), p. xiii.
25. Jacob, *Why Some Customers Are More Equal Than Others.*
26. Alex Markels and Joann S. Lublin, "Longevity—Reward Programs Get Short Shrift," *Wall Street Journal* (April 27, 1995), p. B1.
27. John Schneider, "Putting the Flex in a Flexible Work Force," *Target,* Special edition (1991), pp. 5–13.
28. Bill Fromm and Len Schlesinger, *The Real Heroes of Business, and Not a CEO Among Them* (New York: Currency Doubleday, 1993).
29. Harry V. Roberts and Bernard F. Sergesketter, *Quality Is Personal: A Foundation for Total Quality Management* (New York: Free Press, 1993).
30. Richard Turner, "Is Walt Disney Ready to Rewrite Its Own Script?" *Wall Street Journal* (August 26, 1994), pp. B1–B5.
31. Brian Dumaine, "The Trouble with Teams," *Fortune* (September 5, 1995), pp. 86–92. The integration team concept has a parallel that reaches back into project-management methodology: the integration block on a work-breakdown structure, which accounts for integration of other project modules and gets its own event on a PERT or CPM chart.
32. Robert Tomsho, "Real Dog: How Greyhound Lines Re-Engineered Itself Right into a Deep Hole," *Wall Street Journal* (October 20, 1994), pp. A1 and A10.

33. Stephen J. Frangos with Steven J. Bennett, *Team Zebra: How 1500 Partners Revitalized Eastman Kodak's Black & White Film-Making Flow* (Essex Junction, Vt.: Omneo), p. 54–55.

34. Bob Kantor, "Wiring Teams Together," in "Letters to *Fortune,*" *Fortune* (May 15, 1995), p. 13.

35. Jeff G. Miller, "Supporting JIT Manufacturing with a JIT Organization," *Manufacturing Engineering* (September 1990), pp. 24–30.

36. Jeffrey L. Funk, *The Teamwork Advantage: An Inside Look at Japanese Product and Technology Development* (Portland, Ore.: Productivity Press, 1992), pp. 147–149.

37. David Kirkpatrick, "Why Microsoft Can't Stop Lotus Notes," *Fortune* (December 12, 1994), pp.141–157.

38. Thomas E. Vollmann, "Enterprise Transformation: The Golden Cord to Dominance," discussion draft (March 1995), pp. 179–180.

Chapter 11. A Ten-Year Plan

1. Roy L. Harmon, *Reinventing the Warehouse: World Class Distribution Logistics* (New York: Free Press), p. 328.

2. David A. Garvin, *Managing Quality: The Strategic and Competitive Edge* (New York: Free Press, 1988), pp. 49–50.

3. Some consulting firms have developed their own scoring systems. For example, U.K.-based World Class International has been using a 1-to-6 point scoring scheme involving eight dimensions (structured management, world-class principles and beliefs, customer partnerships, business process management, competitive products and services, world-class manufacturing, supplier partnerships, and employee involvement) and 40 separate measurement questions in assessing clients' "world-class" attainments; "Is Yours a World-Class Company?" *Director* (September 1994).

4. Gary S. Vasilash, "Total Quality at AlliedSignal," *Production* (September 1994), pp. 52–57.

5. Robert S. Kaplan, "The Balanced Scorecard: Measures That Drive Performance," *Harvard Business Review* (January-February 1992), pp. 71–80; also, Robert S. Kaplan and David P. Norton, "Putting the Balanced Scorecard to Work," *Harvard Business Review* (September-October 1995), pp. 134–148.

6. John Hoffecker and Charles Goldenberg, "Using the Balanced Scorecard to Develop Companywide Performance Measures," *Target* (Fall 1994), pp. 5–17.

7. Ibid.

8. The fifth edition of my own textbook omitted all the matter on lot sampling tables, OC curves, and average outgoing quality—with nary a protest from professors using the book; Richard J. Schonberger and Edward M. Knod, Jr., *Operations Management: Continuous Improvement* (Burr Ridge, Ill.: Richard D. Irwin, 1990), Chapter 4.

9. "Ask the QIC: Quality Costs," *On Q* (June-July 1995), p. 10.

10. Shawn Tully, "Raiding a Company's Hidden Cash," *Fortune* (August 22, 1994), pp. 82–87.

11. Karen Bemowski, "Three Electronics Firms Win 1991 Baldrige Award," *Quality Progress* (November 1991), pp. 39–41.

12. Marvin L. Patterson, *Accelerating Innovation: Improving the Process of Product Development* (New York: Van Nostrand–Reinhold, 1993), p. 20.

13. Gary Hamel and C.K. Prahalad, "Strategy as Stretch and Leverage," *Harvard Business Review* (March-April 1993), pp. 75–84.

14. Henry Mintzberg, *The Rise and Fall of Strategic Planning: Reconceiving Roles for Planning, Plans, Planners* (New York: Free Press, 1994).
15. Art Byrne, "How Wiremold Reinvented Itself with Kaizen," *Target* (January/February 1995), pp. 8–14.
16. For example, Carolyn Burstein and Kathleen Sedlak, "The Federal Quality and Productivity Improvement Effort," *Quality Progress* (October 1988), pp. 38–40.
17. Peter F. Drucker, *Post-Capitalist Society* (New York: HarperCollins, 1993), pp. 36–39.
18. Richard A. Melcher, "How Goliaths Can Act like Davids," *Business Week* (Enterprise 1993, special edition), pp. 192–201.
19. Personal visits to the company (which shall go unnamed), first to conduct a seminar and later to commiserate with the president and brains behind the growth strategy (early 1990s).
20. Art Byrne, "How Wiremold Reinvented Itself with *Kaizen*," *Target* (January-February 1995), pp. 8–14.
21. Robert H. Hayes and Gary P. Pisano, "Beyond World-Class: The New Manufacturing Strategy," *Harvard Business Review* (January-February 1994), pp. 77–86.

Index

A.T. Kearney, 72
Abdon, Johnny, 78
Activity-based costing (ABC), 17, 76, 95, 97, 98, 100, 104–107
Adams, J. Stacy, 99
Adelman, Phil, 214
After-sale service data, 41
Aggregate forecasting, 145
Agile manufacturing, 127, 129–132
Airbus Industrie, 30, 84
Alcatel Network Systems, 67, 82, 89, 239
Alcoa-Australia, 99
Allen-Bradley, 168, 171
AlliedSignal, 67, 72, 76–78, 88, 227–228
American Airlines, 95
American Customer Satisfaction Index (ACSI), 12–13
American Express, 213
American Productivity and Quality Center, 69
American Society for Quality Control, 230
Amtico Limited, 45–46, 211, 213
Anderson, Robert, 56
Anderson Consulting, 78, 122, 222
Apple Macintosh, 125
Applicon, 41
Arcs, in assembly lines, 158–160
Association for Manufacturing Excellence (AME), 172, 236
Association of Southeast Asia Nations (ASEAN), 117
AT&T, 9
Australian Engineering Excellence Award, 73

Bain & Company, 209, 213
Balanced scorecard, 228–229

Baldor Electric, 67, 74–75, 88, 167–168
Baldrige Quality Award, x, 9, 33, 39, 51, 68, 142, 183, 227
Barrett, Jim, 77
Bartell, Bud, 31
Basket-of-values concept, 37, 99, 188–191
Bausch & Lomb, 144
Baxter Healthcare, 67, 71–72, 88, 98, 171, 186
Becton-Dickinson, 196
Benchmarking, 16, 20, 30, 50, 56, 65, 69, 71, 85, 100, 147
Benetton, 140, 141
Beninati, Marie, 120
Bernard Manufacturing Division of Dover Industries, 35–36
Bertain, Leonard, 37, 203, 215
BFR (Belgarde-Fisher-Raynor) group, 76
Bibeault, Donald B., 150
Bidder, Gerald W., 87
Billesbach, Thomas, 35, 218
Black & Decker, 4, 237
Blanton, Alexander, 107, 109, 173, 175
Blue Shield of California, 207
Boeing, 29–30, 44, 120–121, 127, 136, 146, 195, 216–217
    Welded Duct plant, 67, 84–85, 89
Boër, Germain, 95
BOGOS (buy one, get one free), 144
Bonuses, 17, 28, 191
Boothroyd, Geoffrey, 33, 119, 121
Borham, Roland S., Jr., 74
Bossidy, Lawrence, 77
Bowman, Hank, 123
Bradford, Bill, 97
Brand names, 15
Bräsler, Peter, 87

267

Bray, Dennis, 119, 132
Breakthrough management, 22
Brief therapy method, 204
Briggs & Stratton, 159, 160
Broad-band pay systems, 17
Burgmaster, 2
Burnham, Dan, 77
Burroughs-Wellcome, 171
Busamante, Alejandro, 158
Butenhoff, Peter, 165–166
Byrne, Arthur P., 242

Calsonic, 122
Campbell Soup, 157, 230
Canfield, Wayne, 86
Capacity
    principles-based management and,
        26–27, 43–46, 56
    unconstrained, 173–175
Capture team, 221
Cardiff Business School, 122
Carnaud Metalbox, 6, 7
Carole Little, 120
Carter, John, 72
Case, Ken, 81
Caterpillar, 4, 172, 173, 234
Cell formation, 168
Cellular manufacturing (cells), 23, 28, 65,
        66, 71, 78, 86, 111, 141, 202, 231
Chandler, Alfred, 206
Chandler, Richard, 80, 197
Channel stuffing, 139
Charles Machine Company, 8
Chavis, Charley, 78
Check sheets, 104
Chetak-Bajaj, 133
China, 117
Chow, Chee W., 95
Circle of Truth, 217
Clark Equipment, 110
Clausing, Don, 123
Clorox, 12
Coca Cola, 7, 117, 157
Colgate Palmolive, 12
Collins, Paul, 106
Commerce, Department of, 237
Competitive analysis, 30
Complacency, 20, 30, 65, 100, 239
Concurrent engineering, 73
Consultants, 86, 87, 235
Conti, Tito, ix
Control Data, 22, 194
Conveyor removal, 158
Conway, Bill, 83
Coopers & Lybrand, 77
Cost allocation, 104–107, 110–113

Cost-containment center, 103
Courtaulds, 211
Covey, Stephen, 22
Crafted with Pride Council, 165
Criticon, 237
Crosby, Philip, ix, 71, 75, 85, 142
Cross-careering, 16, 196
Cross-docking, 17
Cross-training, 76, 196, 198, 199
Crown Cork & Seal, 6
CSI Feedback Form (Solectron), 10, 11,
        29
Cummins Engine, 3, 4, 183
Customer-focused principles: *See*
        Principles-based management
Customer-focused production units, 28–29,
        57–58
Customer satisfaction, 9, 19, 29
    broad-based customer data, 9–12
    pooled customer data, 12–13
Customer stability, 209–213
Cycle-time-based costing, 100

Daily financial report, 102–104
Dana, 6, 241
Data-based performance: *See* Principles-
        based management
Davey Products, 67, 72–74, 88, 211
Day, Pat, 84
Deere and Company, 4, 5, 72
Defense, Department of, 228
Delaware Valley Industrial Resource
        Center (DVIRC), 237
Delta Point, 84
Demand forecasting, 145
Deming, W. Edwards, ix, 35, 39, 66, 75,
        83, 92, 191, 204, 235
Deming Prize, x, 64, 227, 234
Dempster, Barrie, 72, 74, 211
Dennis, Pam, 69
deShazer, Steve, 204
Design, principles-based management and,
        24–25, 33–34
Design-built team, 29
Design for manufacture and assembly
        (DFMA), 16, 33, 73, 119–121
Design for service operations (DFSO), 33
Destra Consulting, 69
Dewhurst, Peter, 33, 119, 121
Dial, 12
Die Change Challenge, 31
Digital design, 17, 41
Doricchi, Ruby, 214
Dover Elevators, 67, 78–80, 88
Dover Industries, 4, 35–36
Drucker, Peter, 93, 181, 209, 211, 240, 241

Du Pont, 2, 3, 30, 99, 102
Du Pont Furnishings, 57–58

Eastman Kodak, 3, 4, 187, 209–211, 213, 218–219
Eaton Corporation, 2–5, 14
Economy of multiples, 125
Edict, management by, 20
EDS, 207
Efficient customer response (ECR), 135, 143–144
Eisner, Michael, 216
Electronic Controls Company, 102, 180–181
Electronic data interchange, 16, 17, 41, 46
Ellis, Christian, 189
Emerson Electric, 2–4, 83
Emery Air Freight studies, 185
Emery, F. E., 160
Employee alienation, 189
Employee-driven performance: *See* Principles-based management
Employee stability, 213–214
Employee stock ownership, 17
Employee suggestions, 40, 178, 185, 190
EPS (earnings per share), 14
Equipment flexibility, 31, 45
Equipment maintenance, 44, 45, 56, 86
Esso Chemical Canada, 51
Ethical principles, 22
Ettlie, John, 65
European Quality Award, 9, 39
European Union, 117
Everyday low pricing (EDLP), 151
Exxon Baytown, 51, 67, 81, 89, 125

Fail-safing, 186–187, 205
Faull, Norman, 87
Federal Express, 182
Federal Reserve, 173
Ferguson, 137
Fill-and-pack sector, 156–158
Final-demand-based bridge building, 140–141
Finance era, 15
Fishbone charts, 104
Fisher, George, 209–211
Five Pillars of the Visual Workplace: The Sourcebook of the 5S Implementation (Hirano), 85
5 S's, 44, 85, 202
Fletcher, Doug, 75–76
Flex force, 213
Flexible production, 166–170
Floyd, Ray, 81, 125
Fluke Corporation, 57
FMC Corporation, 69

Follow-through, ten-year plan and, 233–235
Ford Electronics, 67, 82–83, 89
Ford Motor Company, 2–5, 14, 15, 72, 117, 184, 206
Forecasting, 145
Fornell, Claes, 12, 13
Forward buying, 144
Four P's of marketing, 46
Four Seasons, 121
Fox, Colin, 84
Franklin Electric, 74
French manufacturers, 6–7
Fulford, Bob, 203
Funk, Jeffrey, 222

Gain sharing, 17, 79, 91
Galvin, Robert, 102, 182
Garvin, David A., 226
Gates Rubber, 67–70, 88
Gelb, Tom, 81
General Agreement on Tariffs and Trade (GATT), 118
General Electric, 3, 4, 69, 73, 77, 86, 95, 188, 230, 232–233
General Motors, 4, 14, 31, 32, 93, 119, 121, 126, 128, 144, 183–184, 195
    Antilock Brake Systems division, 186
Germany, 12, 68, 122
Gerstner, Lou, 22
Giddings & Lewis, 132
Gilbarco, 185
Globe Metallurgical, 51
Greif, Michael, 202
Greyhound, 217
Griggs, Jonathan, 193
Grimes, Paul, 173
Groupe Schneider, 118

Hall, Robert, 127, 130–131, 202
Hallmark Cards, 33–34
Hambrick and Quist, Inc., 137
Hamilton, Hap, 79
Hamilton Standard, 172–173, 204, 237
Hammer, Kenneth A., 150
Handley-Walker, 70
Harley-Davidson, 28, 188
Harmon, Roy, 78, 128, 158, 226
Harrington, Joseph, Jr., 58
Harris Corporation, 220
    Farinon Division, 188
Hawk, Elizabeth, 189
Hawkins, Joy, 240
Haworth, 8, 64
Hay, Edward, 81
Hayes, Jim, 74

Hayes, Robert H., 243
Health-care products, 171
Herman Miller, 64, 69
Herrera, Isidoro, 249
Heuring, George, 187
Hewlett-Packard, 8, 9, 15, 38, 39, 102, 105, 106, 119, 186, 190, 193, 194, 213, 214, 222, 232
Hexapod, 119, 132
Hicks, Donn, 31
Hirano, Hiroyuki, 85, 202
Histograms, 104
Hitler, Adolf, 240–241
Hoffman, Kelly, 83, 84
Honda, 122–123
Honeywell, 4, 125
Honeywell-Scotland, 67, 70–71, 88
Hon Industries, 4, 5
Horizontal promotion, 196
How to Lower Health Care Costs by Improving Health Care Quality: Results-Based Continuous Quality Improvement (Sloan), 202
Human resource management, 177–200
    motivation and reward, 184–192
    principles-based management and, 24–27, 36–39
    role changes, 178–184
    work force upgrades, 192–199

IBM Corporation, 3, 4, 9, 15, 22, 72, 117, 119, 171, 175, 207, 213, 229
IBM LaserPrinter, 120
Imai, Masaaki, 85
India, 117
Industry Week Best Plant, 40, 71, 81, 82, 107
Ingalls & Snyder, 107, 173
Ingersoll Milling Machine Company, 119, 132
Ingersoll-Rand, 109–110
Institute for Productivity Improvement, 36–37
Intel, 8, 175
Internal Revenue Service (IRS), 240
International Harvester, 15
International Learning Systems (ILS), 69
Inventory turnover, 2–9, 13, 14, 19, 79, 173, 232–233
Investor's Business Daily, 109
Ireland, 55, 187
Ishikawa, Kaoru, ix
ISO-9000, x, 68, 82, 171

Jacob, Rahul, 210
Japan, 1, 63, 84, 85, 95, 117, 121–123, 239

Japanese Manufacturing Techniques (Schonberger), 14, 81
Jay Medical, 197
Jessen, Mogens, 46
JIT Factory Revolution: A Pictorial Guide to Factory Design of the Future (Hirano), 202
Job classifications, 195–197
Johnson, H. Thomas, 2, 97
Johnson Controls, 67, 85–86, 89, 119
Johnson & Higgins, 222
Johnson & Johnson, 2–4, 36, 41, 97, 146
Jostens Diplomas, 65, 67, 75–76, 88, 188, 190–191
Juran, Joseph M., ix, 75, 204, 226
Just-in-Time Manufacturing: An Aggressive Manufacturing Strategy (Lubin), 85
Just in time (JIT), 16, 34, 35, 65, 75, 77, 138, 231
Just-in-time training method, 25, 37, 69

Kaizen, 71, 172, 198, 204, 236–237
Kaizen: The Key to Japan's Competitive Success (Imai), 85
Kanban, 16, 41, 85, 86, 111, 159, 167, 202
Kantor, Bob, 219
Kato, Yutaka, 95
Katzenberg, Jeffrey, 216
Kearns, David, 182
Kenmex, 158
Kennametal, 144
Kernodle, Jeff, 164
Kmart, 143
Knowledge sharing, 181
Kohlberg, Kravis, Roberts, 2
Kolind, Lars, 222–223
Komatsu, 234
Kone Oy Liftworks, 40
KPMG Peat Marwick, 228, 229
Kreitner, Robert, 185
Kurt Salmon Associates, 120, 142

L.L. Bean, 30
Labor relations, 195
Lackey, Charles, 36
Latin America, 54, 117
Lauger, Dave, 197
Leadership, 181–183
Lean manufacturing, 4, 41
Le Carbon-Lorraine, 6
Lee jeans, 163
Lego Systems, 46
Legrand, 6, 7
Lemco Miller, 203
Lewis, Joe, 85

Limited, The, 141
Linearity index, 17
Logical cell, 218
Looney, Barbara, 242
Lot sampling, 229–230
Lubin, Richard, 85
Lucas Industries, 6, 71
Luthans, Fred, 185

Machine That Changed the World, The
    (Womack, Jones, and Roos), 125
Mack Trucks, 101–102
Magma International Incorporated, 28
Mak, Lee, 82
Malcolm Baldrige Quality Award, 9, 33,
    39, 40, 51, 64, 68, 100, 137, 142, 183,
    227, 232
Management modes, 20
Manufacturing Extension Partnership
    (MEP), 237
Manufacturing performance, 1–17
Maquiladoras, 54–55, 161–162
Marketing Corporation of America, 152
Marketing era, 15
Marks and Spencer, 163
Mars Inc., 196
Martin Marietta, 159
Maruchek, Ann, 72
Maskell, Brian, 87
Mass customization, 115, 117, 122
Mass production, 115–133
    agile manufacturing, 127, 129–132
    auto assembly, 125–127
    component costs, 118–121
    image of, 116
    Japanese and German mistakes,
        121–123
    rejuvenation of, 116–117
    scale economies, 124–125
    standardization, 127–128
    trade pacts resize production volumes,
        117–118
    usage-rate production, 128–129
Materials requirements planning (MRP),
    56
Matsushita, 121, 123–124
May, Bob, 207–208
Mazak USA, 169–170
Mazda, 169
McDonnell-Douglas, 120, 230
McDonnell Douglas Helicopters, 94, 202
McDougall, John, 70
Megatrends (Naisbitt), 2
Menke, William C., 149
Mercedes-Benz, 126
Merck, 213

MERCOSUR, 117
Mexico, 54–55, 158, 161, 162
Microelectronics Modules Corporation,
    150
Microsoft, 23, 28, 29, 220
Microsoft-Ireland, 187
Midland Communications, Inc., 186
Milas, Gene, 190
Miller, Robert, 69
Miller Brewing Company, 157, 181–182
Milliken, Roger, 142, 182–183
Milliken and Company, 5, 40, 51, 98, 121,
    125, 136, 141–142, 152, 155, 180,
    182, 185, 186, 191
Mintzberg, Henry, 234
Miracles technique, 204–205
Mississippi Department of Education, 78
Mitsubishi Electric Company, 222, 223
Mitsui, Toatsu, 155
Miyamori, Yukio, 122
MK Electric, 41
Modular assembly, 126–127, 131
Modular production system (MPS), 166
Modular sewing, 163, 165–166
Monthly financial report, 100, 104
Morcott, Southwood J., 241
Motivation, 97–99, 184–192
Motorola, 2–4, 8, 15, 22, 39, 102, 119, 137,
    182, 185–186, 229
Multicompany planning, 141–145
Multi-echelon collaboration, 135, 136,
    140–145, 152, 153
Multifunctional-internal collaboration, 136,
    140, 141, 147–151
Multifunctional teams, 147–151, 179,
    199–200
Multimodal freight carriers, 16
Multinationals, 117

NAFTA countries, 117
Naisbitt, John, 2
Nakagawa, Shin-ichi, 146
Nakajima, Seichi, 85
Nashua Corporation, 35, 83
National Bureau of Standards and
    Technology, 237
National Center for Manufacturing
    Sciences, 126
National Quality Research Center, 12
National Science Foundation, 165
National skills standards, 193
Natural teams, 215–216
Negative reinforcement, 186–187
Nestadt, Kevin, 74, 249
New Shop Floor Management, The
    (Suzaki), 127

Next-echelon collaboration, 136, 140, 141, 152, 153
Nippon Denso, 6, 72
Nishimura, Les, 9, 11
Nissan, 71, 122
    Kyushu plant, 169
Non-value-adding waste, 32, 98, 105
Northern Telecom, 67, 85, 89, 188
Nypro, 39, 46–47, 149–150, 209, 213, 241

Occupational Safety and Health Act, 82
O'Donnell, Tom, 198
O'Guin, Michael, 221
Oldsmobile, 131
Omni-Circuits, Inc., 149
Omron, 123
Operations, principles-based management and, 24–25, 34–36
Operations and control, information for, principles-based management and, 26–27, 41–43, 59
OPW Fueling Components, 36
Organizational learning, 20, 21
Organization charts, 180
Oticon, 222–223
Outboard Marine, 3, 4, 14
Outsourcing, 206–208

Panasonic bicycle division, 130
Pareto diagrams, 104–105, 202
Parker Hannefin, 109
Partnership era, 15
Pay, 37, 76, 184, 188–192
Pechiney, 6
Peer performance appraisal, 17, 188
PepsiCo, 4, 5, 7
Performance appraisal, 17, 187–188, 191
Performance Measurements for WCM (Maskell), 87
Personal quality checksheet, 215
Peters, Tom, 208
Peterson, Leroy D., 78
Peugeot, 6–7
Pharmaceutical Manufacturers' Association, 193
Physio Control, 207–208
Pineau-Valencienne, M., 118
Pisano, Gary P., 243
Pittiglio Rabin & McGrath (PRTM), 120
Plamex, 158
Plant design, 121, 155–175
    arcs in assembly lines, 158–160
    conveyor removal, 158
    flexible production, 166–170
    production line design, 156–157
    production support, 170–173
    station cycle times, 161–166

    unconstrained capacity, 173–175
Plant Engineering magazine, 72
Plant-in-a-plant, 29, 141
Plastic Omnium, 6, 7
Point-of-sale data technology, 16, 41, 46, 142, 143, 145
Policy-based management, 20, 21
Ponder, Quentin, 74
Pope and Talbot, 29
Powell Electronics, 237
Pratt & Whitney, 237
Precor, 55
Principles-based management, 19–47
    capacity, 26–27, 43–46, 56
    design, 24–25, 33–34
    general, 23–25, 28–33
    human resources, 24–27, 36–39
    information for operations and control, 26–27, 41–43, 59
    operations, 24–25, 34–36
    promotion and marketing, 26–27, 46–47
    quality and process improvement, 26–27, 39–40
    research project, 50–66
    scoring against, 245–253
    scoring scale, 49–50
    shift to, 20–22
Prioritization, 104–106
Procedures-based management, 20–21
Process benchmarking, 100
Process capability index (C_{pk}), 39
Process control charts, 104
Process flow charts, 104
Process industries, 51, 59, 64, 121
Proconseil, 6, 202
Procter & Gamble, 12, 128, 151
Product costing, 92–97
Product development, target costing and, 93, 94–95
Product families, 23, 28, 57
Production-distribution misconnection: *See* Strategic linkages
Production era, 15
Production lines design, 156–157
Production support, 170–173
Productivity, Inc., 236
Productivity Connection, 203
Product line, cost information and, 95–97, 107
Profit sharing, 17, 83, 191
Project teams, 179–180, 199–200, 219–222
Promotion and marketing, principles-based management and, 26–27, 46–47
Provost, Lloyd, 81
Pursuit of Excellence program, 80

Quaker Oats, 139, 151–152
Quality, 201–223; *see also* Stability
   miracles technique, 204–205
   principles-based management and,
      26–27, 39–40
   visual management, 201–204
Quality, speed, flexibility, and value
   (QSFV), 30–32, 42–43, 57, 59
Quality College, 75, 85
Quality costing, 17, 229–230
Quality era, 15, 16
Quality function deployment, 16, 73
Quality-improvement process (QIP),
   69–70
Quality Is Personal (Roberts and
   Sergesketter), 215
Queen City Treating Company, 136, 149,
   209
Quickie Designs, Inc., 67, 80, 89, 197–199
Quick response, 16, 31, 46, 135, 141–143,
   145, 152, 165, 231
Quick Response Manufacturing (QRM),
   78–80
Quick-setup expertise, 174
Quiñones, Raúl, 249

R.A. Jones, 173
Rabinovitz, Leonard, 120
Rapid prototyping, 17
Rate-based scheduling, 36, 41, 128, 202
RCA, 137
Real Heroes of Business, The (Fromm and
   Schlesinger), 214, 215, 240
Recognition, 37, 38, 75, 184, 185–186
Reengineering, 16, 28, 96, 103, 138–142,
   147, 216
Reichheld, Frederick, 213
Reinventing the Factory (Harmon and
   Peterson), 78
Remanufacturing, 121
Renault, 6–7
Repetitive motions, 161
Response ratio, 17
Return on stockholder equity (ROE), 14
*Revolution in Manufacturing, A: The
   SMED System* (Shingo), 174
Rewards, 37, 75, 98, 184–192, 213
Rhomberg Bräsler Pty, 67, 87, 89
Riegel, Joe, 85–86
*Rise and Fall of Strategic Planning:
   Reconceiving Roles for Planning,
   Plans, Planners* (Mintzberg), 234
Roberts, Harry, 215
Robos, Gary, 80
Rosemount Pressure Products, 67, 83–84,
   89
Roth, Aleda, 72

Saturn, 126, 144, 195
Scale economies, 124–125
Scattergrams, 104
Schlumberger's Well Services division, 97
Schneider National, 143
Schonberger, Richard J., 35, 70, 78, 83, 87
Schonberger seminar, 70, 71, 76, 78,
   80–83, 86
Schwarz, James E., Sr., 149
Scorekeeping, 227–233
Scott Paper, 213
Seagate Associates, 194
Sealed Air Corporation, 132
Sears, 143
Selby, Bill, 84, 85
Seminars, 70, 71, 76, 78, 80–83, 87, 235,
   237–238
Sentrol Corporation, 42–43
Sergesketter, Bernard, 215
777 passenger aircraft, 29, 120–121, 136,
   146, 217
Sheldon, Paul, 132
Shingo, Shigeo, 174
Shingo Prize, 40, 51, 64, 67, 82, 108, 227
Shinijutsu, 237
Simons, René, 202
Simulation models, 171–172
Sloan, Daniel, 201–202, 204
SMED system, 79, 174
Smith, Adam, 195
Smith, Fred, 182
Smith, Jack, 119
SmithKline, 171
Socio-technical systems, 160
Solectron, Inc., 9–12, 29, 175, 241
Sony, 162
Sood, Rakes, 137
Soucy, Art, 172–173
South Africa, 54
Southern Pacific Rail Corporation, 207
Springfield (Missouri) Remanufacturing
   Company (SRC), 102–103
Square D, 118, 188
Stability, 205–223
   customer and supplier, 209–213
   employee, 213–214
   project cohesiveness and, 219–223
   team, 215–219
Stack, Jack, 102, 103
Stalk, George, Jr., ix
Standardization, 127–128
Standard Motor Products, 121
Starbuck's, 214
Star system, 181–182
Station cycle times, 161–166
Statistical process control (SPC), 66,
   81–83, 194, 220, 229

Steelcase, 8, 64
Stenger, Ed, 149
Strategic benchmarking, 100
Strategic CIM (computer-integrated
    manufacturing) Alliance, 171
Strategic linkages, 135–153
    multi-echelon collaboration, 135, 136,
        140–145, 152, 153
    multifunctional-internal collaboration,
        136, 140, 141, 147–151
    next-echelon collaboration, 136, 140,
        141, 152, 153
Stretch goals, 231–233
Stride, Phil, 45
Stronach, Frank, 28
Sue, Craig, 190
Sunoco, 72
Sunrise Medical, 80, 197
Sunrise Pursuit of Excellence program,
    197
Supplier partnerships, 16, 71
Supplier stability, 209–213
Suzaki, Kiyoshi, 32, 127
Swanson, 156–157
SWAT-team concept, 168
Sweden, 12
Synchronization, 35–36

Tanguay, Pierre L., 238–239
Target costing, 16, 93, 94–95
Taylor, David, 81
Taylor, Frederick W., 240, 241
Teams, 23, 28, 29, 40, 120, 146–151,
    178–181, 197–200, 214–216,
    219–222
Team stability, 215–219
*Team Zebra: How 1500 Partners
    Revitalized Eastman Kodak's Black &
    White Film-Making Flow* (Frangos),
    218
Telefunken, 137
Temps, 213–214
Ten-year plan, 225–243
    follow-through, 233–235
    scorekeeping, 227–233
    value, 226–227
Texas Instruments, 8, 15, 72, 119, 229
Textile Clothing Technology Corporation,
    165
Thomas Group, 78
Thompson, Martin, 71
Thomson, 137
3COM Corporation, 229
3M Company, 85, 99, 150–151, 170–171
Thriving on Chaos (Peters), 208
Throughput, 231

Timken Company, 4, 40, 107–108, 186,
    213
Titles, 180–181, 200
Total preventive maintenance (TPM), 16,
    44, 56, 66, 72, 85, 86
Total quality control, 1, 16
Total Quality Leadership, 77
Total quality management: *See* TQM
Total Quality Maturity Path, 227–228
Toyoda, Tatsuro, 169
Toyo Kogyo (Mazda), 32
Toyota, 234
Toyota-Kyushu, 169
Toyota system, 1, 4, 8, 84, 159, 170
Toys R Us, 151
*TPM: Introduction to TPM, Total
    Productive Maintenance* (Nakajima),
    85
TQM, 47, 59, 64, 65, 68, 69, 72, 75, 79–80,
    98, 104, 138, 139, 140, 152, 153, 180,
    183–184, 220, 240
Trade loading, 139, 144
Trade pacts, 117
Traditional accounting system, 99–100, 106
Training, 1, 36–37, 66, 73, 75, 77, 83,
    183–184, 189–190, 193–194, 198,
    240–241
Trinova, 109
Trist, E. L., 160
TRW, 4–6, 195
TSS (Toyota sewing system), 163, 165,
    166

Unconstrained capacity, 173–175
Unilever, 12
Union Carbide Ethyleneamines, 51
Unisys, 40
United Auto Workers, 31, 101, 182, 195
United Electric Controls, 40
U.S. Postal Service, 72, 95, 239–240
U.S. Shoe Company, 165
U.S. Steel, 72
University of Cambridge, 122
Usage-rate production, 128–129

Valeo, 6, 7
Value, 16, 31–32, 91–113, 226–227
Value pricing, 128
Vanbeu, Lee, 70–71
Varian Ion Implant Systems, 203
Varian NMR Instruments, 67, 82, 89
Variax, 132
Vecellio, Anthony, 126
Vendor-managed inventory (VMI), 135,
    143–144, 152
VF Corporation, 163

Virtual stability: *See* Stability
Visionary thinking, 22
Visual Factory, The: Building Participation Through Shared Information (Greif), 202
Visual management, 16, 43, 74, 100, 201–204
Vollmann, Thomas, 222–223

Waaramaa, Finn, 94
Wainwright Industries, 40
Walker Systems, 242
Wal-Mart Stores, 29, 136, 143, 146, 151, 152, 163
Walt Disney Company, 216
Western, Dan, 183
Westinghouse, 15, 85
Wheelabrator, 56, 238–239
Wheeler, William, 81
Whirlpool, 2, 3, 123, 124, 230
Wien, Byron, 14

Wilson, Walt, 11
Wiremold Company, 236, 242
Work-life security, 189, 192
World Class International (WCI), 45, 70, 106, 249
World Class Manufacturing (Schonberger), 35, 47, 70, 78, 83, 87
Wrangler jeans, 163, 164

Xerox Corporation, 11, 15, 30, 147, 182, 229

Yamaha, 122–123
Young, John, 232
Young Presidents Organization (YPO), 80

Zangwill, Willard, 122
Zarrella, Ronald, 144
Zero working capital, 230–231
Zytec Corporation, 33, 100, 102, 104, 232